CAROL TATOR, FRANCES HENRY,
WINSTON MATTIS

Challenging Racism
in the Arts: Case Studies
of Controversy and Conflict

UNIVERSITY OF TORONTO PRESS
Toronto Buffalo London

© University of Toronto Press Incorporated 1998
Toronto Buffalo London
Printed in Canada

ISBN 0-8020-0808-9 (cloth)
ISBN 0-8020-7170-8 (paper)

Printed on acid-free paper

Canadian Cataloguing in Publication Data

Tator, Carol
   Challenging racism in the arts : case studies of controversy and conflict

   Includes index.
   ISBN 0-8020-0808-9 (bound)   ISBN 0-8020-7170-8 (pbk.)

   1. Racism in art – Case studies.   2. Arts – Ontario – Toronto – Case studies.
   I. Henry, Frances, 1931–   .   II. Mattis, Winston.   III. Title.

   NX513.T67T37 1998   700'.45203   C97-932783-0

University of Toronto Press acknowledges the financial assistance to its
publishing program of the Canada Council for the Arts and the Ontario Arts
Council

Contents

Acknowledgments

There are a number of people whose support and effort made this book possible. We wish to thank Jeff Henry, who first conceived of a project to document and analyse the events surrounding *Show Boat*. Jeff's vision, passion, and dedication to the arts, and to racial and cultural equity in cultural production, has inspired people working in all areas of the arts. Karen Warner assisted us by doing many of the interviews that inform our analysis. Tim Rees generously offered his ideas and suggestions for revisions. Eva Mackey's support and careful reading of the manuscript helped us focus, clarify, and sharpen our analyses. Cecil Foster and Roger Rowe, despite the pressures of work, took the time to do a critical reading of the chapter on *Show Boat*. Matthew Kudelka, our copy editor, provided invaluable help.

We are deeply appreciative of the many people who participated in individual and group interviews and who generously shared with us their time and reflections. We have attempted to accurately incorporate their observations, stories, experiences, knowledge, and insights in every chapter of this book. We think it is appropriate at this time to say how personally enriching it was to meet with so many gifted Canadians who have made such a contribution to Canadian culture and identity, despite the barriers they must constantly confront in their personal and professional lives.

Especially, we want to acknowledge Glenn Jordan and Chris Weedon, authors of *Cultural Politics: Class, Gender, Race and the Postmodern World* (1995), published by Blackwell. The authors heartened us with their knowledge and scholarship, and underscored for us the commonalities of the struggle over cultural production experienced by minorities within postmodern societies.

Finally, we thank our families for their love, patience, and support.

CHALLENGING RACISM IN THE ARTS

Introduction

This is a book about the quest for identity, representation, and affirmation in a multiracial, multicultural society, and the struggle against the power of a dominant culture that is still significantly influenced by the legacy of its Eurocentric heritage. One of the key assumptions of this book is that culture is a key site in the political struggle to transform power relations. We set out to document how ideas and images about racial and ethnic minorities are seamlessly woven into various forms of cultural production including literature, theatre, music, the visual arts, and the media. We seek to uncover the cultural politics buried in the norms and practices of cultural institutions such as museums and galleries, publishing houses, artists' associations, arts councils, and broadcasting networks.

In the past ten years more and more controversies have been arising over the issue of race and representation in Canadian cultural production. In this book we employ a case study approach to analyse these conflicts and their consequences. These cases provide a means of mapping new forms of cultural and racial politics in Canada. We believe that these case studies reflect an emerging crisis in representation in which cultural institutions are being scrutinized, challenged, and redefined as to their role, function, and meaning. The specific cultural events we explore, as well as the crisis over Quebec, show that race, culture, and identity are very important sites of struggle within the context of constructing a national identity.

The case study methodology allows us to provide detailed and very specific information about a number of cultural situations and events, and then explore and expand on the issues raised by those events. The case studies we use in this book are based on actual cultural events that took place in Toronto between 1985 and 1995. These events were:

1985–96   Efforts to establish a Black/dance music FM station to serve Metropolitan Toronto.[1]

1989   *Into the Heart of Africa*: An exhibition at the Royal Ontario Museum of cultural African artifacts, photographs, drawings, weapons, and other objects collected by Canadian missionaries and soldiers.

1993   *Miss Saigon*: An American musical produced by Mirvish Productions.

1993   *Show Boat*: An American musical produced by Live Entertainment (Livent) Productions.

1994   The Writing Thru Race Conference: A conference of First Nations writers and writers of colour in Vancouver.

1995   The Barnes Collection: An exhibition at the Art Gallery of Ontario of eighty-three Impressionist and Post-Impressionist paintings that were part of a vast art collection that had its origins on four continents, owned by Dr Albert Barnes.

Analysis of these events suggests that there are fundamental tensions in democratic liberal societies that are perhaps most visible in the struggles over cultural representation. Some of the tensions examined in this book are these:

• Homogeneity and anglo-conformity versus heterogeneity and the politics of difference.
• Concepts of truth and history as immutable and absolute versus multiple, changing interpretations of truth and history.
• Eurocentric aesthetic values and standards versus those of other cultural traditions.
• Freedom of expression of élite cultural producers and institutions versus the freedom of ethno-racial communities to express dissent and resist racist representation.
• Art as consumer product versus art as a vehicle for self-discovery.
• Art as an apparatus of economic power versus art as a vehicle of social empowerment.
• Finally, the tension between multiculturalism as a vehicle for affirming racial and cultural diversity and an instrument of social transformation, versus multiculturalism as a mechanism for containing cultural and racial differences and as an instrument of hegemonic control.

These tensions are expressed in racialized discourse – that is, in the repertoire of words, images, texts, stories, conversations, explanations, and everyday practices which, threaded together, produce an understanding of the world and of the status of people of colour in that world. Discourse is used to communicate deep and powerful meanings about people of colour, and to construct forms of social organization and social practices that in turn structure institutions. Discourse influences individual thinking, feeling, and behaviour, as well as cultural policies, organizational planning processes, and decision-making. Discourse is language put to social use, but it is often invisible to those who use it (Fiske, 1994).

In this book we intend to explore the systems of discourse and meaning that are embedded in each of the above cultural representations; these systems support patterns of domination, exclusion, and marginalization. We argue that the rhetoric of racism is expressed in popular/mass culture as well as 'high' culture. 'Codes of recognition' such as stereotypical representations are woven into radio and television news production and programming, advertisements, the print media, the visual arts, literature, the music industry, and the theatre. Both high culture and mass culture provide the elements out of which individual, communal, and national identities are created. The arts, film, music, and the print and broadcast industries provide us with a sense of what it means to be a woman or man, poor or privileged, Native Canadian or African Canadian. Cultural production provides the lens through which we view the world and communicates powerful messages about the core values, norms, cultural hierarchies, and central narratives of mainstream society.

We explore representational systems as a process of establishing undesirable 'otherness' – the polarization of society into 'we,' 'birthright Canadians' (Dabydeen, 1994), or 'Canadian Canadians' (Mackey, 1996), and 'they,' 'visible minorities,' 'ethnics,' 'immigrants,' 'new Canadians.' Labelling the 'others' becomes part of the formation of individual and collective identities. We believe that one measure of racism in a society is the extent to which cultural and racial differences mark one's position and status as 'other' within the processes of cultural production.

Our analysis of the case studies shows how discourse on race and racism converges with questions about national and cultural identity, and with democratic liberal values such as freedom of expression, truth, individualism, and tolerance. Covert forms of racism are hidden in the values, assumptions, and dispositions of literary art critics, curators and trustees of museums, theatrical producers and directors, journalists and editors, government bureaucrats, and politicians.

We contend that racial exclusion is reinforced by the dominant culture, which controls marginalized groups' access to and participation in the arts. Mainstream cultural institutions and cultural 'authorities' have the power to render invisible and inaudible the images, stories, and voices of ethno-racial minority communities, their artists, and their activists. We argue that a racially influenced discourse helps determine what gets defined as 'great' literature, music, art, and what gets labelled as 'primitive,' 'exotic,' 'unauthentic,' 'ethnic,' 'community' art.

The case studies illustrate how cultural productions and creative processes define and structure meaning, articulate and communicate authoritative messages, and embed powerful and negative images of ethno-racial minorities into the collective psyche of Canadian society. The cultural institutions we examine in this book have repeatedly demonstrated an inability to recognize and respond to the concerns and aspirations of ethno-racial communities. There appears to be an unwillingness to really listen to those who are now part of Canadian society, or to establish meaningful dialogue and relationships across racial and cultural boundaries.

We will attempt in this book to show how cultural production can be the source, site, and inspiration for radical forms of social change. We will also argue that the arts and popular culture offer the possibility of new constructions of Canadian identity, new forms of social relations, and a new, transforming multiculturalism.

In each of the case studies, the phenomena examined reflect a struggle over identity at the level of the individual, the group, and the community, and ultimately address the issue of national identity. We look at how the dominant culture both proposes and imposes identity on the 'others' – that is, on people of colour and on other nondominant cultures. At the same time, we look at how those designated as 'others' are seeking to reclaim their right to choose how they will be recognized, defined, and represented in relation to their individual and collective identities. These ethno-racial minorities are seeking to express these identities in different forms of cultural practice; they are also determining the conditions and tools necessary for resistance.

We analyse how ethno-racial communities, individual artists, cultural critics, and cultural activists attempt to redefine the concepts of 'mainstream,' 'margins,' 'differences,' 'otherness,' out of a deep commitment to the principles and ideals of democratic society (West, 1990).

All but one of the events we examine took place in the same six-year period – a period characterized by sweeping social, cultural, economic, and political changes in Canadian society. Each of the events served as a cultural flashpoint that sparked important issues and provided important insights.

However, cultural production is a complex process that cannot be fundamentally altered by any single event or cultural practice. It follows that individual acts – producing *Show Boat* or *Miss Saigon*, writing a book, holding a conference, developing an exhibition, trying to establish a Black/dance music station – are less significant than the absence of theatres that reflect and represent the stories and memories of non-European Canadians, the dearth of creative art forms in the public domain by Native peoples and artists of colour, and the neglect by the media of voices, music, and perspectives reflecting different cultural traditions and heritages (Wallace, 1993). It is the connections underlying these absences and exclusions that are analysed in this book.

The fact that each of the cultural events we describe in the case studies occurred within a short period demonstrates one of our central points: resisting racism is no longer simply a matter of challenging racist individuals and institutions; instead, there is a growing recognition that if racist discourse is embedded in the fabric of culture, and if cultural productions are an expression of that discourse, then resistance must be directed at challenging those forms of cultural production which reinforce racist ideologies.

The case studies suggest that cultural products and practices mirror the larger social processes: cultural representations echo social realities. Thus, all forms of cultural production must be understood in the context of how they were produced, by whom, at what historical moment, and with what social, economic, and political impact. Cultural practices cannot be separated from the environment within which they find expression.

We share Marlene Nourbese Philip's view (1993) that cultural racism becomes more blatant and pervasive during periods when people of colour are more assertively claiming their rights. Our premise is also similar to that of Pieterse (1992), who notes that while 'othering' and oppression have a history as old as representation itself, the processes of both are expanding and intensifying in this age of mass communications.

In each of the case studies, the media acted as the main conduit through which the events described were filtered and explained. The media were always present to interpret what was 'real.' Yet the issues and concerns of ethno-racial minorities are rarely included in the conventional explanations of 'reality' (Fiske, 1994).

We examine the linkage between the media's White or Eurocentric values and the political, social, and corporate élite groups that play such a central role in cultural production. Our interest in the role of the mass media is linked to the fact that they have nearly exclusive control over the resources required to produce popular opinion, especially in the area of race and ethnic relations (Fleras and Elliot, 1992; Van Dijk, 1991; Hall, 1973).

These case studies of cultural production demonstrate that ethno-racial minorities do not have control over systems for producing images and discourse about themselves. We contend that the systems that do exist have been constructed by the dominant culture, which promotes, supports, and affirms forms of exclusion. For both the dominant culture and ethno-racial minorities, cultural productions and processes are embedded with conflicting meanings. The production of images and icons, symbols and stories, myths and metaphors, is part of the process of creating meaning; and meaning is developed across the boundaries of cultural and racial difference, as well as across other social markers such as gender, sexual orientation, and class (Rutherford, 1990). But the meanings of any one cultural form, artifact, or event are neither fixed, nor true, nor immutable. Postmodern thinking affirms the validity and value of the struggle over meanings.

One of our aims with this book is to expose the contours, meanings, and methods of racialized cultural representations. We also want to provide the reader with some understanding of the significance of the struggle now being waged against those cultural productions which form an integral part of the social processes of exclusion and oppression (Foucault, 1980).

Cultural politics – that is, the politics of difference – creates new and explicit demands, which have a ripple effect on all of our social, cultural, economic, and political institutions. The debates over cultural production described and examined in this book touch on fundamental and deeply felt issues about who we are, and what we want to be, and what we might become.

Some of the key questions about the relationship between culture and power that we address in this book are as follows:

• How are cultural products produced, legitimated, and disseminated, by whom, and with what political, social, and economic implications?
• How is social inequality legitimated through culture, cultural institutions, and cultural practices?
• How is it established whose culture is the official one and whose is to be subordinated? Whose cultural traditions are regarded as worthy?

- How do power relations determine access to culture and cultural practices? What are the tools of cultural hegemony?
- How do cultural institutions perpetuate cultural racism? How is power maintained by the dominant culture within cultural institutions, and with what consequences? What barriers do artists of colour encounter that result in lack of access and equity?
- How is power manifested in systems of representation? Which images of cultural life are projected, and which are marginalized? Whose voices are heard, and whose are silenced?
- How are marginalized and oppressed people empowering themselves? How does resistance operate? How have the arts become a tool in the struggle against marginalization and oppression? What are the forces facilitating/impeding resistance?
- How do the cultural politics of difference influence our understanding of the principles and practices of a cultural democracy, a society based on the notions of liberalism, multiculturalism, and humanism?
- What new forms of discourse, what new cultural models or paradigms are required that will allow us to create a society in which the hermetic seal that divides Canadians into 'us' and 'them' is broken? Can some form of critical/transformed multiculturalism provide Canadians with a new vision of collective identity? (Jordan and Weedon, 1995; Berger, 1992)

We study each cultural production in this book from both the position of the mainstream and the terrain of marginality. But as bell hooks (1990) points out, the margin should not be viewed solely as a site of exclusion and oppression. It can also be a site of possibility, the catalyst for 'radical perspectives from which to see and create, to imagine alternatives, new worlds ...' (150), and for transforming change. Marginality itself becomes a strategy in the construction of one's own identity as well as a sense of collective identity. Those who are obligated to negotiate both 'margin and centre' are well placed to deconstruct dominant discourses and systems of representation (ibid.).

In this book we have provided a discursive space – that is, an opportunity for those on the margins to share their perspectives. Individuals involved in producing non-mainstream cultural works – cultural and community activists, advocates, critics, artists, writers, performers, directors, musicians, and others – talk about their struggles to find space for their work on the 'representational stage' of Canadian culture (Mackey, 1996: 903). We document their efforts and those of their communities to shape the process of cultural exchange, to create new forms of cultural expression, to fundamentally alter cultural institutions, and to gain control over the production of racist images and representations that permeate Canadian mainstream culture. This 'cultural politics of difference' – a term coined by Cornel West (1990) – represents the distinct expressions of talented contributors to culture who seek to empower themselves and their communities, and to engage in forms of social action that lead to the expansion of freedom and democracy.

In our study we suggest that ethno-racial minorities are placed outside the 'imagined community' and culture of Canadian society (Mackey, 1996; Walcott, 1993; Anderson, 1983), and we point out some of the ways they are trying to find their way into the centre of mainstream culture.[2] We also describe the failures of the dominant culture to 'imagine' racism as a defining characteristic of Canadian society – of its collective values, beliefs, and norms. 'Racism as imagination has a grammar and syntax ...' (Srivastava, 1991: 34), but one that is often invisible to those identified with the dominant culture.

As we noted in an earlier work, *The Colour of Democracy* (Henry et al., 1995), Canada suffers from historical amnesia. Its citizens and institutions are functioning in a state of collective denial, having obliterated from their collective memory the racist laws, policies, practices, and ideologies that have shaped Canadian social, cultural, political, and economic institutions for three hundred years. This country's individuals, communities, organizations, and institutions, and the Canadian state itself, are influenced by two competing ideologies: democratic liberalism and racism (ibid.).

We recognize that in this book we are in some ways trespassing on sacred ground. The debates over culture, cultural representation, and cultural identity deal with fundamental and deeply felt issues about who we are as a country and as a people. We are presenting for scrutiny, interrogation, and criticism our society's hierarchy of cultural values, cherished beliefs, and aesthetic practices. The notion of transforming our public culture challenges deeply held assumptions and traditional forms of cultural practice and rhetoric of the kind employed in democratic liberal societies.

Terminology

One of the most significant challenges facing those who wish to write about identity, culture, race, and racism relates to appropriate terminology. Williams (1976) makes the point that not only do words change, but their historical context affects how they are used. Moreover, the radical changes that words undergo suggest that there is no fixed, correct, or reliable meaning for any term. Apple (1993: 25) expresses the challenge of language in this way: 'Concepts do not remain still very long. They have wings so to speak, and can be induced to fly from place to place.' One therefore needs to look for the meaning of particular terms in their specific contextual use.

The terminology in cultural studies and discourse analysis, from which the authors draw, can also create problems. Many readers find the language used in cultural criticism elusive and obscure and find it difficult at times to grasp the point being made. For this reason we have tried to demystify the language so as to make it as accessible as possible. Even so, many readers will encounter some unfamiliar terms and concepts. The authors encourage them to use the detailed glossary provided at the end of the book.

We also wish to point out that terms such as culture, race, history, truth, freedom of expression, and universalism, for example, are not neutral concepts; rather, they exist as part of many different social and interpretative frameworks. There are powerful currents that alter interpretations depending on the situation, location, and social context (Lentricchia and McLaughlin, 1990; Fiske, 1994).

Although colour remains the nucleus of the race classification system, paradoxically, it bears little relation to the actual skin tones of human beings. Whites do not consider themselves part of the colour spectrum, but rather identify their group as constituting the universal norm. However, the gradations of colour from white to black associated with various racial groups have social, economic, and cultural consequences. The ideology that defines Whites as superior renders people of different colours inferior. Skin colour therefore has an important relationship to one's status and position in Canadian society. As Joanne St. Lewis (1996: 28) observes: 'In conversations about race, all of my being is telescoped to my skin. The colour of my skin drives the engine of my public life. It defines relationships and sets out possibilities. Attitudes and beliefs make it real.'

For this reason, references to colour in this book are capitalized to reflect this context. The terms 'mainstream,' 'Anglo,' 'dominant group,' and 'core culture' are used interchangeably throughout the book to refer to the group in Canadian society that maintains the power to define itself and its culture as the norm. Phrases such as 'racial minorities' and 'people of colour' appear often in this book and are also used interchangeably. Each of the terms Blacks, African Canadians, Asian Canadians, and Aboriginal or First Nations peoples refers to a highly complex, fluid, and heterogeneous community. For both individuals and groups, identity formation is always in the process of definition and redefinition. Groups exist in a state of constant transformation.

However, in the case studies and in other parts of the book, the authors often allude to these diverse racial and cultural groups in terms of their belonging to a collectivity who share certain common commitments and common sensibilities that cross the particular terrains of class, gender, colour, ethnicity, and individual differences. These new collective racial identities serve as a basis for solidarity and mobilization. They form part of a political process that empowers people of colour to resist and challenge racism.

Perspective

The perspective of this book is influenced by many factors, including the following: the ethno-racial backgrounds of the authors; our genders, and our educational and professional backgrounds; our geographic and social locations; our work as academics and our experience as anti-racism practitioners; our lifetime involvement working in, and with, racial minority communities; and, finally, our commitment to social change, social action, and social justice. We therefore are neither 'neutral' nor 'objective' observers. But then, as we argue later in this book, no piece of writing is ever totally impartial or value free.

Our study of cultural production draws from the theories and concepts contained in the field of cultural studies and attempts to show how these constructions translate into common norms and everyday practices within creative expression and cultural production. We aim to capitalize on the important contributions of cultural theorists who have explored, critiqued, and defined the relationship between culture and power.

Our perspective in this book is congruous with that of writers such as Stuart Hall, who has said that 'the work of cultural studies is to mobilize everything it can find in terms of intellectual resources in order to understand what keeps making the lives we live, and the societies we live in, profoundly and deeply anti-humane' (quoted in hooks, 1994: 3). Our study is also influenced by the outlook of writers such as bell hooks, who views the airing of diverse perspectives as a means for us to educate one another and acquire a sense of 'critical consciousness' (1990: 6).

We have no interest in simply 'trashing' the contributions of any cultural producer; we hope instead to offer a critique of cultural production in Canada that is illuminating and constructive. It is not our intent to label as racist any particular managers, critics, journalists, or others in the cultural field, nor do we see our role as that of 'cultural thought police.' Our concern is not with *individual* prejudicial attitudes. By focusing on this narrow aspect of racism we would be deflecting the problem of cultural representation away from the ideological centres and the historical, political, cultural, and institutional contexts within which racist cultural production has functioned.

Our approach, then, involves examining the various supportive assumptions, familiar beliefs, unchallenged modes of thought, and unquestioned values and norms that are rooted in the ideology of the dominant culture. Our aim is to help uncover what mainstream culture accepts as 'fact' (or 'truth') 'reality' (Foucault, 1988).

We have undertaken this project in order to enrich the reader's understanding of various perplexing and profoundly important issues that are confronting this country (as well as all other postmodern Western industrialized nations) as the new millennium arrives. As we move to the close of one century and the beginning of another, we must search for new paradigms, policies, models, ideas, and undertakings related to cultural production. We are writing this book because we believe that alternatives are possible to the current state of crisis over issues of representation, power, and identity.

We hope this book will help make clear some of the conditions necessary for meaningful exchange, dialogue, and action between ethnoracial minorities who, in their own lives and work, are challenging racist representations, productions, and practices, and the mainstream White culture that has largely controlled the parameters of the debate on this subject. Our aim in writing this book is to cast light on a subject that has remained largely in shadow: culture as the site for altering the fundamentally unequal power relationships that structure difference, including race, culture, gender, and other social categories.

For this book we have many audiences in mind: students, artists, writers, performers, film-makers, cultural activists, and people working in cultural institutions of any kind, whether public or private, from schools to museums and art galleries, to TV stations, to government agencies (the list is practically endless). We also hope that the public at large – that is, individuals who enjoy the products of cultural production and who have been perplexed by the controversies described in the case studies – will find that this book helps illuminate the complex issues underlying the protests.

Finally, in writing this book we have meant to document the efforts of artists of colour and racial minority communities to transform cultural production. We believe that underlying these struggles is the search for cultural and political values and norms more appropriate to a pluralistic, multiracial country and a democratic culture.

A Note on Methodology

The analysis that informs this book is based on a rigorous inquiry into a multidisciplined body of knowledge drawn from cultural studies, discourse analysis, aesthetics, sociology, anthropology, history, and mass communications. This study of systems of cultural representation has also been guided by a multifaceted methodology.

Besides carefully reviewing the academic cultural-studies literature, the authors collected and analysed published materials written by artists, producers, playwrights, arts administrators, and others whose lives are devoted to the practice of art and culture. Specific attention was paid to literary sources and to magazines such as *Fuse, Border/Lines, This Magazine, and Possibilitiis,* which regularly publish the work of writers and cultural critics from diverse ethno-racial communities.

An intensive interview methodology was also employed. We interviewed almost one hundred of the key players in the case study incidents described in this book. These included museum personnel, senior editors, members of the writers' union, visual artists, performers, applicants to the CRTC, members of the minority public who led demonstrations against cultural agencies, and the leaders of the several protest movements that evolved to challenge productions such as *Show Boat* and *Miss Saigon.* Also, focus group interviews were held with members of the ethno-racial groups directly involved in the protests. Further, the authors interviewed opinion leaders in a number of different communities.

Wherever possible, we have tried to incorporate either direct quotations from those interviewed or excerpts from their published materials in order to directly (without interpretation) communicate to the reader their feelings, thoughts, and words. However, to ensure confidentiality for those who requested it, the interviewees are sometimes not referenced.

Participant observation was also an important tool of the methodology. One of the authors attended the Writing Thru Race Conference, where she interviewed participants, attended all the open sessions, and in general assumed the role of participant observer. This author also joined the picket lines at the two theatrical productions and took note of events, and interviewed participants, including some of the theatre staff and even a few police officers. She also attended the first preview performance of *Show Boat*, and took note not only of the production but also of the many activities outside of the theatre involving demonstrators, the theatre-going public, the media, and the police. The event attracted significant television coverage, and tapings from several newscasts were viewed many times by the authors.

The authors also participated directly in the attempt to license a Black/dance music station. Two of the authors participated in several of the presentations made to the CRTC by one of the applicants. Moreover, one author is a professional musician and has had extensive experience in writing, producing, and performing 'Black music.'

Framework

This book has four main sections. It begins with a theoretical introduction in which we attempt to orient the reader to theories, concepts, and constructs underlying our analysis. The second section consists of the six case studies identified earlier, which form the book's central core. In the third section, we revisit and analyse the dominant themes and tensions explored in the six cultural productions. In the final section, 'Concluding Reflections,' we analyse some of the critical issues that frame the case studies, focusing on cultural production in the context of national identity and multiculturalism.

Notes

1 The case study of the application for a Black/dance music station (see Chapter 5) is somewhat different in both format and focus from the others examined in this book. The other studies in this book deal with issues of race, racist representation, and exclusion, to demonstrate that elements of racism are embedded in cultural production. The analysis of the CRTC's failure, thus far, to license a Black/dance music station in Toronto also deals with the theme of representation, but from the perspective of the CRTC as the administrative agency responsible for an important arena of cultural production. For many, broadcasting and television are crucial areas for analysis, not only because

what is seen and heard influences public opinion, but also because these media also produce and reproduce particular projections of group and individual identity. The analysis considers the cultural politics that surrounded the efforts to obtain a licence, as well as the institutional resistance of the CRTC as the licensing agency.

2 Anderson (1983) uses this term to define the concept of 'nation.' A nation is 'imagined' because the members of even a very small state do not all know one another, yet in 'the minds of each lives the image of their communion' (15). It is also imagined as 'limited' because even the largest nation has boundaries. Moreover, a nation is imagined as a community because 'regardless of the actual inequality and exploitation that may prevail ... the nation is always conceived as a deep, horizontal comradeship' (16).

References

Anderson, B. 1983. *Imagined Communities*. London: Verso.

Apple, Michael. 1993. 'Constructing the "Other": Rightist Reconstructions of Common Sense.' In C. McCarthy and W. Critchlow, eds. *Race, Identity and Representation in Education*. New York and London: Routledge. 24–39.

Berger, Maurice. 1992. *How Art Becomes History*. New York: HarperCollins.

Dabydeen, Cyril. 1994. 'Citizenship Is More than a "Birthright."' *Toronto Star*. 20 September. A23.

Fiske, John. 1994. *Media Matters: Everyday Culture and Political Change*. Minnesota: University of Minnesota Press.

Fleras, Augie, and Jean Elliot, 1992. *Multiculturalism in Canada*. Scarborough, Ont.: Nelson Canada.

Foucault, Michel. 1980. *Power/Knowledge: Selected Interviews and Other Writings, 1972–1977*. Ed. Colin Gordon. New York: Pantheon.

– 1988. *Politics, Philosophy, Culture: Interviews and Other Writings, 1977–1984*. Ed. Lawrence Kritzman. London and New York: Routledge.

Hall, Stuart. 1973. *The Structured Communication of Events*. Birmingham, U.K.: Centre for Contemporary Cultural Studies.

Henry, Frances, Carol Tator, Winston Mattis, and Tim Rees. 1995. *The Colour of Democracy: Racism in Canadian Society*. Toronto: Harcourt Brace.

hooks, bell. 1990. *Yearning: Race, Gender and Cultural Politics*. Toronto: Between the Lines.

–, ed. 1994. *Outlaw Culture: Resisting Representations*. London and New York: Routledge.

Jordan, Glenn, and Chris Weedon. 1995. *Cultural Politics: Class, Gender, Race and the Postmodern World*. Oxford, U.K., and Cambridge, U.S.A.: Blackwell.

Lentricchia, Frank, and Thomas McLaughlin, eds. 1990. *Critical Terms for Literary Study.* 2nd ed. Chicago: University of Chicago Press.

Mackey, Eva. 1995. 'Postmodernism and Cultural Politics in a Multicultural Nation: Contests over Truth in the *Into the Heart of Africa* Controversy.' *Public Culture.* 7(2) Winter. 403–48.

– 1996. 'Managing and Imagining Diversity: Multiculturalism and the Construction of National Identity in Canada.' D.Phil, Social Anthropology, University of Sussex.

Nourbese Philip, Marlene. 1993. *Showing Grit: Showboating North of the 44th Parallel.* Toronto: Poui.

Pieterse, Nederveen. 1992. *White on Black: Images of Africans and Blacks in Western Culture.* London and New Haven: Yale University Press.

Rutherford, Jonathan, ed. 1990. *Identity: Communicating Culture and Difference.* London: Lawrence and Wishart.

St. Lewis, Joanne. 1996. 'Identity and Black Consciousness in North America.' In James Littleton, ed. *Clash of Identities: Essays on Media, Manipulation and Politics of Self.* Englewood Cliffs, N.J.: Prentice Hall. 21–30.

Srivastava, Aruna. 1991. 'Imag(in)ing Racism – South Asian Canadian Women Writers.' *Fuse Magazine.* Fall. 29–34.

Van Dijk, Teun. 1991. *Racism and the Press.* London and New York: Routledge.

Walcott, Rinaldo. 1993. 'Critiquing Canadian Multiculturalism: Towards an Anti-Racist Agenda.' Master's Thesis, Dept. of Education, York University.

Wallace, Michele. 1993. 'Negative Images: Towards a Black Feminist Cultural Criticism.' In S. During, ed. *The Cultural Studies Reader.* New York: Routledge. 118–34.

West, Cornel. 1990. 'The New Cultural Politics of Difference.' In Russell Ferguson, ed. *Out There: Marginalization and Contemporary Culture.* New York: New Museum of Contemporary Art.

Williams, Raymond. 1976. *Key Words: A Vocabulary of Culture and Society.* London: Fontana.

1

Theoretical Perspectives

Postmodernism and Cultural Studies

The theoretical orientation of this book is influenced by trends and developments in the field of cultural studies. This relatively new discipline, an interdisciplinary blend of the social sciences, is closely associated with the philosophical discourse of postmodernism. This book deals with the dynamics of cultural production in a society that can easily be characterized as postmodern.

Canada meets many of the criteria of a postmodern society because it is characterized by rapid population changes and ethno-racial diversity. These features were recognized many years ago by Lyotard (1986) as a condition of heterogeneity and localism rather than homogeneity and universality. This type of society is one in which traditional values are increasingly challenged by the transglobal movement of people and their culture. Like other post-industrial Westernized societies, Canada is characterized by increasing racism, anxieties about its rapidly changing socio-cultural fabric, and nostalgia for traditional values and norms.

Postmodernism has many meanings (which sometimes conflict), but can best be understood as a paradigm for social change: specifically, the change from the modernist view of society that is founded on the theories of the eighteenth-century Enlightenment, with its emphasis on reason, rationality, and individualism. In the postmodern period these values have not been abandoned, but they *are* being redefined by the needs and demands of subjective experience. Postmodern societies in various stages of capitalism are distinguished today by the following:

• Broken geographical boundaries and the dissolution of nation-states.

- Emphasis on transnational and transglobal movement of peoples and cultures.
- Increasing technology of communication.
- Shifting and fragmenting societal values and the challenge to traditional values.
- The fragmentation of individual identities by different social markers – race, gender, ethnicity, sexual orientation, and many other influences – so that identity has become temporal and shifting and no longer fixed.
- The 'conquest' of culture and forms of popular culture by imagery and representation.
- The proliferation of cultural products characterized not by high culture and its aesthetics but by the aesthetics of individual expression.
- The obliteration of the distinction between art and everyday life.
- The erasure of the boundary between high and mass or popular culture. (Featherstone, 1988)

As a postmodern society, Canada is undergoing rapid social and cultural change. Its values are changing, its traditional values are being challenged, and individuals can no longer be slotted neatly into predestined roles. In the same way, its political and economic arenas are characterized by a degree of fragmentation; and its social and political order, once controlled by an anglophone European-descended élite, is also on shifting ground.

Postmodernism, like any developing philosophy, has undergone significant modifications in the thirty years that it has dominated discussions on social theory. In its earlier manifestation, the discourse strongly challenged authority and power relations in society, with particular emphasis on the role of women and ethnic and racial minorities. Later it moved into a phase in which it began to question some of the major values in society, including those values which worked to maintain traditional forms of social and political hierarchies and advantage. As well, postmodernists were distrustful of authority – a major characteristic of the 1960s. Within this framework, concerns about identity, representation, and difference became dominant. While earlier postmodernists had also challenged authority, and had sought to put theory into practice through an emphasis on social and political action, later developments tended to de-emphasize the 'action' component of postmodernist theory. Nevertheless, the politics of identity, or the ways that cultural and subjective identities have become politicized so that they lay claim to

greater resources and benefits, still characterize postmodernist discourse today. Identity politics, along with the idea that 'difference' is
created by race, ethnicity, gender, and other less visible factors, is still
dominant (Derrida, 1985).

One of the main issues challenging postmodernist theories is this: To
what degree can these theories lead to practical solutions? If postmodernist societies are characterized by fragmentation and difference, to
what extent can these theories lead to or define means of overcoming
social inequalities that are rooted in a construction of difference and
identity? Also, does the postmodern condition inevitably lead to more
and more dissolution of boundaries, of nation-states, and ultimately to
social and political chaos?

An economic determinist point of view suggests that as long as the
power of capitalism remains basically intact, societies will continue to
undergo change but not transformation. For politically oriented theorists, the challenge to traditional power relations on the part of the
disempowered remains the most effective means of creating change,
although even the doyen of such theorists, Michel Foucault, suggests
that such attempts contain the seeds of their own destruction (in Sypnowich, 1996: 122).

One serious social concern in this changing historical context is that
racism in all its forms and guises has become even more deeply
entrenched in postmodernist societies. One of the primary objectives of
this book is to provide an analysis of its most overarching form – cultural
racism and its discourse – in a society that is characterized more and
more by cultural and racial diversity and by a 'politics of difference.' The
book sets out to examine how the basic cultural values that shape, regulate, and guide Canadian society are influenced by a racist discourse.

The six case studies demonstrate how cultural practices and cultural
systems of representation are wedded to values that promote social processes of differentiation, exclusion, and domination. These values are
manifested in cultural institutions, and in cultural productions including theatre, music, writing, and museum and artistic exhibitions.

Postmodernist cultural studies have narrowed the traditional gap
between high culture and mass/popular culture by demonstrating that
basic values structure or influence all forms of culture. This is why the
case studies we selected for this book include examples of both high
culture (museum exhibitions and literature) and popular culture (the
efforts to establish a Black popular music station and the mounting of
two musical theatre productions).

Besides showing how racism affected each of the case study situations, this book will highlight the pivotal role played by the media in interpreting and disseminating messages that include a racist discourse. The authors argue that to a significant extent, the case study examples became part of the public discourse not because of their intrinsic interest to large numbers of people, but rather because the media chose to focus on them and in so doing reinforced (and in some instances actually interpreted) the events in ways that would reinforce racist values in the larger society.

The Cultural Studies Theoretical Perspective: Issues and Definitions

One of the most intriguing theoretical developments in the social sciences in recent years has been the growth of a field of inquiry called cultural studies. This approach to the study of culture, strongly influenced by postmodern perspectives, began more than twenty years ago in Great Britain after it was recognized that the traditional disciplines that study culture – anthropology, sociology, history, literature, and so on – had become so fragmented and formalized into separate disciplines that culture was being studied in disparate pieces (Giroux, in During, 1994: introduction). Moreover, traditional academic disciplines and their practitioners were isolating themselves from the public sphere, which is where popular culture – one of the distinguishing characteristics of postmodern society – has its nexus. The field of cultural studies recognizes the relationship between culture, cultural production, and asymmetrical power relations in society and refuses 'to agree that literature and any other cultural object is distinct from politics' (ibid.: 5). It encourages a critical examination of the dominant culture and an effective resistance to its hegemonic control. Cultural studies is inherently oppositional in its approach to dominance. Although it has been difficult to define the boundaries of this field because of its overwhelming subject matter, Bennett (1992: 23) provides a rough working definition when he states that cultural studies functions 'largely as a term of convenience for a fairly dispersed array of theoretical and political positions which, however widely divergent they might be in other respects, share a commitment to examining cultural practices from the point of view of their intrication with, and within, relations of power.'

Lawrence Grossberg and colleagues (1993) argue that cultural studies is 'radically contextual' (90) in that the concept of culture can be understood as operating at many different levels. Anthropologists have long defined culture as the learned, shared, and transmitted way of life of a people, group, or nation. However, the concept has been defined in many other ways; for example, to some people culture refers to artistic/ intellectual activities and is synonymous with 'high' culture. For the purposes of this book, we will apply a definition closer to that of Williams (1976) and Grossberg (1993), both of whom emphasize that culture is a signifying system through which a social order is communicated, reproduced, and experienced.

In this book, which is strongly influenced by a cultural studies approach, we will emphasize 'cultural racism' and the racist discourses embedded in the value system of society.* We perceive 'cultural racism' as a fundamental form of racism because it includes ideas that are deeply embedded in the value system of society – as a part of the invisible network of beliefs, attitudes, and assumptions that define the cultural value system of society.

The Politics of Diversity and Critical Multiculturalism

Central to this area of inquiry are questions relating to the factors of race, national identity, and ethnicity in the transnational new world order. The international/global movement of people and ideas has created conditions of multiculturalism and diversity in countries that had earlier been monocultural; it has also generated concerns centring on race, ethnicity, and the politics of diversity. The rights and privileges of those artists and culture producers and performers who do not subscribe to an ideology of Eurocentric superiority increasingly assume social, political, and cultural importance. Kobena Mercer has recently argued that 'multiculturalism in its broadest sense, as the dilemma of living with difference, is really the decisive issue that cultural studies has to address' (Mercer, 1992: 447).

In its approach, cultural studies breaks with the traditions and conventions of most of the social sciences. For example, it is subjective: it studies culture in relation to how it affects the living experiences of people rather than as an abstraction divorced from the realities of everyday experience. Culture is neither a social construct, nor something to be defined by high culture and its forms.

Cultural studies recognizes the dynamic and changing nature of culture and cultural production – that is, how these change rapidly as new

---

* We use the terms 'cultural racism' and 'racist discourse' interchangeably to refer to a set of values, as well as to linguistic, representational, and textual practices.

influences shape the thought, activity, and agenda of people in society. Moreover, cultural studies engages the facts of societal inequality and analyses the impact of such inequality on the lives of those most affected, such as women and racial minorities. It is very much concerned with diversity, and with the effects of diversity on mainstream traditional institutions and organizations. Earlier, cultural studies concentrated on opposing culture against the state; more recently, it has affirmed the 'other' ways of life in their own terms rather than merely their difference from state sponsored and controlled forms. Cultural studies is now concerned with how ethno-racial and women's groups are committed to maintaining and elaborating their own autonomous values, identities, and cultural products. The emphasis has shifted to the study and analysis of these as independent from the larger mainstream culture or the state.

Thus, cultural studies affirms otherness and difference in what has been called the 'politics of survival' (During, 1994: introduction), or the 'politics of difference' to use West's term (1990). This approach is part of a theory of society in which difference and otherness is central and in which the dynamic of pluralism and heterogeneity is emphasized. First popularized by leading postmodernist theorist Jacques Derrida (1985), the notion of difference relates to dominant values, which attempt to maintain a traditional national and personal identity even while new people and new values are posing an increasing challenge. Groups and persons who are 'different' and who have been excluded from the mainstream because of race, ethnicity, gender, and other traits are now demanding political, social, and cultural recognition and representation.

Such a theory does not necessarily require that the forces of capitalism or a free market economy be the central causes of structural inequality. Rather, it works toward creating conditions of autonomy for all 'othered' groups; thus, society does not need a total revolution in its mode of production, but does need to create conditions of equality and equity.

A postmodernist cultural studies approach leads to a new understanding of the ideology of multiculturalism, and it is such an understanding that guides some of the analysis attempted in this book. Much of what follows can be viewed as a reaction to the delegitimization of the traditional state and to the decline of its dominant system of cultural values. This forms part of the new 'radical or critical' understanding of how multicultural societies function in an increasingly transglobal and diverse world. It recognizes the important political role of culture as a means of disseminating ideology in societies segmented by diverse ethno-racial groups, who are now challenging the central role of the state and its traditional cultural values. Turner (1994: 421) notes that critical multiculturalism 'is essential to a realization of the implicitly revolutionary nature of multiculturalism as a program of cultural, social and political transformation.' Critical multiculturalism is more than the celebration of cultural differences or even their 'hybridization with one another.' It calls for the equality of all cultures within the state, and demands that the traditional political community and its socio-cultural institutions dissociate themselves from a monocultural approach to diversity. It denies the singular or privileged position of the traditional Eurocentric state and its culture, and values alternative forms of culture and their expression. Thus, critical multiculturalism is a movement for change, and provides a theoretical framework for 'challenging the cultural hegemony of the dominant ethnic group ... by calling for equal recognition of the cultural expressions of nonhegemonic groups' (ibid.: 407).

Another significant feature of a cultural studies approach is its opposition to the moral agenda of the 'New Right.' The New Right fears the new and different values brought in by people of 'different' (thus 'inferior') cultures, and places enormous importance on the need to maintain a traditional, monoculturally based society. A homogeneous image of the national culture is celebrated and enforced to counter the alleged dangers of the increasingly global economy. The promotion of a monocultural society with its emphasis on family values, hard work, and traditional gender roles, requires a devaluation not just of other nations and their cultural identities but of the enemies within – those who are 'other' racially, sexually, ethnically, and so on. These beliefs, which are enshrined in the position of the New Right, are challenged by a cultural studies perspective.

Cultural studies also emphasizes the important role of popular culture in the transmission and reproduction of values. The traditional difference between 'high' and 'popular' culture, so characteristic of Eurocentered discourses of the past, no longer prevails. Cultural studies has been defined as a form of 'cultural populism' (During, 1994: 17).

The field of cultural studies strongly emphasizes cultural policy analysis, in recognition that cultural production and distribution requires economic resources. Since resources such as radio and television networks are limited, it is usually government agencies that make licensing decisions. Decisions that affect the distribution of resources are open to traditional forms of bias and often shut out the newer voices in society. Moreover, funding agencies – especially those which dispense public monies – are now facing considerable pressure to follow more inclusive policies. Cultural policy decisions with regard not only to allocating financial resources but also to regulating cultural industries are also part of cultural studies (During, 1994).

From its dynamic beginnings, the role of postmodernist cultural studies was not only to challenge traditional theories and forms of action, but also to define new forms of social action and to provide a new politics of engagement. Recent commentators have, however, criticized the field for its lack of social and political action and for concentrating on the study of texts and concepts 'such as hegemony, resistance, articulation [which] are too sweepingly and uncritically used and are only lightly underpinned by substantive social analysis' (Knauft, 1994: 133).

In a recently published Canadian work on the politics of race, ethnicity, and culture, the point is made that the 'increasing textual preoccupation' of academics and theorists occurs because it has become increasingly difficult 'to launch a politically engaged critique of representational icons' (Amit-Talai and Knowles, 1996: 14). It is safer, therefore, to analyse texts rather than continue the struggle for political change. The authors argue for a 're-energized research project' in which identities are resituated in the examination of power relations and in which discourses are analysed but not 'at the expense of rigorous empirically grounded analysis and an insistence on concrete social change.' They also emphasize, as the authors of this text do, that it is not only systems that must be examined but the people who as political actors play a major role in experiencing and contesting racism. At the same time, the roles of individuals in cultural institutions must be examined with respect to how they make decisions, establish priorities, and exercise power, in ways that effectively marginalize ethno-racial groups and individuals.

The focus of this book is on empirically grounded case studies, all of which reveal the multifaceted dimensions of racist discourse. We hope that by clearly presenting examples of how racist discourse is revealed in cultural institutions even in apparently simple ways, we will be encouraging forms of social and especially political action to counter such inequities.

Theoretical Methodology

Discourse and Discourse Analysis

The notion of 'discourse,' which stems from Foucault's seminal work (1980), has become central to postmodernist perspectives on culture and society. The use of 'discourse analysis' as a methodological tool has become standard practice for social scientists, especially those who are influenced by the theoretical positions of postmodernist and poststructuralist 'cultural studies.' As noted above, these theoretical formulations shape and define our outlook on racist discourse and its expressions in Canadian society.

However, the term 'discourse' is slippery, elusive, and difficult to define. Like 'cultural studies,' it at times includes everything and anything to do with expressive human behaviour. At other times it refers to the specific practices and expressions of people and their institutions. As Fiske (1994) notes, it has been used to refer both to a theoretical position and to the specific practices of a discourse.

Discourse is most closely associated with language and the written or oral text. At this level, it 'challenges the concept of "language" as an abstract system and relocates the whole process of making and using meanings from the abstracted structural system into particular historical, social and political conditions' (ibid.). Discourse is the way in which language is used socially to convey broad historical meanings. It is language identified by the social conditions of its use.

Linguistic discourse thus carries a set of social meanings that usually are politicized in the sense that they carry with them concepts of power that reflect the interests of the power élite. Discourse analysis of language and text is often used as a tool for identifying and defining social, economic, and historical power relations between dominant and subordinate groups.

Discourse analysis does more than analyse the social origins of linguistic forms. It also considers those sets of social relations ordered by a particular discourse; it identifies forms and practices and ways of behaving according to an identifiable discourse. Thus, in addition to texts, there are values, norms, attitudes, and behavioural practices associated with a specific discourse. As Goldberg (1993: 295) notes, the field of discourse involves 'discursive formation,' which is the totality of ordered relations and correlations of subject to each other and to objects; of economic production and reproduction; of cultural symbols and signification; of laws and moral rules; and of social, political, economic, and/or legal inclusion or exclusion.

Because social reality changes so quickly in a postmodern world that is characterized by massive globalization, any particular discourse is also influenced by these changes. Discourses therefore are dynamic, shifting, and ever-changing.

At another level, discourses can be analysed from the perspective of their constituent parts. Several dimensions or components of discourse can be identified (Goldberg, 1993). These include the following:

- A topic or area of social experience to which making sense is applied. Example: The social experience of race and racism in a postmodernist society such as Canada.
- A social position from which this sense is made and whose interests this sense promotes. Examples: Who defines racial discourse, and what position of power do these people and their institutions hold? And how does a racial discourse promote the interests of those in positions of privilege who define it?
- A repertoire of words, images, and practices by which meanings are circulated and power applied. Examples: Exclusionary employment and promotion practices, and media representations of people of colour.

Discourse functions to make sense of the social reality of lived experience. Specific conditions are made sense of within the social relations that structure them. To make sense of the world is to exert power over it, and to circulate that sense socially is to exert power over those who employ that sense in coping with daily life. At times, discourse becomes visible or audible, in a text, speech, or conversation. But it also works silently within the cognitive make-up of individuals as they attempt to interpret their rapidly changing world.

What Is Racist Discourse?

There is a discourse of racism that advances the interests of Whites, and that has an identifiable repertoire of words, images, and practices through which racial power is directed against minorities (Fiske, 1994). Foucault (1980) describes discourse as a technique used by the power élite to exert control over other constituent groups. Most contemporary societies, including Canada, are heterogeneous. Any analysis of such a society's culture must uncover the processes by which discourses repress, marginalize, and invalidate differences/'others'; by which these 'others' struggle for audibility and for access to the technologies of social circulation; and by which these 'others' fight to promote and defend the interests of their respective social formations.

Following Goldberg (1993: 47), racialized discourse includes far more than a set of descriptive representations about minority people, for example, representations of Blacks as 'niggers.' These representations are merely the tip of an iceberg in which are frozen various racist assumptions and ideas, which together constitute the foundation of a racialized discourse. These assumptions and ideas include the following:

- A set of premises about the nature of humankind: that there is a hierarchical classification in which some humans or races are different mentally and physically from others.
- A set of ethical choices that people make, such as to dominate, restrict, exclude, disrespect, or abuse human beings whom they consider lower on the classification scheme than themselves.
- A set of institutional regulations and practices ranging from severe state systems (such as apartheid) to exclusions from and restrictions on equal access to education, services, employment, and the like.

A racialized discourse is expressed in many different ways. For example, the subjects of race, racism, and alleged racial differences are often discussed and analysed by the media, by academics, by members of the legal and justice systems, by agencies of government, and so on. These constructions of expression may well contain elements of racialized discourse. These texts cover a wide spectrum of expressions, including a nation's written history; scientific forms of racist explanation; and economic, legal, bureaucratic, and religious forms of dogma (Goldberg, 1993). Such texts and other expressions may be, and often are, racist themselves. As Goldberg notes (1993: 42), 'the law, moral discourse, and the social sciences can thus silently incorporate racialized language ... while claiming to be *antiracist*.'

Thus, we can identify not only a 'racialized discourse' containing elements of belief, thought, and action, but also a 'racist expression'; both of these have hugely influenced social structures and culture.

Racist discourses and their expressions are cross-cultural, and permeate the language and the central institutions of the Western world. In particular, the media write about events in ways that are culturally racist, that is, by using racist images and stereotypes and representations (van Dijk, 1987).

Racist discourse as a part of culture may be understood as the fundamental form of racism because it includes ideas that are deeply embedded in society's value system. It is part of the invisible network of beliefs, attitudes, and assumptions that define society's system of cultural values.

Every society holds a multitude of beliefs and attitudes that it considers sacred and that help define and regulate the behaviour of its citizens. Examples: democracy is a superior form of societal organization; people are to be judged innocent until their guilt is established by due process of law; all people have an equal right to benefit from society's resources; parents should care for and educate their children. At the more mundane level of everyday behaviour, people should not raise their voices in public, should obey traffic signs, and so on.

Beliefs and values form the core of a society's culture. In North America, one of these existential beliefs is in the supremacy of European culture and civilization. Eurocentrism is one of the central values of Canadian society (and of other European-derived societies). It is a form of racism, therefore, in which certain people and their cultures are perceived to be superior to others, which will always be inferior. This is an important element in the racist discourse that characterizes North American and other Western societies. Because this discourse is so central to the thought and behaviour of people, its effects are deep-rooted and pervasive. Eurocentrism pervades all of the institutions in society and strongly influences the behaviour of the people who work in institutions and organizations, as well as the personal everyday behaviour of the citizenry.

Racist discourse finds its expression primarily in the perceptions, attitudes, and values of those who have always controlled and shaped cultural and organizational life in Canada. A Eurocentric bias provides the screen through which decision-makers in Canadian institutions filter their view of the world, establish priorities, assess ability, and allocate resources. Nowhere is this more apparent than in the arena of culture and cultural production.

Eurocentrism: The Basis of Racist Discourse

Eurocentrism is so pervasive that it is thought by many to be a matter of 'common sense.' Philosophy and literature, two dominant disciplines addressing the realm of human thought and art, are almost always thought of as originating in Europe. 'History' usually begins with an analysis of European history. More often than not, the history of civilization is taught in universities as the history of 'Western' civilization. Art forms such as music, visual arts, and literature are almost always understood to be the products of Europeans and neo-Europeans. In fact, as Shohat and Stam (1994) note, 'The residual traces of centuries of axiomatic European domination inform the general culture, the everyday language, and the media engendering a fictitious sense of the innate superiority of European-derived cultures and peoples' (1).

Eurocentrism, known also as the 'colonizer's model of the world' (ibid.: 2), received its main ideological thrust from European mercantile expansion. Between the fifteenth and eighteenth centuries, European countries were engaged in 'discovering,' exploring, subjugating, colonizing, and exploiting many areas of the world. Colonialism brought with it a way of life and a system of values based on the 'supremacy' of what the Europeans brought with them and on a concurrent dismissal of the 'native way of life.' This system of thought, developed to help maintain European political, military, and economic authority over the 'natives,' has been maintained until the present and is now so deeply ingrained in our value system as to become part of our 'common sense' understanding of the world. As Shohat and Stam (ibid.: 2) outline, Eurocentrism is a complex yet contradictory set of beliefs, which include the following:

- History began in Greece, and Europe alone is the 'motor for progressive historical change.'
- Non-European democracies are to be 'subverted' in favour of Western forms.
- The impact of Western oppressive practices, such as colonialism and slave trading, is to be downplayed as much as possible.
- The cultural and material production of non-Europeans is to be appropriated, the achievements of non-Europeans are to be denied.

The Eurocentrism of today is somewhat softer than earlier forms, but the belief in the innate superiority of European civilization, and of its products, and (above all) of its people, is still widespread and pervades the cultural value systems of most Westernized nations.

The Transmission of Racist Discourse: The Role of the Media

Values of Eurocentrism are embedded in the larger value system of society, but how do these values reach the ordinary citizen, and how do they exacerbate racism? Although values are learned through family and peer group socialization, through societal institutions (including schools), and so on, a key mechanism for transmitting cultural values is the media. For most adults past school age, the media are the main source of information, not only about events but also about their meaning. As a system of representation and a process of mass communication, the media perform a number of different functions, including information processing and reproduction, education, entertainment, employment, advertising. Most important, perhaps, is the role of the media in socialization.

For many people the mass media are a crucial source of beliefs and values, from which they develop a picture of their social world. The media play an important role in guiding and shaping how we perceive the world and how we relate to it as individuals. The print and electronic media have become major transmitters of society's cultural standards, myths, values, roles, and images. Because of the marginalization of minority communities from the mainstream of society, a significant proportion of mainstream people rely almost entirely on the media for their information and understanding of these groups and their communities.

In a liberal democracy, media institutions are expected to reflect alternative points of view, to remain neutral and objective, and to provide free and equitable access to all groups and classes. Journalists, editors, broadcasters, and directors of media organizations are not, however, always neutral, impartial, objective, and unbiased (Hall, 1973; Fleras and Elliot, 1992). Coverage of issues affecting people of colour is filtered through the assumptions of reporters, advertisers, journalists, editors, photographers, programmers, and producers who are mostly White. They have a context, a social location that affects how they interpret the event or situation. This context in turn influences what they choose to air or film, what they select, and what eventually gets included as part of the story (Troyna, 1984). The media also use a unique process of coding information, which is then 'decoded' in specific ways by the reader or viewer. Media representations play a key role in sending encoded messages, which the receiver is then free to 'read' in ways that reinforce the values associated with racist discourse and the promotion of Eurocentrism.

The media often select events that are atypical, present them in a stereotypical or sensational light, and contrast them against a pretext of normative White behaviour (Hall et al., 1975). Media professionals are often guided by a need to focus on the extraordinary, which sells well in the marketplace. It has also been argued that the reproduction of racism in the media – particularly in the press – takes the specific form of 'élite racism.' The media's dominant values are inextricably linked to those of political, social, and corporate élite groups, and it is in their interest to play a role in generating consensus. The mass media have nearly exclusive control over the resources required to produce popular opinion, especially as these relate to minorities (van Dijk, 1991). The case studies in this book demonstrate the validity of van Dijk's analysis of the media's role in reproducing White ideology.

The media have demonstrated a lack of responsiveness to the issues and challenges confronting minorities on a daily basis in relation to their access to mass communication in a multiracial and pluralistic society. 'Common sense' everyday discourse in the media generates images that reinforce cultural racism. Binaristic hierarchies divide society into 'them' and 'us.' 'We' includes members of the White mainstream, who are law-abiding, fair, progressive, rational, unemotional, and homogeneous, and who value and are committed to the values of a liberal democratic society. The 'others' represent the opposite of these attributes; 'they' challenge our most cherished principles and ideals (Shohat and Stam, 1994; Omi and Winant, 1993; van Dijk, 1991). These images help sustain White group dominance.

The media professionals (editors, journalists, broadcasters, producers, and the like) and their institutions control access between the power élites, who, we will argue throughout this book, include cultural producers and the mass audience. By controlling the qualitative aspects of the information that will become the audience's news, and by determining which events will dominate the 'agenda' of news programs, newspapers, and public discussion, and by selecting which 'expert' opinions will be utilized, the media assume the function of gatekeeper or agenda setter (ibid.).

Conclusions

This book focuses on some of the ideas, values, and meanings found at the very core of society's normative value system, and on how this value system emphasizes *difference*, particularly cultural and racial differences. The particular interest of this book is to document how racist discourse is manifested through cultural productions and cultural institutions.

This book looks at new forms of discourse that are being constructed by Aboriginal artists and writers, by writers, artists, and performers of colour, and by other cultural commentators and activists, to challenge and resist racist cultural production. The new cultural politics of difference consists of positive and creative responses to those systems of representation which reinforce the processes of exclusion, domination, and control. In the cultural politics of difference, existing paradigms of diversity and pluralism are re-examined and refashioned, and liberalism and multiculturalism are rearticulated in ways that incorporate the aesthetic agendas, products, and productions of racial minorities and other communities marked as 'others.'

In each of the case studies, the struggle over power is a focal issue. Power is at the centre of cultural politics. Systems of representation and cultural practices involve relations of power, and social power manifests itself in 'competing discourses' (Jordan and Weedon, 1995: 14). Power both enables and disables; it allows or denies individuals and groups opportunities and possibilities for self-realization and group recognition. Power also involves challenging the authority of mainstream cultural producers and cultural institutions. The struggle for power is to be seen in the context of the empowerment of individuals and communities, rather than 'power over' any group. This is a crucial distinction. Ethnoracial minorities are searching for ways to preserve control over their own lives, and the lives of their communities. They are no longer content to stand outside the doors of the museum, art gallery, theatre, radio station, or publishing house. They are demanding not only to enter the public culture but also to transform it. The ultimate goal is to affirm racial and cultural difference as the core of the social, cultural, and political life in Canada (Kulyk Keefer, 1996; Mackey, 1995).

References

Amit-Talai, V., and C. Knowles. 1996. *Re-Situating Identities: The Politics of Race, Ethnicity and Culture.* Toronto: Broadview.

Bennett, T. 1992. 'Putting Policy into Cultural Studies.' In L. Grossberg, C. Nelson, and P. Treichler, eds. *Cultural Studies.* New York: Routledge.

Derrida, Jacques. 1985. 'Racism's Last Word.' *Critical Inquiry.* 12(1) Autumn. 290–9.

During, Simon, ed. 1994. *The Cultural Studies Reader.* London: Routledge.

Featherstone, Michael. 1988. 'In Pursuit of the Postmodern: An Introduction.' In M. Featherstone, ed. *Postmodernism: Theory, Culture and Society* (Special Issue). 5: 195–213.

Fiske, John. 1994. *Media Matters: Everyday Culture and Political Change.* Minneapolis: University of Minnesota Press.

Fleras, Augie, and Jean Elliot. 1992. *Multiculturalism in Canada.* Scarborough, Ont.: Nelson Canada.

Foucault, Michel. 1980. *Power/Knowledge Selected Interviews and Other Writings, 1972–1977.* Ed. Colin Gordon. New York: Pantheon.

Goldberg, David. 1993. *Racist Culture: Philosophy and the Politics of Meaning.* Oxford, U.K.: Blackwell.

Grossberg, Lawrence. 1993. 'Cultural Studies and/in New Worlds.' In C. McCarthy and W. Critchlow, eds. *Race, Identity and Representation in Education.* New York and London: Routledge. 89–105.

Hall, Stuart. 1973. *The Structured Communication of Events.* Birmingham, U.K.: Centre for Contemporary Cultural Studies.

Hall, Stuart, C. Critcher, T. Jefferson, J. Clarke, and B. Roberts. 1975. 'Newsmaking and Crime.' Paper presented at NACRO Conference on Crime and the Media. Birmingham: University of Birmingham Centre for Contemporary Studies.

Henry, Frances, Carol Tator, Winston Mattis, and Tim Rees. 1995. *The Colour of Democracy: Racism in Canadian Society.* Toronto: Harcourt Brace.

Jordan, Glenn, and Chris Weedon. 1995. *Cultural Politics: Class, Gender, Race and the Postmodern World.* Oxford, U.K., and Cambridge, Mass.: Blackwell.

Knauft, B.M. 1994. 'Pushing Anthropology Past the Posts: Critical Notes on Cultural Anthropology and Cultural Studies as Influenced by Postmodernism and Existentialism.' *Critique of Anthropology.* 14: 2. 117–52.

Kulyk Keefer, Janice. 1996. 'Writing, Reading, Teaching Transcultural in Canada.' In H. Braum and W. Klooss, eds. *Multiculturalism in North America and Europe: Social Practices – Literary Visions.* Wissenschaftlicher Verlag Trier.

Lyotard, Jean-Francois. 1986. *The PostModern Condition: A Report on Knowledge.* Manchester: Manchester University Press.

Mackey, Eva. 1995. 'Postmodernism and Cultural Politics in a Multicultural Nation: Contests over Truth in the *Into the Heart of Africa* Controversy.' *Public Culture.* 7(2) Winter. 403–31.

Mercer, Kobena. 1992. 'Periodising Postmodern Politics and Identity.' In L. Grossberg, C. Nelson, and P. Treichler, eds. *Cultural Studies.* New York: Routledge. 424–38.

Omi, M., and H. Winant. 1993. 'On the Theoretical Concept of Race.' In C. McCarthy and W. Crichlow, eds. *Race, Identity and Representation in Education.* New York and London: Routledge.

Shohat, Ella, and Robert Stam. 1994. *Unthinking Eurocentrism: Multiculturalism and the Media.* London and New York: Routledge.

Siddiqui, Haroon. 1993. 'Media and Race: Failing to Mix the Message.' *Toronto Star.* 24 April. D1, D5.

Sypnowich, Christine. 1996. 'Some Disquiet about Difference.' In J. Hart and R. Bauman, eds. *Explorations in Difference: Law, Culture and Politics.* Toronto: University of Toronto Press. 117–36.

Troyna, Barry. 1984. 'Media and Race Relations.' In E. Cashmore, ed. *Dictionary of Race and Ethnic Relations*. London: Routledge.

Turner, Terence. 1994 'Anthropology and Multiculturalism: What Is Anthropology that Multiculturalists Should Be Mindful of It?' In David Goldberg, ed. *Multiculturalism: A Critical Reader*. Oxford: Blackwell. 406–25.

van Dijk, Teun A. 1987. *Communicating Racism: Ethnic Prejudice in Thought and Talk*. Newbury, CA: Sage.

– 1991. *Racism and the Press*. London: Routledge.

West, Cornel. 1990. 'The New Cultural Politics of Difference.' In Russell Ferguson, ed. *Out There: Marginalization and Contemporary Culture*. Cambridge, Mass.: MIT Press.

Williams, Raymond. 1976. 2nd ed. 1983. *Keywords*. London: Fontana.

2

Into the Heart of Africa

Background

The Royal Ontario Museum (ROM) is a highly respected cultural institution of international stature. In November 1989 it mounted an exhibition, called *Into the Heart of Africa*, consisting of about 375 artifacts from Central and West Africa that had been stored by the ROM for over one hundred years. Some of these artifacts had been acquired by Canadian soldiers who participated in Britain's colonial campaigns in the late nineteenth century. Others had been collected by Canadian missionaries between 1875 and 1925, as they worked to bring 'Christianity, civilization, and commerce' to African tribal societies. (So explained the caption of the first panel in the exhibition's Missionary Room.)

The theme of the exhibition, which closed in August 1990, was the role played by Canadians in the European colonization of Africa. The exhibition was divided into five thematic areas: 'The Imperial Connection,' 'Military Hall,' 'Missionary Room,' 'Ovimbundu Compound,' and 'Africa Room.' The first three sections focused on Western views of Africa and included such items as photographs of Canadian missionaries and military stations, reproductions of newspaper articles, period drawings, objects such as scales used to measure gold dust for the colonizers, and spears that White soldiers brought home after their battles against Africans. The displays in the last two sections were designed to highlight aspects of African life and culture. The exhibits for the Ovimbundu Compound were intended to reveal African life as the missionaries would have witnessed and interpreted it. In the Africa Room were displayed cultural forms such as masks, beaded jewellery, and musical instruments, which were displayed as they have conventionally been presented in Western museums (Schildkrout, 1991).

Dr Jeanne Cannizzo, an anthropologist and specialist in African art, learned of the existence of this collection and expressed an interest in developing a museum exhibit. The ROM hired her as a guest curator, and she, working with the ROM's in-house staff, proceeded to research the collection, and plan and design the exhibit.

In explaining the aims of this exhibit Dr Cannizzo suggested that the show was intended to examine both Canadian and African sensibilities. She described the objects of the ROM collection as an expression 'not only of the world view of those who chose to make and use them, but also of those who chose to collect and exhibit them' (Cannizzo, 1991: 151). She stressed that the show's objectives were these: to illustrate the social history that provided the context of the exhibit; to present the collection as cultural texts through which the life histories of the objects in the show could be discovered; to illustrate the complexities of cross-cultural encounters; and to expose the racist assumptions of those Canadians involved in the colonization and missionizing of Africa (ROM Catalogue, 1992).

Cannizzo, in another perspective on this collection, suggested that 'this art was collected as representative of a certain phase of Canadian history. I wanted to use that perspective in some way. It does not reflect the African reality. Rather, it reflects what Europeans found exciting, or horrible, or bizarre in what they encountered – and they brought back these objects' (in Da Breo, 1989/90a: 37).

Da Breo went on to suggest that the exhibition was intended to acknowledge Canada's colonial past by examining these cultural artifacts and the processes by which they had been collected. Also to show that White Canada had a somewhat less than perfect understanding of the richness of complex African societies.

Despite these positive intentions, sadly, 'the museum was unable to recognize the opportunity presented to it to do exactly what it said the show was intended to do' (Nourbese Philip, 1992: 103). Instead, the exhibition became the most controversial and contested show in the history of the ROM.

Those who opposed the exhibition viewed *Into the Heart of Africa* as an expression and demonstration of cultural racism and cultural appropriation, in that objects belonging to others had been seized, and possessed, and then given away. The military took weapons; the merchants took gold, ivory, and crafts; and the missionaries took idols and other sacred objects. 'Collectively, they left nothing in Africa which struck them as valuable' (Da Breo, 1989/90b: 36). In each instance, control of the possessions was maintained by members of the dominant culture.

Through this process of acquisition, the true meaning and significance of these artifacts in the lives of African peoples was decontextualized and lost.

Critics of the exhibition argued that the narrative which held the fragmentary collection together was told from a White, Eurocentric perspective, and that African voices and their interpretations of these events had been silenced. Thus, in a sense, the real story of Africa and its peoples remained untold (Crean, 1991; Schildkrout, 1991; Itwaru and Ksonzek, 1994).

Sequence of Events

In the spring of 1989, after several months of research, planning, and design, the ROM was ready to open the exhibition. As it does for all major exhibitions, the museum set about marketing the event among those who would have the most interest in attending. On the assumption that the Black community would want to attend the exhibition, it hosted a reception in June to which it invited (among others) individuals involved in the arts in the Black community – specifically, the African-Canadian community. A consultant, a Black woman named Sandra Whiting, was hired to help publicize and market the exhibition and to facilitate outreach to the Black community.

Before the exhibition opened, the ROM distributed a promotional brochure. One of those to receive it was a teacher, Elizabeth Parchment, who worked at the Toronto Board of Education. Before the reception she met with Hari Lalla, curriculum adviser for race relations and multiculturalism at the Toronto board, to express her concern about the brochure, which she felt contained stereotypical language. As students and teachers were to be invited to view the exhibition, she felt strongly that the board should respond to what she regarded as the 'alarming nature of the brochure.' This same concern would later be expressed by members of the African-Canadian community. The language in the brochure called attention to the glories of the Imperial Age, and to the heroism of Dr David Livingstone, the missionary explorer who has been romanticized throughout history (though he was viewed in a very different light by Africans). The brochure emphasized that 'trophies of war' would be included as a major part of the exhibition (Da Breo, 1989/90b).

The Toronto Board of Education asked for an interview with the ROM to discuss some of its concerns about both the brochure and the exhibition. At the meeting, which was attended by Parchment and Lalla of the Toronto board and by Dr Cannizzo and two members of her staff, the two board representatives suggested changes both to the brochure and to the design and composition of the exhibition itself. They left the meeting with assurances that their suggestions for changes would be considered (Lalla and Myers, 1990).

The actual outcome of this discussion was that the ROM decided to hold two focus groups following the reception with the Black community, to assess whether the concerns of Parchment and Lalla were shared by others. However, the focus groups were intended to measure the negative impact only of the brochure, not the exhibition itself.

At the reception held on 28 June 1989, which was attended primarily by African-Canadian visual artists and writers, several ROM staff members made presentations describing the completed exhibition. It became clear during the reception that the ROM and the community had two diametrically opposed agendas for the evening. The ROM was really looking for endorsement and support for the exhibition and for help in promoting it in the Black community. For their part, members of the Black community, after a private viewing, had a number of questions and concerns regarding the museum's approach – in particular, the interpretation of the historical events surrounding the acquisition of the cultural objects on display. They were offended by the notion that the exhibition would be seen (as implied in the brochure) through the eyes of Livingstone, the missionary explorer who influenced a steady stream of Christian followers to bring 'the word of God into new and unknown lands' (Da Breo, 1989/90b: 32). Those participating in this discussion made a number of suggestions to the curator about how the exhibition could be altered so as to provide a more unbiased presentation.

They wanted assurances that the exhibition would reflect a balance between African and Western descriptions of the meaning and significance of the artifacts being displayed. They also wanted a commitment from ROM officials that the objects exhibited, and the commentaries attached to them, would be free of bias and stereotyping. They said they expected the displays and accompanying texts to accurately reflect how the objects had been collected. Finally, they felt that the exhibition should provide some insight and critical commentary on Canada's role as 'Defenders of the Empire' during the colonial age (Da Breo, 1989/90b).

There was a wide gap between the responses of the ROM officials and those of the African-Canadian community to the exhibition: 'The community was undergoing a collective seizure. The ROM, by contrast, held onto its business suit for dear life ... One had the impression that like the dinosaurs in their collection, the ROM Directors were clumsily lumbering through unfamiliar, unfriendly territory' (Da Breo, 1989/90b: 34).

After the reception the ROM conducted the two focus groups with members of the African-Canadian community. The one concrete result of these discussions was that the museum decided to rework and reprint the brochures. The same discussions also made it clear to museum officials that they had better hire someone to do some outreach with the African-Canadian community and to develop some programming to showcase present-day Africa. Abdu Kasozi, an African with a doctorate in history, was retained as program director for five months, to help co-ordinate various lectures, workshops, music and dance performances, and screenings of African films. These were to be presented at the museum in February 1990, in conjunction with Black History Month.

In November 1989 the ROM opened the exhibition. From the brochure, deeply offensive wording such as 'dark continent,' 'trophies of war,' and 'mysterious land' had been removed. However, this 'improved' brochure now included a photograph of a bare-breasted, partially painted, barefoot, grass-skirted African woman. This image was as offensive to many members of the Black community as the language had been in the earlier brochure. Also, the image of the woman seemed to bear no relationship to the supposed themes of *Into the Heart of Africa*.

Shortly after the exhibition opened, a group of twelve Black community leaders were invited to view it. Charles Roach, a prominent lawyer and social activist, wrote in the *Toronto Star*: 'As we entered the exhibition we were confronted by displays that immediately chilled us. So upset were some in the group that only four of us completed the tour' (5 June 1990). Others had similar experiences. Susan Crean: 'I left the show feeling nervous and slightly ill' (1991: 26). Marlene Nourbese Philip: 'I came out of the show feeling physically dejected' (in Drainie, 1990).

Artist and writer Natasha Ksonzek (in Itwaru and Ksonzek, 1994) described her walk through the exhibition in the following way: 'The pathways I follow do not acknowledge me. Although knowledge is said to be kept here I do not feel empowered by it. I feel my own life-flesh a trespass against the silence of death here, my frailty against the all-encompassing stone around me, as if I'm trading something of myself for their information' (88).

Clem Marshall, a teacher with the Toronto Board of Education, wrote the following in a letter to *The Globe and Mail*: 'The overall impact of the exhibition is negative because it infantilizes the African peoples depicted, although many of the objects bear testimony to the skill and developed aesthetics of those who created them. In fact the cumulative tone of the exhibition is paternalistic and paternalism is the form of racism we encounter most often in Canadian society' (25 March 1995).

After viewing the exhibition, Molefe Kete Asante, chair of African Studies at Temple University in Philadelphia, denounced the exhibition: 'They have reinforced the same kind of arrogance the missionaries had. The presentation of Africa is not only fragmentary, it is limited and gives a very, very negative impression' (in Crean, 1991: 124).

Over the next several months the protests escalated. Sixteen Black groups formed a coalition calling itself the Coalition for the Truth about Africa. In the spring of 1990 they began demonstrating against the exhibition in front of the ROM. Their demands were straightforward: continue to exhibit the objects but change or clarify the explanatory texts – otherwise, close the show. At the heart of their grievances was this question: 'Why, in the first seventy-seven years history of the ROM, does the first "African" exhibit have to be from a colonial perspective?' (from the CFTA Information Kit). This question received no answer from the ROM, and there were very few changes.

The coalition concentrated its demonstrations on Saturdays, a particularly busy day for the museum. Twenty to fifty demonstrators, carrying signs and placards and distributing pamphlets, would appear early each Saturday. Several of the demonstrators would read speeches, using a bullhorn to attract the crowds. They called the museum the 'Racist Ontario Museum,' and while they did not demand that the exhibition be closed, they urged the museum to change or clarify the offending explanatory texts.

The ROM responded by saying that there were no plans to change the show in any way, that the show was historically accurate and people were simply reacting to it in different ways. The museum's director stated publicly that the museum would stand by its curator and the exhibition. Dr Cannizzo, in the meantime, kept a low profile and declined to speak about the controversy (Butler, 1993).

On at least two occasions, the demonstrations turned violent. In one instance, a few of the demonstrators had raised their voices at visitors trying to enter the museum. Officials called the police, who tried to break up the demonstration. Thirty-five police officers and some fifty demonstrators were involved in a violent confrontation. Two demonstrators were arrested, and two policemen and several demonstrators were hurt. In the wake of this incident, the ROM applied for and received an injunction from the Supreme Court of Ontario forbidding protesters to picket within fifty feet of the museum's entrance. The following day, more than seventy-five people chanting 'ROM is Racist Ontario Museum' gathered to continue the demonstrations.

The exhibition closed nine months later. Following the controversy in Toronto, the exhibition was cancelled in four cities (two in Canada and two in the United States).

Analysis

Racist Discourse

One of the fundamental problems identified with the exhibition was the heavy reliance on irony to deliver the message[1] (Butler, 1993; Hutcheon, 1994). Examples: the exhibition's liberal use of quotation marks around words and phrases charged with meaning such as 'Darkest Africa,' 'the unknown continent,' 'barbarous' people, and White missionaries bringing 'light' to a continent 'full of Muslims, and animists and fetishists.' The quotation marks were meant to caution viewers as to the racist assumptions underlying these labels. The quotation marks around phrases containing demeaning stereotypes were intended to distance the museum from these concepts – as if punctuation could relieve the curator from responsibility for using derogative images of Africa and African peoples (Itwaru and Ksonzek, 1994).

What the curator and the ROM failed to recognize was that the irony of the exhibition's texts required a certain degree of shared knowledge between the curator and the observer (Butler, 1993). Many visitors did not understand that the texts were written to reflect two voices (that of the colonizer/missionary and that of the museum); as a result, they interpreted the images and phrases such as 'barbarous customs' literally. This is reflected in the comment of one visitor (for example), who thanked the ROM for the lovely show on 'primitive Africa' (Crean, 1991: 26). Also, many members of the African-Canadian, Black, and other communities in Toronto, even those who possessed this knowledge and clearly recognized the irony, still felt that the exhibition only reinforced racist stereotypes and assumptions.

What the museum failed to realize was the power of discourse. Words and phrases such as 'Darkest Africa' conjure up different meanings for different people. Readers, viewers, and listeners are likely to understand these concepts in the context of their own cultural frameworks, their own histories, and their respective discursive communities. Words do more than label: they impose an order on perception and create categories of things. The language patterns and habits of a particular cultural community predispose that community to certain interpretations. Words can become weapons, and the misuse of terms can wound, and constitute a form of assault.

Discourse is language in social use (Fiske, 1994). Language is not some abstract system; rather, the process of making meaning out of words is influenced by historical, social, and political conditions. For those who opposed the exhibition, the language it utilized had the effect of erasing the history of domination, subordination, and resistance that was part of the colonial experience in Africa. The discourse of the exhibition also failed to recognize the relationship between those reference points and the experience of racism for African Canadians living in Canada today. At the same time, the story was being told from the perspective of White Canadians: the missionaries and soldiers who were part of the colonization of Africa.

Thus, there were really two alternative discourses, reflecting two radically contrasting points of view. The words or images became so imbued with disparate meanings for different users that whatever the aim of the curator, it became impossible for those words and images to be read and understood 'objectively.' Every discursive community interprets words, images, and actions, and then constructs meanings that make sense to them based on their particular life histories, experiences, and social contexts (Mackey, 1995; Hutcheon, 1994; Schildkrout, 1991).

Regardless, then, of the curator's stated intentions, phrases such as 'Darkest Africa,' 'savage customs,' 'Defenders of the Empire,' and 'unknown continent' supported and preserved racist traditions, and framing them in quotations did not make their use more justifiable (Itwaru and Ksonzek, 1994). In much the same way, the phrase found on the first plaque – 'those who returned brought home "souvenirs" of their journey into the Heart of Africa' – resonated with very different meanings for African-Canadian and Anglo-Canadian viewers.

For many African Canadians, this taking of 'souvenirs' invoked historic memories of cumulative acts of subjugation. The objects represented a legacy of pillage and destruction of a people and a culture (ibid.). But for those who took these artifacts, for the institution that collected them, and for those viewers who shared a similar cultural framework, these images and objects represented the political, cultural, and religious symbols of a particular place and period in history.

Many of the critics of *Into the Heart of Africa*, especially educators visiting the exhibition with their students, expressed concern about the strong likelihood that children would miss the irony of the messages. From the perspective of these educators, the use of irony was clearly an inappropriate learning tool. A Black student commented: 'I look at those spears and shields and all I can think of is how did they get them? By killing Africans, that's how. What am I supposed to feel?' (in Lalla and Myers, 1990).

The school board representatives argued that relying on irony as a vehicle for implying criticism of cultural imperialism and racism was both ineffective and inappropriate: 'Irony is a method of distancing oneself from what one is saying or observing; the sense of superiority inherent in its use is inappropriate in these circumstances' (Lalla and Myers, 1990: 3).

Even the museum's volunteer guides failed to understand the irony. One teacher, who visited the exhibition twice with classes, noted that the unsatisfactory information the tour guides provided only strengthened the negative impact of the exhibition. She found the guides unable to explain or interpret the exhibits without sharing their racist assumptions and understandings of the displays (McClelland, 1990: 10).

For example, one guide told a group of students that 'the missionaries civilized the pagans of Africa,' and that the Zulu were 'an extremely vicious tribe' (ibid.: 10). Another guide, this one for a grade five class, explained that missionaries taught the Africans to carve wood. This same guide offered that a mask was used to practise 'barbaric rituals, vicious, barbaric rituals.' Another guide offered that African girls must have been crazy to put pieces of ivory through their noses (ibid.: 10).

One of the ROM security staff responsible for monitoring the exhibition, who was on duty at least three times a week for the entire ten months it ran, observed that it took him a long time to understand that the show was really only comprehensible to a few, and open to misunderstanding by all others (Fulford, 1991: 25).

Racist Images

At the core of much of the criticism of the ROM's exhibit were the actual images that formed the display. The concern was with how these objects misrepresented and dehumanized African peoples and misinterpreted their history. The Africans in this exhibition were repeatedly depicted as objects. The lens of the camera held by the missionary or colonizer captured the 'object,' but the 'objects' were rendered by the oppressor as powerless, passive, and silent. The exhibition was totally 'devoid of images and voices of resistance' to colonial subjugation (Butler, 1993: 63). The Africans captured by camera lens seemed not to be contesting their oppression in any way.

Yet many times in the history of the colonization and missionizing of Africa, African peoples resisted imperial domination both physically and in writing. This could have been an important part of the narrative. Instead, viewers were confronted with numerous examples of passive Africans seeming to stoically accept their fate.

Among the dozens of controversial images and objects included in this exhibition was a very large engraving (approximately 2 by 2.5 metres), depicting Lord Beresford thrusting his sword through a shield into the heart of a Zulu man. It was labelled with its original caption, 'Lord Beresford's Encounter with a Zulu.' The word 'encounter' here was being used ironically and satirically. Near the engraving was a display of Zulu spears and shields. Beside it was another picture of Zulu soldiers, who were described in quotes as 'savages.'

Another photograph showed a missionary, Mrs Thomas Titcombe, offering 'a lesson in how to wash clothes' to Yagba women in Northern Nigeria in 1915 (from the caption accompanying the photograph). In the information kit distributed by members of the Coalition for the Truth about Africa (CFTA, 1990), this question is posed: 'Did Africans not know how to wash before the arrival of Europeans?' (CFTA, 1990: 1). How do you explain 'the cultural bias and racial arrogance of that image of African women who do not appear to know how to wash clothes to schoolchildren?' (Crean, 1991: 25).

Still another photograph, entitled 'Insights and Illusions,' captured the image of a young African woman. This one was taken by the Reverend A.W. Banfield, a Canadian missionary, who explained in the accompanying text that the woman had to be held while he set up his camera. The 'poor creature thought I was going to kill her with that horrid looking thing, the camera.' Ksonzek suggests that the Reverend is undeterred by her pain and the photograph of the nameless and silenced woman 'appears as the illustration for Banfield's anecdote. And for our amusement.' The Reverend controls her image and voice and the viewers collaborate in this act of violation, gazing at the image he has created (Itwaru and Kzonzek, 1994: 85).

Into the Heart of Africa was filled with uncritical presentations of 'the booty of soldiers and spiritual "exotica" collected by missionaries' (Nourbese Philip, 1992: 104). It seemed as if the taking of these 'mementos' was being celebrated by the museum – as if the having and displaying of these artifacts was more important than the history and manner in which the objects had been obtained (Itwaru and Ksonzek, 1994). There was a bias that informed the entire presentation. The objects themselves were in fact spoils, and not part of legitimately acquired art collections. The people who collected them were part of an invasive process that involved the economic and cultural exploitation of African nations (Lalla and Myers, 1990).

In an exhibit titled 'The Front Hallway of Beverly House,' a wall of war 'trophies' including captured spears and shields arranged with gemsbok and hartebeest horns was prominently displayed. Africa was 'reduced to the decor of a wealthy European, a carefully replicated presence celebrating the cultural violation of the African ... what is African is lost' (Itwaru and Ksonzek, 1994). Here again, the museum missed an opportunity to add its authoritative voice and provide commentary or pose critical questions (Schildkrout, 1991).

Soldiers' artifacts were presented with a kind of nostalgic reverence for the military conquest of Africa. Most disturbing to Susan Crean was the displaying of a military helmet that belonged to her great-uncle John Crean, a professional soldier, a man she described as someone who 'spent his entire adult life in one part or another of the globe killing native people on behalf of God, Queen and Empire. His job was to provide the brute force necessary to keep "Pax" Britannica operating in the interests of the British merchant class' (1991: 23).

Crean was dismayed to find her great-uncle treated as an important historical figure – to see him memorialized, with his military helmet and booty of Hausa weaponry and Asante objects displayed in a glass case (the essential framing device of museums). The positioning of the helmet in the centre of the dark opening gallery unintentionally communicated a sense of reverence or glorification of the object (Hutcheon, 1994; Schildkrout, 1991). The soldier's life was further illustrated with newspaper accounts from the battlefront.

On the same military theme, the photograph of Canadian troops leaving Ottawa was accompanied by a plaque reading 'Defenders of the Empire,' the implication being that these soldiers were heroes, not invaders setting out to kill Africans. It was clear from the photograph, and from the information provided by the plaque hanging next to it, whose interests were actually being represented here. A plaque informed the viewer that the soldiers, as British subjects, were 'campaigning against African peoples who resisted the imperial advance and sometimes against rival European powers.' What was missing was some explanation as to why there was a war, and who was going thousands of miles to another continent, and what reason they had for fighting people on behalf of Britain (Itwaru and Ksonzek, 1994).

One visitor from Uganda, commenting on the central flaw in the exhibition, noted that 'the show gives an overwhelming colonial impression. If the ROM is trying to say that these are historical facts and we're ashamed of them, that message doesn't come through' (in Crean, 1991). Sharing a similar concern, Black broadcaster and writer Robert Payne commented that 'the glorification of colonialism in so multicultural a city as Toronto is colossally bad judgement ... Given our druthers, most of us are a touch reluctant to celebrate the men who raped our grandmothers' (in Crean, 1991: 27).

In the same way, African Canadians saw little point in highlighting the role of Dr David Livingstone, who featured prominently in this exhibition. But what did those who saw this exhibition learn of this man and those who followed him? In a pen-and-ink drawing, 'Livingstone's Last March,' he was not marching at all; rather, he was being carried on a sling by two Africans, which only reinforced the image of Africans as 'inferior' beasts of burden for the White man (Itwaru and Ksonzek, 1994). Again, it was up to the viewer to catch the subtlety and irony here; no help was provided. How many museum-goers understood this curating device and grasped the point?

An audio-visual slide show in the exhibition, 'In Livingstone's Footsteps,' provided viewers with a simulation of a lecture that missionaries might have delivered to a congregation of worshippers in the nineteenth and early twentieth centuries, during the period of the missionization of Africa. The lecture was filled with highly derogatory, culturally racist, and paternalistic language. There was a caption at the entrance to the room and an oral disclaimer by the narrator at the beginning and end of the show explaining that this was a fictional re-enactment; even so, most viewers surely missed this important information, as relatively few people sit through an entire presentation in museum exhibitions. Moreover, the derogatory phrases from the soundtrack could be heard by visitors throughout the first part of the exhibition (Crean, 1991; Schildkrout, 1991).

The last area of the exhibition, the 'Africa Room' was intended to present a picture of African life and to move the viewer from a focus on the history of the collection to an emphasis on the 'varied economies, political or cosmological complexities, and artistry of their African creators' (Cannizzo, 1991: 156). However, as the text at the entrance to this section acknowledged, the artifacts were displayed in a manner that would have been familiar to late-nineteenth-century museum visitors, 'but not to the people who made them. The things are theirs, the arrangement is not.'

The Role of the Museum and Ethnography

One of the central problems in the controversy over *Into the Heart of Africa* was the lack of a critical understanding of how, in a contemporary context, people today might view and interpret the museum's collection. Many people of colour – particularly African Canadians, who did not identify with the world view of those who traditionally have served as curators, board members, and museum staff – felt that the ROM never really comprehended the larger meaning of the collection of artifacts. This exhibition provided some insight into the role that museums have played in *appropriating* exotic objects, facts, and meanings. *Into the Heart of Africa* used 'Africa' as an ethnographic object, that is, as a scientific description of a culture, and a people, from the perspective of a Western cultural institution.

The process the museum employed in conceptualizing and developing *Into the Heart of Africa* was based on the anthropological model of objectification in which the West renders the world as object, or, more specifically, 'the world as exhibition' (Mitchell, 1989: 219–22). This process of organizing and ordering the world is analogous to the processes of colonialism. As is clear from the feelings that many members of the Black community expressed after seeing the exhibition, the outcome of this process was an overwhelming sense of pain, powerlessness, and alienation.

What was missing from the discourse was the social, economic, and political realities and conditions that shaped, influenced, and disfigured the 'object.' The meaning of the African experience within the context of British-Canadian imperial conquest had been lost. As one of the texts, 'The Life History of Objects in the Exhibit,' informed the viewer, the spear (for example) became a trophy, which later appeared as decorative art and eventually was incorporated into a museum collection as an ethnographic object. What the museum failed to document was the significance *of the action itself,* through which these objects became part of this collection (Itwaru and Ksonzek, 1994).

Those who challenged this exhibition were contesting 'the museum as artifact for its uncritical and traditional presentation of these objects – the booty of soldiers and spiritual "exotica" collected by missionaries' (Nourbese Philip, 1992: 105). The critics of the exhibition were challenging the ROM's right to make the continent of Africa an ethnographic object.

In the West, collecting has been a vehicle for the 'deployment of a possessive self, culture and authenticity' (Clifford, 1990: 143). Museum collections create an illusion of an accurate representation of a set of experiences, by cutting objects out of specific historical or cultural context and making them exemplify abstract wholes – using, for example, the display of a tribal mask or other cultural artifact to represent a complex culture.

Even though many of the cultural artifacts displayed in *Into the Heart of Africa* clearly reflected a high level of skill and a well-developed artistic sense on the part of the Africans who created them, the exhibition communicated little information about these objects. For example, the viewer observed a beautiful Asante gold necklace but learned nothing about it, except by whom it was collected. In other words, 'the collector discovers, acquires, salvages objects. The objective world is given, not produced and thus historical relations of power in the work of acquisition are hidden or unrevealed' (Clifford, 1990: 144).

Nowhere in the last section of the exhibition were Africans given a voice, or an opportunity to respond to the demeaning stereotypes and racist commentary quoted in the texts accompanying the displays. Given that the curator had conceived of the exhibition as a dialogue, she should have provided an opportunity for this to happen (Schildkrout, 1991).

In the *Toronto Star,* Charles Roach, a prominent member of the Black community, questioned the ROM's role and objectives in this exhibition: 'I have to ask what is the ROM's objective in presenting Africa in 1990 from the perspective of the missionaries? Why show the colonials trampling through Africa imposing their lifestyle on the people? To me, it's a form of cultural genocide and I put it in the larger context of what's happening to Black people in Toronto – the police shootings and the discrimination we face' (5 June 1990).

In this same context, the CFTA posed a rhetorical question: Would an exhibition on the Holocaust ever be acceptable told from the perspective of the Nazis?

Because it glorified acts like the slaying of the Zulus – which was really the precursor to apartheid and to the enslavement of Africans in their own country – Roach found the exhibition chilling. A related problem was this: 'By presenting the African collection through the history of its donors, by giving pride of place to the personal stories of the white Canadians who happened to bring them to Canada, Cannizzo creates a context in which that history is claimed rather than criticized and rejected' (Crean, 1991: 121).

In his report to the Toronto Board of Education, Myers highlighted some of the historical biases contained in the exhibition, and made the point that 'history' is not 'the past' but what historians 'do' with those traces of the past that have been left (Lalla and Myers, 1990). 'All historical accounts are biased in that they involve a conscious selection of data in order to explain why.'

One might ask: What prevented the museum from taking a more critical approach to the subject? Were they worried about offending their important patrons, some of whom probably donated artifacts to the collection? (Butler, 1993: 57). From a broader perspective, were they worried about offending the significant numbers of museum-goers who belong to the dominant culture, and who expect and want to see a familiar approach to the displays and exhibits? Whatever the museum's stated intentions, what is clear from the above analysis is that the exhibition was essentially developed from a White perspective for a White audience.

Institutional Resistance and Marginalization

The protest by members of the Black community and others was not merely about the discourse and images contained in the exhibition; it also targeted the marginalizing and exclusionary process that the ROM employed in developing the exhibition. Dr Cannizzo had suggested that 'by studying the museum as artifact, reading collections as cultural texts, and discovering life as objects one could have a better understanding of the complexities of cross-cultural encounters' (1989: 92). Yet the ROM missed the opportunity to do just that; they missed the chance to create a meaningful dialogue with a community that had an enormous investment in an exhibition focusing on the African experience – the first such exhibition in the museum's history.

As Nourbese Philip later commented: 'The African Canadian demonstrators and other objectors *outside* the museum were, in fact, an integral part of the cultural text *inside* the museum' (1992: 105). As the same writer went on to explain, the ROM had argued that the exhibition was designed to inform Canadians about a period of Canadian history and a series of events about which Canadians did not know. However, this critical question remained: Which Canadians was the ROM referring to – Canadians of European descent or Canadians of African origin? 'Or was the ROM perhaps defining "Canadian" as someone of European heritage?' African Canadians know the history of Canadian participation in African colonialism and live with its implications and consequences as part of their everyday life (ibid.).

The historical issues and their contemporary application were simply not given adequate representation. The perspectives shaping this exhibition, and the meanings given to the objects, were based on a White Western patriarchical Protestant view of the world. It was this particularized version of life and history that the protesters were criticizing. They were really posing this question: 'Does Western knowledge control the framework of the relevant evidence?' (Townsend-Gault, 1992: 77)

The controversy between the Black community and the ROM reflected two contrary perspectives on the respective roles of curators, anthropologists, and cultural communities in developing exhibitions, programs, and other practices within museums. The traditional view of museums is that the experts – those who are trained and highly educated specialists – should be the arbiters in matters dealing with museum exhibitions and other institutional practices. A more contemporary, populist approach would support the stance taken by those who contested the decisions made by the ROM for *Into the Heart of Africa*: that 'African Canadians who objected to the display were, in fact, presenting a *different*, not an *inferior*, way of knowing from the museum "expert"' (Nourbese Philip, 1992: 106).

There is a growing understanding among some museologists that the community has an important role to play in shaping the content of exhibits; and that curators have a responsibility to involve communities, in a meaningful and substantive way, in the planning and implementation of programs and exhibitions. In multiracial, pluralistic cities like Toronto, there is a huge reservoir of expertise in communities such as the African-Canadian community. Individuals in these groups (quoted extensively in this chapter) could have done much to help contextualize the exhibition, and could have provided critical feedback on how different audiences were likely to respond to the ROM's approach in *Into the Heart of Africa*. However, this would have required going beyond token outreach and consultation. What was needed was a willingness to share institutional power, and an openness to systemic changes at every level of the organization.

The Smithsonian Institute in Washington, D.C., provides an example of an institutional response to the issue of cultural and racial biases reflected in the policies, programs, and practices of cultural institutions. The Smithsonian is America's largest cultural institution. In 1993 a special task force was established to examine the relationship between the Smithsonian Institute and the Hispanic community. It found that Hispanic achievements were grossly underrepresented in exhibits, and that in terms of staffing Hispanics held only 3 per cent of the more than 6,500 jobs at the institute. Robert Sullivan, associate director of public programs, suggested that what was wrong with the Smithsonian and other museums in general was that 'they freeze cultures in time. They depict a colonial lifestyle that is no longer tolerated. What we need is a multiple viewpoint, showing an interconnected global universe' (in Shanahan, 1994).

The Smithsonian has now committed itself to systemic changes – including changes to its mandate, hiring practices, and curatorial practices, and to the exhibits in the sixteen museums that form the institute – in order to better represent and reflect the contributions of Hispanics, African Americans, and Native Americans to American history and culture. For example, the Smithsonian Museum of Natural History has closed its entire African Hall and its 'Origins of People' display because, according to Sullivan, the message to the viewer was that, 'culturally, Africa was the kindergarten and Europe was the graduate school.' The African Hall is to be replaced with 'Africa Thresholds,' a space that will question stereotypes and assumptions held by the American public about other cultures (ibid.). A historian who has been hired at the Smithsonian suggests: 'The Smithsonian is a truly national institution. It needs to change not only the way it thinks about itself, but the way people think about it' (Bretos, in Anderson, 1994).

Community Consultation

In the case of *Into the Heart of Africa*, the protesters were raising many of the same concerns identified in the Smithsonian example. Critics of the exhibition were protesting against the museum for not consulting the community more widely and for not listening to those with whom they chose, in a very limited way, to include in discussions.

While the museum took some steps to involve a few members of the community, in doing so it made several significant errors. In the first place, the community involvement occurred *after* the exhibition had been fully mounted and *after* brochures and flyers describing the exhibition had already been printed. Second, it invited a few representatives of the Black artistic/cultural community, but did not seek the views of a broader cross-section of the Black population. Third, it ignored the recommendations made by those who were consulted regarding the exhibition itself; in other words, the museum refused to share its institutional power (Mackey, 1995). Once the Black community coalition was formed and began demonstrating, the museum seemed to dig its heels in, demonstrating little openness to the perspectives of the Black community and of others who shared its concerns. Instead, the board and other officials reaffirmed their support of the exhibition and appeared to take offence at the community's attempts to 'interfere' in museum and curatorial roles.

In an article published three years after *Into the Heart of Africa*, T. Cuyler Young, who served as director of the ROM at the time of the controversy, analysed the events surrounding the exhibition. He suggested that there was probably a very small group of radicals who 'had some other political agenda unrelated to the exhibition,' and that the vast majority of Blacks understood and appreciated the intent and the message of the exhibition (1993: 181). With reference to the efficacy of community consultation, Young continued to reflect the brand of cultural arrogance and élitism that was at the heart of the controversy. In identifying some guidelines, he stated: 'First, you consult only when you think there is a good reason to do so, which I suspect will be rarely. Second, you remember that it is impossible to consult a community. Such things do not exist ... Third, you do not consult with people who you suspect have a narrow and particularistic axe to grind. You do not consult with the radical wing of the Coalition for the Truth About Africa on an exhibition about Africa. You consult African-Canadians (and even Africans) broadly. Fourth, you consult in a manner and to a degree commensurate with issues ... Fifth, you listen carefully and endeavour to sort the wheat from the chaff' (ibid.: 184).

This inability to truly understand and respect the views and the knowledge held by a given community was reflected in the curator's lack of responsiveness to the criticisms directed at the exhibition. When Dr Cannizzo finally broke her silence and attempted to justify the exhibition, she exhibited a major shift in thinking from her stated approach described in the catalogue, in which she commented: 'The meaning and significance of an object change according to the circumstances in which it appears and is understood. That transformational power [of context] is particularly evident in museums, which, like anthropology, are essentially "fictional" in their nature. The meaning of their collections is generated between the curator, the object, and the visitor' (1989: 12).

But seven months after the show was launched, instead of acknowledging the possibility and legitimacy of different interpretations of the exhibition depending on one's context, she wrote in the *Toronto Star* (5 June 1990) that 'the exhibition does not promote colonialism or glorify imperialism ... it should help all Canadians to understand the historical roots of racism' (quoted in Mackey, 1995).

In a similar failure of understanding, John McNeill (a former acting director of the ROM) was quoted as saying that the 'controversy which surrounded the exhibition and led to the cancellation of this tour impinges on the freedom of all museums to maintain intellectual honesty, scientific integrity and academic freedom' (Nourbese Philip, 1992: 103).

According to Susan Crean, *Into the Heart of Africa* was in some respects 'a classic case of a cultural institution unable to see its own bias and unprepared to examine its own cultural assumptions. What the situation called for was a bit of ordinary humility; what we got was a stone wall and that, in my book, was adding insult to the original injury' (1991: 127).

This lack of a meaningful institutional response by the ROM board and staff to the concerns and criticisms of the Black community indicates a massive failure of understanding; clearly, there is an 'invisible, but omniscient "we" that such institutions continue to embody to this day' (Tchen, 1993: 4). In a pluralistic society made up of people from diverse cultural systems, the notion of 'we' is increasingly fraught with tension and conflict. Those marginalized communities that have long been excluded from definitions of the normative self and culture, and excluded from the dominant cultural institutions, are increasing their demands for inclusion and representation.

John Evans, a former president of the University of Toronto, observed in a speech to the Museum Trustees Association in Santa Fe, New Mexico: 'It is fundamental that those who belong to a culture play a seminal role in planning and interpreting exhibitions and educational programs about that culture. *Outside interpreters, expert and well meaning,* rarely have the same perspective. The content needs to be considered in the context of the historical and social constructions that pertain to the exhibit' (1990).

In planning *Into the Heart of Africa*, the ROM failed to address many fundamental questions such as these:

• What political and moral criteria are used to validate and ensure responsible collecting practices?
• How, in a pluralistic and globalizing society, do museums determine whose collections, memories, interpretations, and meanings should be represented?
• How can curators present diverse points of view and multiple voices, and convey a body of knowledge, while at the same time accommodating the public's expectations of hearing a curatorial voice?
• How can a museum exhibition locate a culture in a particular social/environmental context without reinforcing demeaning Eurocentric stereotypes?
• How can a museum help viewers gain a real understanding of non-Western cultures when the spectator's own cultural context and biases so strongly influence the way he or she sees reality?
• How can museums create and disseminate new forms of knowledge that reflect the realities of contemporary society when their primary goal has been to function as a chronicler of the past?
• How does the fact that the men and women who work at the ROM continue to be selected almost exclusively from one cultural and racial background, influence institutional values, priorities, and practices? (Schildkrout, 1991; Clifford, 1990; Tchen, 1993)

The Role That Other Institutions Played in the Debate

There is often a close relationship between cultural institutions and the practices of other social systems. For example, in controversies related to cultural practices and cultural production, the mainstream media often have a strong polarizing influence. In their coverage of these events, the media generally provide uncritical support for the institutions of the dominant culture (Nourbese Philip, 1992).

As the controversy over the ROM exhibition intensified, the media vigorously defended the authoritative voice and claims of the museum. The museum and many journalists argued from a shared perspective that promoted 'a single authoritative truth, not a multiple reading of truths in contexts' (Mackey, 1995: 422). While supposedly maintaining a posture of neutrality, the cultural critics writing for the Toronto press were, for the most part, highly critical of the protesters, who were commonly characterized as bullies, blackmailers, terrorists, and revisionists, and as a threat to the fundamental values of a liberal democratic society, and as 'dangerous to all things "our" society holds dear – academic freedom, the integrity of history, and even cultural pluralism' (ibid.: 423).

Gina Mallett (1990), writing in the *Toronto Star*, noted that an award should be given to 'the soft core liberals who accommodated the Coalition for the Truth About Africa's bullying.' Christopher Hume (1990), the same newspaper's art critic, wrote: 'The price of popularity must sometimes be paid for at the cost of integrity.' He added that 'foremost among the coalition's half-truths is the contention the show was racist. It's anything but.' Sid Adilman (1990), another *Star* writer, noted that the denial of 'freedom of expression' was the central issue: the ROM's 'wishy-washy board stood inert in the face of loud protests by black activists against its superb exhibition.'

Journalists in most of the mainstream newspapers and magazines dismissed the protest as the work of 'radicals' and the 'self-righteous left.' Christie Blatchford (1990), a feature writer for the *Toronto Sun*, concluded her condemnation of the coalition with this comment: 'Why are we so bloody eager to be held hostage by the ravers from the political left? They won big on this one, you know.' Michael Valpy (1993) commented in the *Globe and Mail* that the protesters against *Into the Heart of Africa* who tried to shut the show down were proposing censorship, 'the death of memory,' and the death of education.

Such statements are commonly found in majority discourse about minorities. Both museum spokespersons and the media largely dismissed and belittled the experience of African Canadians, ignoring the systemic structural inequalities affecting daily life in the community. In this kind of discourse the minority group is constructed as the problem within an otherwise harmonious, unified, multicultural society (Mackey, 1995).

One criticism levelled at the community by the media and other social commentators was that the protesters wanted to ignore this important chapter in history. Donna Laframboise (1990) in the *Toronto Star* suggested that the coalition believed there was only one truth – their version – and observed: 'There is something truly appalling about believing that only you have the right story.'

However, from the perspective of those who were critical of the exhibition, the central question was *Whose history is being told?* The coalition believed that the story being told was from a White, Eurocentric point of view; at the same time, the perspectives, interpretations, and voices of Africans were being ignored and silenced. Illustrating this point, Charles Roach (1990) commented: 'The recorded history, culture and the museums of people are necessary expression of exploitation and justification of the ascent to power of that people's ruling class. The victors are the ones who get to write history and control museums.'

For the Black community and its coalition representatives, the exhibition merely confirmed that 'as long as institutions and individuals fail to understand how thoroughly racism permeates the very underpinnings of Western thought, then despite all the good will in the world, catastrophes like *Into the Heart of Africa* will continue to happen. Intentions, particularly the good ones, continue to pave the way to hell. And to Africa' (Nourbese Philip, 1992: 107).

In terms of the impact of the exhibition on educational institutions, it is clear from the many references to the Toronto Board of Education appearing in this case study that the ROM exhibition was generally unsuccessful as an educational experience for students. Despite the comprehensive set of learning materials contained in the school group kits produced for teachers, and despite the program of performances, films, and videos, some of which were appropriate for young people, the Toronto Board of Education had significant concerns about the biases that were present in both the learning resources and the exhibition itself.

The board's report on the ROM exhibition suggested that the exhibition was 'incomplete' in terms of its educative function, as it assumed that the viewer brought a neutral perspective to the viewing. This was unrealistic: 'Those of us of European descent are susceptible to stereotyping.' The board felt that the strong reliance on irony was not effective and that for words such as 'savage' and 'barbarous,' it would not help either students or adults separate myth from reality. The board concluded that *Into the Heart of Africa* 'had no direct curriculum function for elementary school students, and secondary school classes would need extensive and carefully planned preparation.'

Most important, the problems with the exhibition demonstrated the need for museums to be more sensitive in their role as educators. Meaningful consultation with school boards and/or ministry of education representatives, and with members of the community, would have helped museum staff plan the exhibition so that it took into account the backgrounds and experiences of all those coming to view their work.

The third social institution to become involved in this cultural production of the ROM was the police. The Metro Toronto police appeared in significant numbers at the demonstrations. From the perspective of many in the Black community, the police used unnecessary force. During the demonstration of 5 May 1990, two Black men who were attempting to enter the museum and see the exhibition were 'jumped by about eight police officers ... and were choking him ... One policeman even drew his gun ... Two people who were arrested were pulled indiscriminately out of a crowd, verbally and physically abused by the officers, and arrested on false charges' (from the Coalition Information Kit). In a conflict on 2 June 1990, a riot squad of fifty police officers was called in and eight demonstrators were arrested and charged (Lakey, 1990). From the perspective of many in the community, the confrontations between the police and the protesters were symptomatic of the everyday forms of oppression and harassment experienced by members of the Black community in their 'encounters' with the police. This point was made by Charles Roach, who emphasized the importance of understanding how the struggles with the ROM and the Metro Toronto police were welded together. The police were seen by many in the Black community as provocateurs who used unnecessary force: 'Inside the ROM is institutional racism and outside is the brutal reality' (Roach, 1990).

As a final institutional strategy, the museum attempted to use the power of the civil court system, suing the coalition for $160,000 in damages. The suit was eventually dropped (Young, 1993).

Conclusions

The controversy over *Into the Heart of Africa* provided the ROM with a missed opportunity to break new ground with respect to meaningful and accurate cultural representation. The exhibition challenged the ROM to engage in a process of exploring what it believes it is and how this affects its collections, staffing, and organizational life. However, the museum failed to engage in a process of critical examination.

This case study has crystallized many of the issues related to racial and cultural bias as reflected in the institutional values, ideologies, and practices of many cultural organizations in Canada. At the heart of the ROM controversy are changing beliefs about the role and function of museums and other cultural institutions in relation to who should have the power to represent and control images created by 'others.' One of the key factors that contributed to the conflict between the ROM and the protesters was the unequal power relations that heightened the polarization between the dominant culture and a marginalized one.

By definition, marginalized communities operate from a position of unequal power and authority. Institutional power further isolates already marginalized groups and weakens them further. Polarization between dominant and marginal cultures deepens as a result, and two solitudes emerge. The museum officials stood inside, resolute and fixed in their certainty that the exhibition was historically accurate and that little else mattered. African-Canadian protesters demonstrated outside the museum, watched over by dozens of police officers who were 'preserving law and order.' Mainly White viewers 'enjoyed' an exhibition that was planned and executed by White staff in order to 'celebrate the rich cultural heritage of African life' (a phrase taken from newspaper ads promoting the exhibition).

The bureaucratic inertia and institutional resistance of the ROM at every stage demonstrates that because of their traditional values, customs, and practices, institutions such as museums are difficult to change.

The ROM controversy illustrates how the past converges with the present. The protesters saw a relationship between on the one hand the symbolic domination reflected in the colonial images and discourse used in the exhibition, and on the other hand the sense of powerlessness experienced every day by Black people living in modern Canada. In other words, the protesters sought to gain freedom from the past and to begin the process of creating a new egalitarianism by insisting that the museum provide a space for their historical experiences and memories.

This case study has examined two levels of resistance: institutional resistance, and the resistance on the part of the Black community. Regarding the former, museum spokespersons including the executive director, the associate director, the curator, and the publicity manager ignored and/or dismissed the perspectives and the expertise that members of the Black community and other concerned individuals presented to them. The board and staff of the museum did not possess sufficient understanding of the invisible but omniscient 'we' that such an institution represented.

In the final analysis, the exhibition *Into the Heart of Africa* failed. It was a classic example of a situation where the basis for growth, change, and synergy was lost to the moment, as the cultural power of the museum and other institutions was used to preserve a tradition of silencing and marginalization. The ROM, as a 'historical-cultural theatre of memory'

(Clifford, 1990), chose to respect and showcase one set of life histories – that of the 'defenders of the Empire.' In so doing, it discarded the experiences of Africans and the histories of African Canadians. Thus, the exhibition did not really go into the 'heart of Africa' but gave pre-eminence to the story of those Canadians who went 'out of Africa' taking home 'souvenirs' of the journey.

Note

1 The *Oxford English Dictionary* defines irony as follows: 1. A figure of speech in which the intended meaning is the opposite of that expressed by words used; usually taking the form of sarcasm or ridicule in which laudatory expressions are used to imply condemnation or contempt. 2. A condition of affairs or events opposite to what was, or might naturally be expected; a contradictory outcome of events as if in mockery of the promise and fitness of things.

References

Adilman, Sid. 1990. 'Bad Guys Discrediting Integrity of the Board.' *Toronto Star*. 24 December. C5.

Anderson, Paul. 1994. 'New Era Looms for Hispanics at Smithsonian.' *Miami Herald*. 28 December. A1.

Blatchford, Christie. 1990. 'A Surrender to Vile Harangues.' *Toronto Sun*. 30 November. 5.

Butler. S. 1993. 'Contested Representations: Revisiting "Into the Heart of Africa."' Master's thesis, Department of Anthropology, York University.

Cannizzo, Jeanne. 1989. Catalogue for *Into the Heart of Africa*. Toronto: Royal Ontario Museum.

– 1990. 'Into the Heart of a Controversy.' *Toronto Star*. 5 June. A17.

– 1991. 'Exhibiting Cultures: Into the Heart of Africa.' *Visual Anthropology*. 7(1). 150–60.

Clifford, James. 1990. 'On Collecting Art and Culture.' In Russell Ferguson, ed. *Out There: Marginalization and Contemporary Culture*. Cambridge, Mass.: MIT Press.

Crean, Susan. 1991. 'Taking the Missionary Position.' In Ormond McKague, ed. *Racism in Canada*. Saskatoon: Fifth House.

Da Breo, Hazel. 1989/90a. 'Da Breo Interviews Dr. Jeanne Cannizzo.' *Fuse*. Winter. 36–7.

– 1989/90b. 'Royal Spoils: The Museum Confronts Its Colonial Past.' *Fuse.* Winter. 28–36.

Drainie, Bronwyn. 1990. 'Black Groups Protest African Show at "Racist Ontario Museum."' *Globe and Mail,* 24 March. C1.

Evans, John. 1990. 'Minorities Should Help Plan Exhibits.' Quoted from a speech delivered to the Museum Trustees Association. *Toronto Star.* 1 November. A23.

Fiske, John. 1994. *Media Matters: Everyday Culture and Political Change.* Minneapolis: University of Minnesota Press.

Fulford, Robert. 1991. 'Into the Heart of the Matter.' *Rotunda.* Summer. 19–28.

Hume, Christopher. 1989. 'ROM Looks into the Heart of Darkness.' *Toronto Star.* November 17. E3, E22.

– 1990. 'Rejection of ROM Show Not A Defeat for Racism.' *Toronto Star.* 29 September. F3.

Hutcheon, Linda. 1994. *Irony's Edge: The Theory and Politics of Irony.* London and New York: Routledge.

Itwaru, Arnold, and Natasha Ksonzek. 1994. *Closed Entrances: Canadian Culture and Imperialism.* In Toronto: TSAR.

Laframboise, Donna. 1990. 'ROM Protesters Miss Own Point.' *Toronto Star.* 22 October. A23.

Lakey, Jack. 1990. 'Demonstrators Clash with Police.' *Toronto Star.* 3 June.

Lalla, Hari, and John Myers. 1990. *Report on the Royal Ontario Museum's Exhibit 'Into the Heart of Africa' for the Toronto Board of Education.* 9 May. Toronto Board of Education.

Mackey, Eva. 1995. 'Postmodernism and Cultural Politics in a Multicultural Nation: Contests over Truth in the *Into the Heart of Africa* Controversy.' *Public Culture.* 7(2) Winter. 403–31.

Mallett, Gina. 1990. 'When Culture Resists the Mainstream.' *Toronto Star.* 15 December. G3.

Marshall, Clem. 1995. Letter to the Editor. *Globe and Mail.* 25 March.

McClelland, J. 1990. 'Uncovering a Hidden Curriculum.' *Role Call.* 10 April.

Mitchell, T. 1989. 'The World as Exhibition.' *Society for Comparative Study of Society and History.* 31(2). 217–36.

Nourbese Philip, M. 1992. *Frontiers: Essays and Writings on Racism and Culture.* Stratford: Mercury Press.

Roach, Charles. 1990. 'Into the Heart of the Controversy.' *Toronto Star.* 5 June. A17.

– 1990. *Toronto Sun.* 10 June.

Schildkrout, Enid. 1991. 'Ambiguous Messages and Ironic Twists: Into the Heart of Africa and the Other Museum.' *Museum Anthropology.* 15(2). 16–22.

Shanahan, Michael. 1994. 'Exhibiting Political Correctness.' *Toronto Star.* 7 September. A17.

Tchen, J.K.W. 1993. 'What Are We Doing Now for the Year 2010?!? Museums and the Problems of Technospeak, Possessive Individualism, and Social Alienation.' *Getting to 2010: Directors and Educators Visualized the Future.* Fort Worth, Tex.: Association of American Museums.

Townsend-Gault, Charlotte. 1992. 'Stereotypes under De(construction).' *Border Crossings.* 76–7.

Valpy, Michael. 1993. 'The Storm around Show Boat.' *Globe and Mail.* 12 March. A2.

Young, T. Cuyler. 1993. 'Into the Heart of Africa: The Director's Perspective.' *Curator.* 36(3). 174–88.

3

The Barnes Collection

Background

In September 1994 a collection of eighty-three Impressionist and Post-Impressionist paintings arrived in Toronto. They were part of a vast and important art collection acquired by Dr Albert Barnes over the course of his lifetime, from the early 1900s until his death in 1951. Barnes collected Old Masters, including paintings by Tintoretto, El Greco, Titian, and Rubens; and 'New Masters,' including works by Daumier, Renoir, Cezanne, Matisse, Monet, Manet, Rousseau, Van Gogh, Degas, Utrillo, Modigliani, Soutine, and Seurat; as well as African sculptures, Greco-Roman carvings, Chinese paintings, Islamic art, Native American rugs, and other works of art.

Barnes's private collection of some 2,500 works from four continents was regarded in America as very important (Greenfield, 1987). One art historian observed that 'the depth of the Barnes collection is so extraordinary that it defies imagination' (in Graham, 1994: 64).

Barnes was controversial in life and in death. He was respected for his extraordinary knowledge and for his skill in amassing what some art critics considered an incomparable collection of modern art. However, he was also known, and somewhat less admired, for his unorthodox ideas about the role of art in society. In his view, 'great' art did not emerge from one culture but was the product of diverse cultures and different ages. This view never really gained significant support among other art critics and historians.

In the early 1900s, after his pharmaceutical business began to flourish, Barnes organized his employees into a six-hour workday and had them attend art classes at the factory. Both Black and White workers participated in these sessions. The curriculum included studies in philosophy and art. He displayed hundreds of paintings on his shop floor, which interested employees could buy at cost. Barnes also established a circulating library of modern literature for his employees (Wattenmaker, 1993; Greenfield, 1987).

Barnes then began to expand the informal factory seminars. In 1922 he merged his two loves, art and education, and established the Barnes Foundation 'to promote the advancement of education and the appreciation of the fine arts' (Greenfield, 1987: 73). In March 1925 he opened the Foundation Gallery in a twenty-three room limestone mansion in Merion, Pennsylvania, a suburb of Philadelphia. The gallery was used as a laboratory for the art school; every year as many as three hundred students studied aesthetics, having paid a tuition of between 100 and 200 dollars. Barnes restricted access to his collection almost entirely to those with little opportunity to visit mainstream galleries and museums, such as Blacks, working-class Whites, and the foundation's students.

The building's exterior incorporates several African architectural motifs. The main entrance is framed by a wall decoration modelled after a door relief of a mask and a crocodile made by the Akan peoples of the Ivory Coast and Ghana. On the lintel are sculptures of seated female figures modelled after figures made by the Senufo peoples of the Ivory Coast and Mali. There are carvings of crocodiles, masks, and birds. These exterior motifs and the African sculptures signal to the gallery's visitors the centrality of African art in the collection and its importance in the history of modern art (Wattenmaker, 1993).

The formal opening of the Barnes Foundation's new buildings took place on 19 March 1925. John Dewey, the famous American philosopher and educator, was invited to give the dedication address at the gallery's opening. The gallery in which those ceremonies were held was filled with masterworks of the French tradition, which were displayed below a border of abstracted African masks. Dewey in his speech identified the important role that African Americans had played in the development of Barnes's personal and aesthetic vision:

Members of the Negro race, of people of African culture, have also taken a large part in the building up of the activity which has culminated in this beautiful and significant enterprise. I know of no more significant, symbolic contribution than that which the work of the members of this institution have made to the solution of what sometimes seems to be not merely a perplexing but a hopeless problem – that of race relations. The demonstration that two races may work together successfully and cooperatively, and that the work has the capacity to draw out from our Negro friends something of that artistic interest and taste ... We may rejoice at every demonstration of the artistic capacity of any race which has been in any way repressed or looked upon as inferior. It is the demonstration of this capacity for doing beautiful and significant work which gives the best proof of the fundamental quality, and equality, of all people. It serves ... the cause of bringing all people from all over the world together in greater harmony. (Quoted in Wattenmaker, 1993: 12)

Barnes's views and actions as an art collector were guided by three central principles. The first was that great art is not limited to Western aesthetics, nor is it the exclusive product of one tradition or one civilization. Rather, aesthetics reflect a process of cultural synergy – that is, the harmony and integration of elements of diverse cultures. Barnes was convinced that many European artists owed a huge debt to African culture and to the art of other cultures.

In his catalogue introduction, Barnes called attention to the influence of African sculpture on many European artists and sculptors, including Modigliani, whose 'inspiration came from his devotion to the spirit of Negro art' (in Wattenmaker, 1993: 12). He believed that the work of African sculptors and Chinese masters widened the horizons of European artists and provided a powerful demonstration of 'what ought to be ... a commonplace of aesthetic criticism – the continuity of great art through the ages' (Barnes and de Mazia, 1943).

In the early 1920s, Barnes began to collect African tribal sculpture, much of which he purchased from Paul Guillame, the Parisian art dealer who was a trail-blazer in the study and promotion of these works. Barnes then began providing financial support to African-American artists. His interest in and enthusiasm for African art led him to become both a patron and a historian of African-American art. Barnes wrote in 1925: 'We have to acknowledge not only that our civilization has done practically nothing to help the Negro create his art but that our unjust oppression has been powerless to prevent the black man from realizing in a rich measure the expression of his own rare gifts' (Barnes, 1925).'

Barnes's second principle was that the Barnes Foundation was to serve as a force for education and social action. The gallery's opening ceremony emphasized that the foundation was not a museum, but an educational institution. Barnes's third principle was that art was as significant for the processes it nurtured as it was for its products (Owusu, 1988). In this sense, art was a powerful instrument for challenging racism. Barnes believed that an appreciation of the rich cultural heritage of Africa, and of African-American art, could help change the perceptions, stereotypes, and biases of White America. A primary role of the Barnes Foundation was to demonstrate the universal capacity of all cultures to produce significant creative cultural products; in doing so, the foundation would be illustrating the fundamental equality of *all* people.

During the 1920s, Barnes was among the few White Americans who actively supported the New Negro Movement, also known as the Harlem Renaissance. This movement set out to affirm the positive values of the Black heritage and to demand full social and political equality. In 1926, Barnes contributed to *The New Negro*, an anthology of writings edited by Dr Alain Locke, the chief mentor of the Harlem Renaissance. This book examined every phase of recent Black cultural and social achievements; these in turn formed the ideals and goals of the movement. The same year, the Barnes Foundation published one of its first books, *Primitive Negro Culture*.

Barnes was actively involved in the National Urban League, an interracial organization that strove to improve the living conditions of American Blacks. He made generous donations to the organization and vigorously supported its monthly magazine, *Opportunity*. In a promotional flyer soliciting subscriptions for the journal, he wrote: 'I can see in the journal abounding evidence of the high intellectual and aesthetic status of the Negro' (Greenfield, 1987: 139).

Barnes considered, but later abandoned, the idea of developing a centre for the study of Black culture under the direction of the National Urban League. In a pamphlet distributed to residents of Merion Township he provided his reasons for creating such a project, stating that such a national centre would offer 'comfortable living accommodations, freedom from oppression, and instruction by skilled educators of both races, all supplemented by the art resources available.' The goal was to ensure that prejudice did not limit the artistic gifts of African Americans and their capacity to contribute to a richer and more intelligent American society.

When Barnes died he entrusted the foundation and its governance to Lincoln University, a distinguished Black college. His bequest stipulated that no part of the collection was to be sold or put on tour; that no charge could be loaned; and that the gallery's art displays were not to be altered in any way. The foundation's by-laws stated: 'It will be incumbent on the Board of Trustees to make such regulations as well as ensure it is the plain people, that is, men and women who gain their livelihood by daily toil in shops, factories, schools, stores and similar places, who shall have free access to the art gallery upon those days when the gallery is open to the public' (in ibid.: 75).

The foundation's closed-door policy toward visitors ended in the early 1960s after a long battle with the state of Pennsylvania concerning its status as a tax-exempt institution. A new policy was developed allowing public access, but in limited numbers for two-and-a-half days a week.

Events

By the early 1990s the foundation building that housed the Barnes collection was in need of extensive repairs and costly renovations. Richard Glanton, the foundation's president, persuaded the courts to allow the foundation, as a funding-raising strategy, to take some of the collection on a limited world tour. Initially the tour was to include Washington, Paris, Tokyo, Philadelphia, and Fort Worth. When it became apparent that the renovation costs would not be met by this limited tour, an extension was sought. The Art Gallery of Ontario (AGO) successfully lobbied the foundation to be the sixth city. The AGO 'won' its place on the tour by persuading the foundation that Toronto, one of the most culturally diverse cities in the world, would benefit greatly from the art collection and from its underlying philosophy. Financing the exhibition in Toronto required a $3.7 million guarantee. An equal amount of money had to be raised to cover transportation, insurance, and the costs necessary to mount the show. The AGO lobbied the Ontario government, which agreed to contribute about 55 per cent of the required operating revenues.

The AGO claimed that the exhibition would attract hundreds of thousands of visitors, generate significant funds for the economy, produce jobs, and gain the interest of the private sector; this in turn would help reduce the gallery's large operating debt (Graham, 1994).

Little wonder, then, that the Barnes Exhibit arrived in Toronto with great fanfare, excitement, and anticipation. The AGO's success in attracting the support of the private and public sectors was widely applauded. Some saw Toronto's 'victory' over other major international cities as a testament to the passion, tenacity, and resourcefulness of the AGO.

However, the touring Barnes Exhibit left some parts of the community feeling frustrated and disappointed. While it contained many extraordinarily beautiful and important works of art, it was also missing something significant. The touring collection included only the French 'masters,' and none of Barnes's African, Asian, and Native American art and artifacts. The only reference to the art of other cultures was a large photographic panel of one of the actual walls from the Barnes Foundation. The *picture* (our italics) clearly showed the integration of art from a variety of cultural traditions and civilizations. The enlarged photograph showed nineteenth and early twentieth century European paintings interspersed with African, Asian, and Native American work. The key question relating to this omission was this: 'If Barnes was a "pioneer in the area of cross-cultural study of the visual arts" and passionately committed to the concept of integration of art forms from different cultural traditions, why was his collection displayed in such a way that the viewer is unable to see the formal connection between works created continents and centuries away? Why do we end up with a display of only French painters, which undermines what Barnes was trying to accomplish?' (Drainie, 1994).

The director of the AGO, Glenn Lowry, claimed that the foundation denied his request to include some of the art from other cultures with the European collection. In his view, 'even though the exhibit contained only European masterpieces, they were so universal in quality that they would naturally lead the viewer's mind to the richness of visual creation that has come out of all the world's cultures' (ibid.).

Members of the Black community disagreed with this perspective. For many, the Barnes Exhibit at the AGO was an example of cultural racism. They argued that one of the main arguments the AGO had used in winning the exhibition was that Toronto was one of the most multicultural cities in North America. No surprise, then, that many thought that the multicultural nature of the collection would have been highlighted. Ironically, while the AGO was using Toronto's racial diversity to land the exhibition, it was simultaneously rejecting efforts by Toronto's Black community to mount an exhibition of Black/African art for Black History Month. The AGO had also rejected a bid by Asian artists in Toronto to exhibit Asian art forms.

Cultural and antiracist advocates noted that the AGO was centred firmly in the tradition of European art, which it used as its sole criterion for measuring aesthetic 'excellence.' In an article in *Share*, a Toronto African-Canadian newspaper, Richard Kidane (1994) observed: 'While Director Glenn Lowry and Board member Joe Rotman were mobilizing their networks ... to get the exhibit so that, in Glanton's words, "these works may be seen and studied by people in one of the most culturally diverse cities in the world" – the AGO was rebuffing approaches by minority communities, who have long campaigned for the AGO to progress from its monocultural stance.'

Throughout December, until the Barnes Exhibit closed, members of the Black community calling themselves the African Canadian Artists Against Exclusion by the AGO protested against the show.

Analysis

The Creation of Racist Discourse in an Art Gallery

Given the content of his art collection and Barnes's own commitment to a culturally symbiotic approach to art, the exclusion of African and Asian art forms from the exhibition raised important questions about the relationship between power and culture. Power provides some individuals and groups with access while marginalizing and excluding others. The unequal distribution of power in society is at the centre of cultural practices and politics.

The lack of representation of the art of other cultures in this exhibition shed light on how cultural institutions reflect and reinforce the cultural boundaries and racial hierarchies embedded in Eurocentrism. The controversy in Toronto over the Barnes Exhibit demonstrated how historical and current aesthetic values, standards, and norms within art galleries and museums reflect the victory of one version of culture – the Western version – over all others. Definitions of 'quality,' 'excellence,' 'authenticity,' 'beauty,' 'a masterpiece,' and 'universalism' are colour- and culture-coded, and arrived at through the lens of Eurocentrism. They are part of a discourse whose meaning is established and understood based on European-derived traditions.

Art as Consumer Product

The racial diversity of Toronto had a 'market value' to the AGO, which it used strategically, to increase its profitability. In this way, the philosophy underscoring the Barnes collection was sacrificed to the 'bottom line.' The Barnes Exhibit blatantly demonstrated the link between cultural production and consumerism, and the role economics plays in validating racist institutional practices.

Increasingly, culture is being defined and constituted by economic forces. There is a new intersection between commerce, advertising, and consumption. The penetration of commodity culture into every aspect of daily life has become a major axis in the relationship between mass culture and high culture. The gap between these two worlds is rapidly diminishing (Becker, 1994).

One consequence of this trend is that the value of a particular art form or cultural practice is now measured by its mass appeal and 'entertainment' value. The desire to increase profitability has become a central factor when cultural institutions make decisions and set priorities. Associated with this new pattern is a closer marriage with mass culture when it comes to identifying common objectives, ideals, and discourse (Rosler, 1994).

That the AGO treats art as an entertainment product is demonstrated by the fact that the Barnes Exhibit was the most heavily promoted event in its two-hundred-year history. Its advertising budget was $1 million. In the four months that the exhibition ran, nearly 600,000 people spent an hour viewing the show. It became 'the basis for an elaborate affirmation of Toronto's most intoxicating dreams, a high-culture equivalent of the Blue Jays' World Series victories' (Fulford, 1995: 60). The Barnes Exhibit was promoted as a 'blockbuster' show, and much of the hype and hoopla was the same as characterized the 'selling' of *Miss Saigon* and *Show Boat*. It is interesting to note that theatrical producer David Mirvish offered free admission to the Barnes Exhibit with every full-price ticket purchased for *Miss Saigon*.

Coverage of the opening of the exhibition was intense and overwhelmingly positive. This point was clearly made: 'Given what the advertising dollars stand to gain when events like this are staged, too much griping is not just bad manners, it's bad business' (Connolly, 1995: 34). The media provided extensive coverage of a lavish opening party (costing $1.5 million) for 1,700 guests held at the AGO, hosted by Guskin Sheff & Associates, the private sponsors of the exhibition, who also provided a million-dollar donation (Fulford, 1995: 61).

When the AGO went to the Ontario government for funding, it had to harmonize its strategy with the present climate of fiscal restraint. The economic climate was unstable: in 1994 the government had severely cut back its funding of the arts – in particular, it had chopped the AGO's operating budget. The government now had to be convinced that the exhibition would provide a tangible return: 'The pitch, therefore, had almost nothing to do with either "excellence" or "international[ism]." It was all about "cultural tourism" and "economic spin-offs," with the AGO as an exciting new "product" in one of the province's most lucrative industries' (Graham, 1994: 65).

From the perspective of economics and cultural consumerism, the

AGO was accurate in its analysis of the likely economic benefits of the Barnes Exhibit. The investment paid significant dividends in terms of tourist revenues and other consumer spending. A study commissioned by the government of Ontario found that 600,000 people attended the exhibition during its sixteen-week run, and spent about $75 million in doing so. Provincial taxes resulting directly from the Barnes Exhibit totalled $6.5 million (Kirchoff, 1995).

Media coverage of the event focused almost exclusively on economics: 'The Monets, Renoirs, Seurats, van Goghs, Picassos and Matisses were spoken of as if they were convertible currency. They had become number and dollar signs, translated as "anticipated gate receipts," and "projected deficit reductions" ... the exhibition [became] a story where the players were not so much canvases coming to the walls but the supporting cast of "limited tickets," "advance orders," and "three-way partnerships between the gallery, the government, and the private sector" that would put them there' (Rhodes, 1994).

Economic forces did more than anything else to influence the selection of works chosen for the tour. Criticisms that African, Chinese, and Japanese art had been omitted from the exhibit were dismissed by Christopher Hume, the art critic of the *Toronto Star*: 'The sad truth that Dogon masks don't have the mass appeal of a Renoir or a Picasso is to be lamented, but it doesn't make the gallery racist' (1994).

In challenging this assumption that the AGO was not contributing to racism, we must consider two questions: First, what cultural values and standards motivated the decisions taken with respect to the exclusion of what Barnes himself considered a central and significant part of his collection? And second, while African masks and Chinese drawings may not necessarily have 'mass appeal' for those who are White and of Anglo or European background, might they not have attracted a different and much wider audience?

It is not difficult to imagine that a more inclusive exhibition would have broadened public participation to include many of the hundreds of thousands of non-Europeans living in Toronto. As well, many tourists might have been attracted to an exhibition that represented the art of other cultures. In the climate of bottom-line economics and Eurocentric values, these opportunities were lost.

Racial Hierarchies in the Art World

The touring exhibit reaffirmed and reinforced the racial hierarchies that are well established in the art world. In a racially stratified society, the social organization of artistic creation and production mirrors the inequalities found in other social processes. Peter Li contends that in such societies, the means by which works of art are produced, and the aesthetic values and standards by which they are measured, are often mediated by racial differences: 'One way by which art works and cultural creations become racialized is when they are systematically evaluated from the vantage point of a racially-based cultural hierarchy that upholds the primacy of artistic standards and cultural values that flow from the dominant group' (1994: 5).

The decision to exclude African and Asian art and Native American art motifs from the Barnes tour is an example of how the works of African, Caribbean, Asian, and Aboriginal cultures are largely ignored by art museums and galleries in the West. The aesthetic products of these cultures are not seen as part of the living heritage and traditions of the modern world. Marginalization and ethnocentrism determine how the work of artists of colour is evaluated. Eurocentric aesthetic standards are used to separate the dominant art forms from those created by non-European artists; the consequence of this differentiation into 'them' and 'us' is the unequal status and power of racial groups involved in cultural production (Li, 1994).

Yet Barnes clearly demonstrated that Western art has been profoundly influenced by the art and cultural practices of non-European cultures. This is why he questioned and challenged the traditional role, attitudes, and practices of mainstream art museums.

Susana Leval, a curator, art historian, and writer, points out (1992) that cultural, ethnic, and racial groups whose work seems most distant from the treasured European canon are beyond the narrow parameters established by mainstream cultural institutions for inclusion and participation. The West tends to view works of art as the creative products of specific individuals with whom there is a cultural connectedness. Thus, Western mainstream art can be understood as 'a mosaic of contributions made by individuals we know, whose works can be distinguished and whose personal lives – and the way they are related to their age – are worthy of our attention' (Price, 1989: 65).

Art produced outside of the Western culture lacks this cultural connectedness. As one result, the art produced by people of colour – be it Aboriginal sculpture and totem poles, African carvings and masks, or Chinese paintings and pottery – is 'othered,' and the descriptions of their work are assigned the labels that denote how the dominant culture understands their societies: as 'ancient,' 'primitive,' 'tribal,' 'quaint,' and so on. The anonymous artist thus comes to represent an entire community, and is seen as unreflectively conforming to the precepts and practices of his or her tradition. The Western gaze obliterates the presence of an individual human creator (ibid.). The cultures themselves are not seen as being made up of individuals, but rather represent collectivities. These cultures' practices and aesthetic forms gain identity only when they are appropriated by Western museums and galleries (Miller, 1991).

'We' clearly do not know the name of the African artist who produced a particular piece of work displayed in an art museum. Nevertheless, 'individual hands are recognisable in Igbo sculpture, as in African art in general, and the artists have been, and continue to be, well known in the areas in which they live' (Herbert Cole and Chike Aniakor, quoted in Jordan and Weedon, 1995: 404).

This denial of identity is largely the result of the cultural appropriation that took place over the last one hundred years as European and Euro-American settlers, soldiers, merchants, missionaries, colonial administrators, and anthropologists 'stole or "purchased" for a song the art, artifacts and sacred objects of people of colour all over the world, who put the "primitive" and "tribal" cultures of the world on display in the museums of the great western cities' (Jordan and Weedon, 1995: 416).

The Concept of Primitivism as Racist Discourse

Primitivism is a biased term that is not applied to the Greek 'classics' or to the cultural practices of the Roman Empire. Rather, *primitive* as a descriptor is applied to non-European societies. The effect of labelling a society primitive is to freeze its cultural development at a point in time.

In the late nineteenth century, European artists began showing an interest in 'primitive' cultures. The 'myth of primitivism' in modern art is part of the Eurocentric ideology that perceives societies as occupying levels in hierarchical order, with European society and culture at the top and all other societies classified as inferior. The 'primitive world,' the world of the 'other,' is seen and interpreted through the distorting lens of Eurocentrism. Western culture's understanding of other cultural beliefs and practices is reflected and refracted through the representations and misrepresentations that it selects as its interpretation of primitive cultures.

The myth of primitivism in modern art is connected to the perpetuation of a Eurocentred belief system that sees non-European cultures not as autonomous peoples but rather as inferior societies (Brett, 1991). The ideas and attitudes developed in nineteenth-century Europe are still with us today. Primitivism is used to 'to define and fix the positions of non-European peoples in such a way that they are deprived of their active and critical functions in contemporary cultural practices' (Araeen, 1991: 166). The concept of primitivism has been an integral part of art historical scholarship and discourse for almost 150 years (ibid.). It has led to a system of classification and categorization in which 'White art' has been the only form of authentic art.

John Ruskin, one of the most revered figures in the British art world, openly expressed his belief that there is 'no art in the whole of Africa, Asia or America' (in Hiller 1991: 172). The historian Kenneth Clark (1969) dismissed the possibility that African and Asian art influenced Western culture: 'To the Negro imagination [the spiritual] is a world of fear and darkness, ready to inflict horrible punishment for the smallest infringement of a taboo. To the Hellenistic imagination, it is a world of light and confidence, in which the gods are like ourselves, only more beautiful.'

Clark's world-view was rooted in the assumption that Western culture and art is superior to all others; it glorified the history of civilization through the prism of Western culture. This has long been the dominant world-view, and it has strongly influenced art historical scholarship and discourse ever since the nineteenth century (ibid.).

This marginalization and devaluation of cultures outside the dominant culture is what constitutes the myth of primitive cultures. Primitivism has led to two alternative understandings of the art world in general, and of the Barnes Exhibit in particular.

First, primitivism can be interpreted as an ideology that promotes the formation and polarization of the images of 'us' and 'other.' It leads to the construction of a two-tiered art world, with the upper tier composed largely of White, male, European-influenced and centred artists. Subordinate to this level is the work of anonymous artists operating outside Western traditions.

In the second construction, the 'primitive' cultures are not dismissed – rather, they are romanticized. Western artists develop an 'appreciation' of the 'primitive' elements of other cultures – of magic, ritualism, harmony with nature, and mythological imagery and symbols, and so on – and begin to weave these elements into their own work (Clifford, 1990). Paul Gauguin is acknowledged by many art historians as the first European artist to develop an interest in 'primitive' cultural forms, and as the precursor of a different relationship between Western art and that of other cultures (Araeen, 1991). In an interview published in the *Echo de Paris* on 23 February 1891, Gauguin explained why he left France and travelled to Tahiti to paint: 'I only desire to make a simple, very simple act. In order to do this it is necessary for me to immerse myself in virgin nature, see no one but savages live, live their life, with no other thought in mind but to render the way a child would, the concepts formed in my brain, and to do this with nothing but the primitive means of art, the only means that are good and true' (in Varnedoe, 1984: 187).

Cultural Appropriation

It is clear that Gauguin was searching for unspoiled nature. He longed to escape from Western society and to 'discover' the paradise that modern Westerners had lost. This view of primitivism promotes a kind of 'imperialist nostalgia,' a yearning for the exotic, erotic, pastoral, and simple life of the 'native,' 'while forgetting that we have come to know and appropriate the 'other' through imperialism, colonialism, and racism' (Jordan and Weedon, 1995: 421).

Ever since the nineteenth century, the romanticizing of the 'primitive' spirit has been leading Western artists to borrow or appropriate the creative traditions of other cultures. This process has become a significant force in modern European art; in particular, it influenced many of the artists featured in the Barnes Exhibit.

It is clear that in one of Gauguin's paintings in the Barnes Exhibit, *Haere pape*, the artist freely assimilated images based on Polynesian religion and folklore. He also drew upon images of Buddhist relief carvings. Gauguin appropriated motifs from these sources to generate imagery for his art. At the same time, he imposed on these figures new meaning. His meaning was transported to the West, where it became accepted and glorified. Yet 'a kind of fiction persists even in the artist's genre paintings, for he maintains the figure of a pristine landscape devoid of the encroaching presence of European civilization in Polynesia' (Prather, 1993: 166).

The question not explored here is whether, in his representation of elements of Tahitian culture and his depiction of a Polynesian woman, Gauguin in this painting relied upon limiting and objectifying stereotypes generated by the dominant culture. It has been argued that in the Western artistic and cultural imagination the Polynesian woman represents innocence, beauty, exoticism, and sensuality – that she is a creature of a Garden of Eden. That being true, in this example of Gauguin's work we are not really looking at a 'slice of life' drawn from Tahitian culture (Brett, 1991). The image Gauguin created is quite incongruous with the self-representations of those from this culture. In effect, Gauguin 'discovered' Tahiti through his Western lens, by turning his mind to 'interesting and exotic objects.'

John Roberts, an art critic, explains this phenomenon: 'Modernism's assimilation of the "primitive" from Gauguin to Abstract Expression certainly acknowledged the reality of accultural difference. But because of the nature of the process of assimilation – the idealised projection of non-Western cultures as free of the corruption of bourgeois rationalism ... was reproduced in a new form: the FETISHISATION OF THE EXOTIC AS OTHER' (in Jordan and Weedon, 1995: 410. Emphasis in original.).

It can be argued that modern European artists' enthusiasm for and fascination with 'primitive' art did not fundamentally alter the relationship between Western art and other cultures. It did not improve the status of these cultures in Western consciousness; rather, its effect was to reflect and perpetuate Europeans' collective consciousness of the 'other.'

Another artist represented in the Barnes Exhibit was Modigliani, whose portraits of women were strongly influenced by non-Western aesthetics. For example, in *Girl with a Polka-Dot Blouse* Modigliani quite clearly drew from the images and style of a variety of African masks, including Fang, Yaure, Baule, and Marka models. 'By the time of the Barnes portrait, these sources were fully assimilated and difficult to discern' (Weiss, 1993: 224). One wonders if Barnes would concur with this conclusion – that the African influence was 'difficult to discern.' The androgyny evident in the same painting can be traced back to early and ancient Egyptian carvings.

For Barnes, the relationship between European artists and non-Western art forms was blatantly obvious, as illustrated by the *photograph* included with the touring exhibit. The print shows, as the focal point of a wall, a cabinet containing eighteen African sculptures in two rows: seven masks, six figures, and five bone or ivory figurines. Above the cabinet is a long relief from Madagascar, topped by a carved European triptych with eight figures. On either side of the cabinet and relief are paintings by Modigliani that echo the elongations and distortions derived from the African sculptures and Bamana masks in the cabinet. In the same photograph are two Picasso portraits with masklike features. These canvases also relate to the masks in the cabinet and to the Kota figures hanging on each end of the wall. Wattenmaker observes that 'the interspersion of elegant and rugged, both African and European, obliges us to examine our preconceptions about the traditions of sculpture' (1993, Figure 8: 21).

However, the relationship between European and 'primitive' artists does not alter the premises upon which mainstream Western art is based. The Western artist admires and appropriates certain elements within the culture of the 'others,' while at the same time maintaining complete control over the creativity, innovation, and adaptation to the content or style of the original aesthetic form (Jordan and Weedon, 1995). In this way the 'primitive' artists serve as a vehicle for new ideas and approaches in the Western art world. Yet at no time do people from those 'other' civilizations become active subjects in defining or changing the course of art history: 'It is commonly believed that African peoples themselves were unaware of the aesthetic qualities of what they were producing and that it was the west which "discovered" these qualities and gave the African "objects" the status of art' (Araeen, 1991: 166).

By allowing African masks to be 'named' as art, Western art historians and critics permit them to enter their history, their cultural institutions; but these objects do not change what is a singular universal course of art history, which is dominated and controlled by Western traditions and cultural practices.

In interpreting Gauguin's and Picasso's paintings, art historians generally agree that primitivism should be understood in terms of stylistic innovation and the artists' own avant-gardism, rather than in terms of the influence of artists of 'other' cultures (Phillippi and Howells, 1991). Western cultural assumptions continue to reinforce racist ideas in 'popular consciousness, institutions, and scholarship' (Araeen, 1991: 167).

The Role of Contemporary Mainstream Cultural Institutions in Maintaining Cultural Hegemony

Although the artistic response to colonialism is not well documented, scholars such as Susan Hiller (1991), Guy Brett (1991), and Rasheed Araeen (1991) have recently begun to document the intrinsic importance of these art forms, and their relationship to current aesthetic norms.

Beginning with Robert Goldwater's book *Primitivism in Modern Art* (1966), there has been a growing body of scholarship focusing on the importance of non-European artists in art history. The influence of African, Mexican, Asian, and First Nations artists on modern art cannot be overstated. Yet this influence has not transformed the policies and practices of cultural institutions.

In recent years there have been some changes in North America. One artist, Adrian Piper, attributes some of these changes in the United States to Michael Brenson, an influential *New York Times* art critic, who began to review regularly the work of African-American artists. These reviews, from such a highly respected authority, brought about a significant change in the conventions of Eurocentric art criticism: 'By approaching African-American art with the same attention, respect and critical standards he applied to Euroethnic art, Brenson singlehandedly exposed the tacit racism of ignoring African-American art that had prevailed among virtually all other Euroethnic art critics' (Piper, 1994).

Some art museums have shown an interest in developing exhibitions of the art of 'other' cultures. However, 'a subtle Eurocentrism has shaped the prestigious exhibitions, which have recently brought together in the West some of the finest examples of non-European art' (Brett, 1991). Similarly, notions of connoisseurship and quality are intimately linked to familiarity. Cultural blinders and Eurocentric assumptions often prevent Anglo viewers and museum curators from recognizing the quality of the art produced by other cultures (Leval, 1992). Picasso and Matisse are given main galleries in the Museum of Modern Art; the important works of African Americans and Latin Americans are often hung in the hallways.

The location of art is very telling. For example, a painting called *The Jungle* by Lifredo Lam, a Cuban-born artist of Chinese and African-Cuban heritage, was allowed into the Musuem of Modern Art. However, it has been hung in an inconspicuous passageway near the cloakroom, far from the main galleries where the works of the European and American 'masters' are found (Yau, 1990). In this way the museum has assigned to the work a secondary status. This is the result of numerous assumptions that almost every force – galleries, museums, art historians and critics, art magazines – in today's mainstream art world takes for granted. The dominant culture has consistently devalued, suppressed, and ignored attempts by culturally hybrid artists to give visual expression to their cross-cultural experiences and identities.

The issue of location as a means of marginalizing work by nondominant artists was explored in an analysis of a more recent exhibit at the AGO, *The Oh! Canada Project* (Walcott, 1996). The exhibition, which followed the Barnes Exhibit by three years, was divided into two major areas: eight exhibits of the work of the Group of Seven, and a 'community-based arts group' component that included works by Aboriginal, Latin-Canadian, African-Canadian, Chinese-Canadian, and other non-

European Canadian artists. This show was intended to consider the question of landscape and nations from different social contexts. The writer noted that the 'community based' installations were relegated to the perimeter of a separate gallery down the hall from the main gallery rooms, in which the Group of Seven works were being shown. The works by 'community based' artists were hung in a space that was also occupied by educational materials developed for the exhibition, including computer terminals, a fax machine, and a blackboard for 'graffiti' responses, which the visitors were encouraged to share as part of this exhibition's interactive approach.

The difference in the two locations was 'both a symbolic and actual representation of the organization of the nation,' and reflected the tensions between the representations of the dominant culture and the marginalized position of the cultural products of minority artists (Walcott, 1996: 16).

Resistance and Identity Politics in the Arts

In the postmodern world, in Canada and in other countries, non-European artists from Aboriginal, African, Caribbean, and Asian cultures are no longer willing to accept being marginalized and excluded. They are seeking ways to cast off the labels of 'minority artist,' 'primitivism,' and 'ethnic arts' and are insisting on their right to self-representation. Artists of colour and of diverse cultural backgrounds are challenging monocultural assumptions, values, and institutional practices and are asserting their right to create alternative aesthetic representations that reflect their own identities and histories, and to define their own meanings and connections to living traditions. They are demanding recognition of their talents and contributions, unfettered by the demeaning classifications associated with 'minority arts' and 'folkloric arts.' They are challenging the policies and practices of national, provincial, and municipal art agencies and funding bodies. Viewed from another perspective, this need for both access and recognition, which is felt by artists from diverse racial and cultural backgrounds, will only be met when the dominant culture and its institutions acknowledge their role in perpetuating systems of inequality within the art world. However, there are many examples of the powerful backlash that often follows any attempt to alter the dominant culture's control of the art world in any significant way.

The introduction of identity politics into the art world has often meant that a handful of artists of colour are drawn into the system for a brief period of time and may be included in a show or even have a show of their own (Becker, 1994). However, 'sweeping in the margins leaves the white power structure of museum curatorial staffs and those above them relatively untouched' (67).

In the context of the art of indigenous peoples, this point can easily be illustrated. After the Second World War, Inuit craft-production co-operatives were set up in Northern Canada, and everything they produced had to meet an aesthetic standard, which was that the carvings had to be 'primitive.' To this end, the government employed crafts experts, who weeded out 'unsuitable' works. The Innuit were denied the right to appropriate forms from the West or to draw from modern representations, for in doing so they would be diluting their 'primitivism.'

Operating on the same set of assumptions, at Expo 67 in Montreal the Canadian government determined that it could not allow Native Canadians to control a space in the projected 'Indians of Canada' pavilion because they might use it to draw attention to their current struggles, especially over land claims (Brett, 1991).

In 1988, in conjunction with the Calgary Olympics, the government of Canada mounted an exhibition of North American art at the Glenbow Museum called *The Spirit Sings*. The Lubicon Cree of northern Alberta, who were involved in a billion-dollar land claim dispute with the federal and provincial governments, boycotted the exhibition (Brett, 1991).

In each of these cases, the dominant culture with its institutions and bureaucracies maintained control and power, not only over the form and content of the cultural productions, but also in a significant way over the lives of the communities from which these artists emerged.

The pervasiveness of discrimination by American museums was documented in a research study presented at the Agencies of Survivial Conference at Hunter College (Pindell, 1989, quoted in Cruz, 1992).* The findings of this study clearly demonstrated that most major American museums have almost totally excluded artists of colour from the mainstream art world. Between 1980 and 1987, there were seventy-three exhibits at the Guggenheim, and fully 100 per cent of the artists represented were white. At the Metropolitan Museum, out of 208 exhibitions there was one solo exhibition by an artist of colour. The 242 exhibitions at the Museum of Modern Art included two one-person exhibitions by artists of colour. At the Whitney Museum of American Art, 156 exhibi-

---

* Note that to the authors' knowledge, no such study has been conducted in Canada.

tions were presented, and 92 per cent of them represented artists of European descent.

The former deputy director of the Studio Museum in Harlem investigated a sample of museums, private collections, and corporate collections to update the information in this report and found that the figures had not changed substantially as of 1992. She also pointed out that those who were accumulating this data in their own institutions were surprised by the numbers and what they implied (Cruz, 1992).

Despite all the coercive patterns of marginalization, oppression, and exclusion as indicated by this kind of data, artists of colour and diverse cultural backgrounds have continued to make art – to paint, sculpt, photograph, and, more recently, create new art forms.

One of the first art institutes to provide a space for the work of non-European artists was the Whitney Museum of American Art. The Whitney's Biennial Exhibition began in 1993, when for the first time artists of colour were included as a central focus. The show also departed from tradition by exhibiting films, videos, photography, and other nontraditional art forms. A further change was related to some of the subject matter: many of the works in the exhibit dealt with issues of sexism and racism.

The heterogeneity of this exhibition (both of artists and art forms) set off a huge backlash. The fact that the Whitney was for the first time refusing to leave certain communities outside the door of the institution created 'a feeding frenzy' in the popular press and among art critics, who perceived a new kind of domination of the show by artists of colour (Becker, 1994).

The dominant culture's resistance to artists of colour takes many forms. In a contemporary context, the concept of 'primitivism' shifts to the notion of 'ethnic' arts – that is, to the aesthetic forms produced by 'minority' artists. As Li points out, the impact of cultural hegemony in Canada is that racial minorities have to accommodate themselves to the artistic standards established by the dominant culture, while at the same time accommodating themselves to the articulation of their own culture as defined by the preferences imposed by the dominant group. Western-based values suggest that since racial minorities are fundamentally different, 'they are seen naturally as in the possession of folk arts and exotic cultures which are traced to their remote origin' (6). These assumptions have had a profound impact on artists of Asian, African, and Caribbean background, who are seeking to establish themselves as full participants in an art world that rejects their need and right to self-representation.

Stan Douglas, the first Canadian artist to be shown at the Whitney Museum, wrote about the effects of marginalization and stereotypical images on his own identity as a Black Canadian: 'The doubt, that pronounal doubt, doubt of the certainty of an I, is the *a priori* of my work. And it's a doubt which is understood by people who are outside of the dominant representation' (Douglas, 1994).

Conclusion

Like the case study of the Royal Ontario Museum, this analysis of the the Barnes Exhibit provides further insight into the often invisible values and ideological assumptions that operate within cultural institutions and shape museum and gallery practices. When we reflect on Barnes' aesthetic philosophy and how it influenced the way in which he set about developing one of the finest and most inclusive art collections in North America, it is clear how limited was his impact on contemporary aesthetic practices within the mainstream art movement.

The touring exhibition was selected and developed on the basis of decisions that reflected Eurocentric conventions and values. The exclusion of non-European art from the exhibition was not the result of an explicit policy decision, nor was it a carefully planned act. Rather, it was rooted in a history of modern art that has reflected Eurocentric biases and discrimination based on a categorization and classification system that perpetuates racial and cultural hierarchies. Objects collected from European/Western sources are viewed as highly valued works of art, as 'masterpieces' by individuals whose names are known. At the same time, objects created by non-Western artists remain largely unnamed, and are seen as 'interesting,' and 'exotic' – as 'cultural artifacts' associated with 'primitive' collective cultures.

Racism in the history of mainstream art does not totally deny the presence of the art forms produced by the 'others,' by those identified as 'outsiders' or 'primitives'; rather, it appropriates many of their visual ideas and images, which then come to be labelled 'primitive art.' And by creating their own interpretations of the meaning of these works, and by imposing their own cultural assumptions about the cultures and peoples that produced these 'objects,' White Western artists, curators, historians, and art critics have contributed toward erasing the contributions and representations of African, Asian, Caribbean, and Aboriginal artists.

So it was quite in keeping with tradition for the Art Gallery of Ontario and the other five museums that were part of the tour to mount an exhibition that included only European 'masterpieces'; to assume that those who saw the exhibition would be White; and to assume that it would be necessary to leave at home all examples of Barnes's extraordinary collection of 'masterpieces' from the non-European art world.

References

Araeen, Rasheed. 1991. 'From Primitivism to Ethnic Arts.' In Susan Hiller, ed. *The Myth of Primitivism: Perspectives on Art*. London and New York: Routledge. 158–82.

Barnes, Albert. 1925. 'Negro Art and America.' *Survey Graphic*. March.

Barnes, Albert, and de Mazia. 1943. *Ancient Chinese and Modern European Painting*. In Glanton (see below).

Becker, Carol, ed. 1994. *The Subversive Imagination: Artists, Society and Social Responsibility*. New York and London: Routledge.

Brett, Guy. 1991. 'Unofficial Versions.' In Susan Hiller, ed. *The Myth of Primitivism: Perspectives on Art*. London and New York: Routledge. 113–36.

Clark, Kenneth. 1969. *Civilization: A Personal View*. Harmondsworth, U.K.: Pelican. 15.

Clifford, James. 1990. 'On Collecting Art and Culture.' In Russell Ferguson, Martha Gever, Trinh T. Minh-ha, and Cornel West, eds. *Out There: Marginalization and Contemporary Culture*. New York: Museum of Contemporary Art. 144–64.

Connolly, Kevin. 1995. 'Barnes Razing.' *This Magazine*. February. 31–5.

Cruz, Pat. 1992. 'Race, Ethnicity, and Culture in Visual Arts.' A Panel Discussion. 8 January. New York, Whitney Museum of American Art.

Douglas, Stan. 1994. In Scott Watson. 'Making History.' *Canadian Art*. Winter. 30–7.

Drainie, Bronwyn. 1994. 'A Rare Exhibit of Political Incorrectness.' *Globe and Mail*. 6 October. C1.

Fulford, Robert. 1995. 'Lords of the Grange.' *Saturday Night*. June. 60.

Glanton, Richard. 1993. In *The Great French Paintings from the Barnes Foundation*. New York: Alfred Knopf in association with Lincoln University Press. vii–ix.

Goldwater, Robert. 1996. *Primitivism in Modern Art*. Rev. ed. New York: Vintage.

Graham, Ron. 1994. 'Barnes or Bust.' *Toronto Life*. September. 62–8.

Greenfield, Howard. 1987. *The Devil and Dr. Barnes: Portrait of an American Art Collector*. New York: Penguin.

Hiller, Susan, ed. 1991. *The Myth of Primitivism: Perspectives on Art*. London and New York: Routledge.

Hume, Christopher. 1994. 'Racism Charges against AGO a Bizarre Spin on Barnes Show.' *Toronto Star*. 15 December. H6.

Jordan, Glenn, and Chris Weedon. 1995. *Cultural Politics: Class, Gender, Race and the Postmodern World*. Oxford, U.K., and Cambridge, U.S.A.: Blackwell.

Kidane, Richard. 1994. 'AGO Gains on Back of Blacks.' *Share*. 8 September. 8.

Kirchoff, H.J. 1995. 'Barnes Show a Big Money-Maker for Ontario.' *Globe and Mail*. 27 April. C1.

Leval, Susana. 1992. Art Panel. Whitney Museum of American Art.

Li, Peter. 1994. 'A World Apart: The Multicultural World of Visible Minorities and the Art World of Canada.' *Canadian Review of Social Anthropology*. 31(4).

Locke, Alain., ed. 1926. *The New Negro*. Cited in Richard Glanton. 1993. *The Great French Paintings from the Barnes Foundation*. New York. Alfred Knopf in association with Lincoln University Press.

Miller, Daniel. 1991. 'Primitive Art and the Necessity of Primitivism to Art.' In Susan Hiller, ed. *The Myth of Primitivism: Perspectives on Art*. London and New York: Routledge. 50–70.

Owusu, Kwesi, ed. 1988. *Storms of the Heart*. London: Camden Press.

Phillippi, Desa, and Anna Howells, 1991. 'Dark Continents Explored by Women.' In Susan Hiller, ed. *The Myth of Primitivism: Perspectives on Art*. London and New York: Routledge. 238–60.

Pindell, Howardena. 1989. *New Art Examiner*. (Quoted in Cruz; Arts Panel.)

Piper, Adrian. 1994. *A Journal for Women Artists of African Descent: At the Cross-roads*. Summer/Fall.

Prather, Marla. 1993. *The Great French Paintings from the Barnes Foundation*. New York: Alfred Knopf in association with Lincoln University Press.

Price, Sally. 1989. '"Others" Art – Our Art.' *Third Text*. 6. 65–79.

Rhodes, Richard. 1994. *Canadian Art*. Fall.

Rosler, Martha. 1994. 'Place, Position, Power Politics.' In Carol Becker, ed. *The Subversive Imagination: Artists, Society, and Social Responsibility*. New York: Routledge. 179–99.

Varnedoe, Kirk. 1984. 'Gauguin.' In William Rubin, ed. *'Primitivism' in Twentieth-Century Art*. New York: Museum of Modern Art.

Walcott, Rinaldo. 1996. 'Lament for a Nation: The Racial Geography of "The Oh! Canada" Project.' *Fuse*. 19(4) Summer. 15–23.

Wattenmaker, Richard. 1993. 'Dr. Albert Barnes and the Barnes Foundation.' In *Great French Paintings from The Barnes Foundation*. New York: Alfred A. Knopf in association with Lincoln University Press. 3–28.

Weiss, Jeffry. 1993. 'Amedeo Modigliani.' In *Great French Paintings from The Barnes Foundation*. New York: Alfred A. Knopf in association with Lincoln University Press. 218.

Yau, John. 1990. 'Please Wait by the Cloakroom.' In Russell Ferguson, Martha Gever, Trinh T. Minh-ha, and Cornel West, eds. *Out There: Marginalization and Contemporary Cultures*. New York: New Museum of Contemporary Art and Massachusetts Institute of Technology.

4

The Writing Thru Race Conference[1]

Introduction

In the summer of 1994 the Writers Union of Canada (TWUC) sponsored the Writing Thru Race Conference. It took place in Vancouver and brought together 180 First Nations writers and writers of colour for a three-day conference. Participation in the conference's daytime events was by invitation and was restricted to writers of colour and First Nations writers. (The evening sessions, however, were open public meetings.) This small group of writers managed to capture national attention for six months. The conference was important enough that it was debated in the House of Commons. Dozens of articles and editorials were written about it, and it led to intense public discussion among some of the country's leading writers.

Writing Thru Race raised important questions about representation, cultural and racial identity, cultural appropriation, and racial and cultural barriers to access in the cultural industries. The conference challenged the power of the White writing and publishing establishments. As such, it posed a threat to the dominant culture and to some of its cherished cultural traditions and practices. The Writing Thru Race Conference symbolized the desire of Aboriginal writers and writers of colour to be recognized for their creativity and for their contributions to Canadian culture and the literary landscape.

First Nations writers and writers of colour have been publishing some of the most vital and relevant contemporary texts of our time. Yet they continue to face racial barriers that prevent them and their works from being recognized. The central catalyst for the conference was the need to bring writers, critics, and cultural workers from across the nation together in a supportive environment in which they could address the critical issue of 'race' as it relates to all aspects of the literary arts.[2]

Events

The Writing Thru Race Conference had its origins in 1989, when two First Nations writers, Lenore Keeshig-Tobias and Daniel David Moses, began raising their concerns at the TWUC annual general meeting (AGM). Keeshig-Tobias and Moses were probably the only First Nations members of the union, which at the time had only a handful of writers of colour in its membership. The two writers requested that a task force be established to examine access to publications and training, as well as broader questions of artistic authenticity and of outreach to First Nations writers and writers of colour. A formal motion was made at the 1989 meeting to create such a task force.

During the often heated discussion that followed the motion, a writer of South Asian heritage stated that although he was not against the motion, the proposers did not really know what they were talking about. This criticism led some White members to vote against the motion, since it had already been disparaged by a writer of colour. Although the vote was close, TWUC rejected the motion. At the same AGM a highly controversial panel discussed issues of access for writers of colour. One noted publisher contested the view that there was differential access for writers of colour, arguing that at his publishing firm, 'they were all colour blind.'

Some White members of TWUC, as well as the writers of colour, argued that it was time to place on the union's agenda issues such as appropriation of voice and culture, ethnocentrism, and unequal access to publishers and funding.

This 1989 meeting clearly showed that TWUC as a whole was not ready to take any kind of collective action; however, an ad hoc committee was formed to study the question of access and appropriation affecting writers of colour and their craft. (See the analysis of cultural appropriation later in this chapter.) The union developed a questionnaire and distributed it to its members. This questionnaire included questions on jury selection at the Canada Council and other funding bodies and on a variety of other issues of concern to writers of colour. The Association for Native Development of the Fine and Visual Arts assisted in this research.

The study's findings were presented in 1990, and the ad hoc committee was formally established. One of the first tasks the committee under-
took was to plan a conference at which First Nations writers and writers
of colour could come together and discuss shared concerns.

In 1992, Susan Crean was elected chair of TWUC. During her campaign, she had declared her unwillingness to chair a union that refused
to address issues of race and racism experienced by writers of colour
and First Nations writers.

In May 1992 the ad hoc committee, with the support of TWUC, sponsored 'The Appropriate Voice,' a three-day retreat in Geneva Park,
Ontario. The goal was to identify common areas of interest that required
further examination and discussion. It was considered a great success:
seventy writers discussed candidly and emotionally, for the very first
time, their feelings and experiences with racism. During these sessions a
number of issues surfaced related to empowerment, cultural and racial
identity and representation, and personal, community, and collective
equity. Many of the participants viewed the Geneva Park session as a
momentous event and a turning point for First Nations writers and
writers of colour.

The committee brought several motions from their Geneva Park session to the 1992 AGM, including the idea of holding a national conference
for writers of colour and First Nations writers. This recommendation was
highly controversial and divisive. Some writers in the union, including
Margaret Atwood and Graeme Gibson, strongly supported the initiative.
Others reacted with anger and hostility. Some members found it difficult
to understand why 'these people' needed to go off on their own to talk
about the writers' union. Pierre Berton, for instance, stated that he represented 'the society for continuing anachronism.'

Keeshig-Tobias was moved to tears by some of the racist comments.
In an interview, writer Althea Prince shared her responses: 'I felt at that
meeting that some writers were given the opportunity to reclaim their
humanity and took it and some will never change and don't care ... but
they voted the motion in – but I have never been convinced that the vote
reflected a total feeling or the most important feeling. I believe some
White writers felt that they were being invaded, although I was the only
writer of colour to have joined the union that year' (interviewed by the
author, 14 July 1994).

A number of members objected to the ad hoc committee tabling a
motion on the 'appropriation of voice.' One writer stated, 'Do you
mean that from now on, I can't write what I want to write about? That's
censorship!' Some contended that minority writers were objecting

because they were not very good writers. One White writer commented, 'If you can't write well, then the thing to do is monopolize the topic – by having this monopoly whatever you write must be accepted and published because you are the only authority on the subject.' According to Prince, this was 'an incredible definition of the appropriation of voice issue.'

In a strange twist, the issue of appropriation of voice was itself appropriated and turned into an issue of censorship. One notable writer, in his keynote address to the dinner, said that he had always appreciated being a writer in Canada because he was free to write about whatever he wanted. Now he felt that his freedom was threatened.

Despite the contentious atmosphere, a White writer moved that the ad hoc committee be renamed the Racial Minority Writers' Committee (RMWC) and be established as a formal advisory committee of TWUC. The motion was passed, and the newly structured committee polled writers of colour and First Nations writers to identify topics for discussion at a conference. The topics chosen were these: appropriation of voice, access to publishing, publishing in first languages, and the selection process for reviewers.

In June 1993, at the next AGM of the writers' union, a motion to provide $5,000 to the Racial Minority Writers' Committee to investigate the feasibility of holding a national conference on 'race' and writing was passed.

Over the next few months the RMWC, chaired by Roy Miki, met with many writers, artists, filmmakers, curators, performing artists, and other cultural workers to explore the idea of the conference. Miki reported a high level of support from ethno-racial writers, although some were concerned about the conference being associated with the union and its race politics (McFarlane, 1995: 27).

A conference planning committee was subsequently established. It included First Nations writers and writers of colour who were not members of TWUC. This committee's job was to facilitate outreach and representation, develop guidelines and objectives, obtain funding, and determine the content of the conference. A conference policy was established limiting the enrolment to First Nations writers and writers of colour. 'Conference organizers supported the ideas that a conference for First Nations writers and writers of colour would reflect valuable private gatherings that have taken place throughout the history of this land, producing particular needs not produced in a conference or social space organized within an all-inclusive paradigm' (McFarlane, 1995: 28).

This committee planned three public preconference events for November 1993, March 1994, and April 1994. Two of these events focused on racism in TWUC, barriers to publication of minority writers' works, coalition-building within and across diverse communities, and the overriding issue of appropriation. These two meetings were open only to writers of colour and First Nations writers.

The third preconference event was open to the public. It was held just prior to the 1994 annual general meeting of TWUC. Roy Miki chaired this panel discussion, which included writers Makeda Silvera, Larissa Lai, Susan Crean, and Lenore Keeshig-Tobias. After the presentations by panel members, the forum received comments from the audience. Speakers from the floor crowded to the two microphones. One participant cynically commented: 'My cousin is married to a Chinese – does that mean she can go to sessions and he can't? So you are splitting up families.'

Pierre Berton said he thought it was great that this conference was being held, and that in fact it should have been held years ago. However, he added that he was against the use of union money for this purpose. Berton suggested that 'the writers' union cannot officially support anything that excludes people on the basis of the colour of their skin' (Conference Report). He observed that the union's constitution forbade holding a meeting that was closed. He went on to suggest that a meeting should take place, but 'Don't ask for taxpayer's money!' Audience members applauded Berton's comments. Makeda Silvera, a writer of colour and union member, responded that she too paid taxes. She expressed her disgust with the people who had cheered Berton's comments, and left the stage.

Some White writers, hoping to distinguish their views from Berton's, observed that women often meet without the presence of others. Some stated that if the aim was to bring together writers of colour from all over the country, then clearly more than a three-hour meeting was required. Some supporters noted that the conference had already been voted on, and that a repeat discussion on the subject was therefore useless.

At the next day's AGM, a motion was tabled to deny the conference TWUC's financial support. This motion was subsequently amended to read that the union would support *this* conference but would never again support a special-interest-group conference. This motion was defeated by a free vote.

Althea Prince said that the process reminded her of plantation life and society, where African people were not allowed to meet in groups larger than three and their talking drums were banned. Once again, centuries later, at a meeting in Canada, African and Native voices were being silenced (Conference Report, and interview, 14 July 1994). Panellist Lenore Keeshig-Tobias talked about how her genre – story telling – was not considered fiction by mainstream writers, who were forgetting that writers cross genres all the time. She remembers that some mainstream members of the union saw this kind of comment 'as an attempt by unspecified, anonymous thought police to tell people what they could write about. But I never heard in all my life about preventing somebody from writing about something. They are not asking writers in this country to never mention Aboriginals or have any Aboriginal people in their writings. They were just saying prepare to get criticized. It was an attempt by native communities to protect copyright' (interview, with Susan Crean, 2 July 1994).

Planning for the Vancouver conference continued, but the union was faced with another difficult problem. A controversy erupted when the union invited June Callwood to be keynote speaker at a dinner. Members were angry at this decision because Callwood had once been accused of racism as a result of her activities at Nellie's, a hostel for women that Callwood had helped found in Toronto. It is important to note that these critics were White writers: no writers of colour wrote against the decision to have Callwood speak. Callwood did address the meeting, but later resigned from the union. A number of other writers resigned with her.[3]

In the weeks leading up to the conference, another controversial move made more headlines. Under intense pressure from the Reform Party in Parliament, the federal Heritage Minister, Michel Dupuis, withdrew federal funding for the conference on the basis that his government could not support an 'exclusive' conference. Roy Miki, the conference chair, said that he learned of the cancellation of funding by reading about it in the newspaper (interview, 2 July 1994). Neither he nor any other member of the union was ever officially informed by Heritage Canada.

The Canada Council, the City of Vancouver, and the Ontario Arts Council maintained their financial support for the conference, despite mounting public pressure against the event. Union members began raising funds on their own, with both executive members and those in the RMWC taking an active fund-raising role. Several high-profile members, including Margaret Atwood and even such critics as Pierre Berton, made substantial contributions. All told, this effort managed to raise more than the $22,000 that Heritage Canada had initially promised. On 30 June 1994, despite all the obstacles, the Writing Thru Race Conference convened in Vancouver.

The Conference

The opening evening was a public event and attracted about 225 people, including some members of the media. The participants were an extraordinarily diverse group; there were many artists of First Nations, African-Canadian, South Asian, and Southeast Asian origin. (Also, a handful of Whites would choose to attend the evening meetings.) Lenore Keeshig-Tobias chaired the event. She described this meeting as the second step in a ground-breaking process, the first having been the 1990 Geneva Park meeting where fifty First Nations writers and writers of colour came together. She continued: 'It feels good, doesn't it? Don't you feel good? And, as I invite the chair of the writers' union to come up, I want you all to close your eyes and take a deep breath, and I want you to realize that you are a breathing part of this prophecy and together we are going to make the prophecy come true.'

William Deverell, the chair of TWUC, began by thanking Michel Dupuis and the Reform Party for their 'unintended' contribution. This was an ironical reference to the withdrawal of support by Heritage Canada. Deverell noted that more than twice the promised grant had been raised as a result of last-minute fund-raising, with support coming from individuals, cultural organizations, and unions. He also thanked the media, who 'so smugly rose to the attack.'

On a more serious note, Deverell then reflected on the absence of so many gifted First Nations writers and writers of colour in the Canadian cultural landscape, paraphrasing American writer Richard Wright: '"If African Americans had been allowed to participate in the vital processes of our country, what would have been the texture of our lives, the pattern of our traditions, the routine of our customs, the state of our arts, the code of our laws? America would have been stronger and greater." And that speaks for the Canadian experience – you will make Canada stronger and greater through your efforts this weekend on this birthday of our country.'

Roy Miki spoke next. He discussed his own involvement in minority issues and his desire to be part of this cultural movement. He also referred to the enormous attention the media was paying to the event and to certain writers and journalists, who seemed to have unfettered access to repeat themselves over and over again. At the same time, writers of colour, after one article, were being told they had had their say. Miki added that the alienation of cultural and racial communities from the literary sphere was overwhelming. Because of the continued racism in Canadian society and the general exclusion of people of colour, it was not until the 1970s that writers were able to begin reclaiming their narratives and histories. Despite a creative outpouring, the literary arts remained exclusionary and racist. Miki reminded the group that the 'Appropriation of Voice' conference at Geneva Park had been the first step in analysing the conjunction of race and writing and was the origin of the present conference. Dionne Brand, Daniel David Moses, and Lillian Allen then took turns reading from their own work, mesmerizing the large crowd as they did so.

The atmosphere was jubilant. People were elated that they had translated a vision into reality, and had overcome so many obstacles in their path. As one person said, 'It's here, it's happening, we did it!' The same spirit of celebration characterized the first morning session. To Cecil Foster, the defining moment at the Vancouver conference occurred when writer/publisher Makeda Silvera paused in her address on publishing to ask everyone to stand and hold hands: 'And as everyone rose, and held hands, there was an audible sigh, a collective let-down, as if the worst was indeed over. And it was' (Conference Report, appendices).

The second and third evenings were both devoted to public readings. The second evening was opened by Sunera Thobani, then chair of the National Action Committee on the Status of Women, who gave a rousing presentation in which she expressed her outrage at Heritage Canada's decision to withdraw funding for the conference. As before, people cheered as individual writers read from their works. Every person and every event was marked by the same enthusiasm. Cyril Dabydeen, the poet, later described the nights of readings as 'memorable moments with the range of power of words, the effusion of language, the blood-beats of dialect, passion and tenderness. And a profusion of mother tongues and their resonances: Urdu, Punjabi, Spanish' (Dabydeen, 1994: 24).

During the day sessions, panels and workshops were held on a wide variety of diverse themes, including the following: Emergence of First Nations Writers and Storytellers in a Multicultural Urban Environment; Reading and Writing Thru Race: Theory and Practice; The Teaching of Canadian Minority Writing; Writing for Children; The Effects of Racism; Finding One's Own Identity; Access, Equity, and Publishing; Writing in One's Mother Tongue; The Politics of Writing; The Politics of Editing; Bridging Cultures Through Visual Art and Text; First Nations Peoples' Estrangement and Marginalization in the Publishing Industry; First Nations People and Storytelling; and Race and Sexuality in Writing.

The Closing Plenary Session

The last plenary focused on strategies for the future. Several recommendations were passed. One major recommendation, that a separate writers' union be created, was rejected. It was decided that another bureaucracy should not be created because the resources, time, and energy to create a separate union were lacking. Instead, there was agreement to work within TWUC, to take a proactive role in shaping its priorities, structures, and agenda, and to increase minority membership in the organization.

The responsibilities of a racial minority coalition were also delineated. It was recommended that this group act as an umbrella for all writers of colour. The group decided to meet at least once a year. Particular interest was expressed in developing smaller regional groupings. Other recommendations from the conference dealt with issues such as the accessing of resources for writings in languages other than English (or French), and the creation of better communications and publishing networks.

The plenary ended with a unanimous vote of thanks to the writers' union for its support of the conference.

Analysis

Issues of Identity, Representation, and Recognition

Identity and difference were the two central themes at this conference, which provided a forum for exploring a number of critical issues: the fluid and transforming nature of identity; the ways in which these various selves serve as a critical resource in the creative process; the potential conflicts and tensions between an individual's various identities (including race, ethnicity, gender, class, and sexual orientation) that the writer/artist must negotiate; the boundaries and barriers of colour and difference that limit the range of possibilities and opportunities; and the need for writers of colour and First Nations writers to define their own issues, agendas, priorities, visions, and values, instead of simply responding to the interests and demands of the dominant culture.

The conference provided a safe space for First Nations writers and writers of colour to assert their need and right to have their identities and differences recognized, respected, and affirmed. The participants sought an acknowledgment of their distinct cultural, racial, linguistic, and other defining characteristics. They hoped to discover collective strategies for dismantling those ideological, attitudinal, organizational, and institutional barriers that block writers of colour, First Nations writers, and writers from nondominant cultural backgrounds from full and equal participation in the mainstream of Canadian culture.

The conference was a unique opportunity for First Nations writers and writers of colour to name those assumptions and practices that diminish their words, experiences, and aspirations, that marginalize their work, and that restrict access to resources available to writers from the dominant culture.

Writer Lee Maracle (1992) continues to dream about a time when there will be no need for 'postcolonial conferences on literature, no conferences on Indigenous sovereignty and no one asks, "What do you Indians want anyway?"' She believes, however, that in the real world, colonialism is still the primary condition of First Nations peoples and that Canadian literature reflects this state of being: 'We search your institutional hallways for evidence of ourselves.' But there is no 'meeting place,' no place or space in the fortress (created and occupied by members of the dominant culture) for those whose lives and writing are shaped by colour and difference (15).

Bharati Mukherjee found her 'otherness' defined in Canada by the gradation of her skin colour – so much so, that she ultimately left the country. She asserts that 'to be a third world woman writer in North America is to confine oneself to a narrow, airless tightly roofed area' (Mukherjee and Blaise, 1977: 285).

The conference, because it directed its attention to issues of identity, difference, and racism, posed a significant threat to the Eurocentric values, assumptions, and beliefs that have formed the central core of Canadian cultural identity and aesthetic representations. This is reflected in a statement by fourteen White authors who a few months before the conference, in an attempt to silence the debate on racism in Canadian literature, wrote that fellow members of TWUC should 'shut the f--k up' on the issue (Clarke, 1994).

The decision to stage an event that was designed to challenge the power and privilege of the dominant White culture, and to empower those who had been ignored, marginalized, or silenced by cultural traditions and practices, created a sense of 'moral panic' among significant figures in the cultural world. Dionne Brand, in analysing the backlash to the conference, observed in one of its opening sessions: 'I think there is a real panic in the intellectual life of this country. That is the panic of the "white" intellectual elite. It now hears other opinions and experiences of the people of colour in the country who challenge its definitions of what the country is and what it looks like. And that panic you can also see in the everyday social life of the country' (McFarlane, 1995: 20).

At another level, the resistance, conflict, and anger expressed at the meetings of TWUC, which spilled out across the pages of the national media and found its way into the speeches and acts of politicians, reflected a deeper state of political and cultural tension, uncertainty, and anxiety. It drew attention to issues that have become increasingly burdensome and problematic in these last decades of the twentieth century. Among its other contributions, the conference brought these questions into sharp focus:

- What is Canadian culture?
- What does it mean to be Canadian?
- Who is included in the construction of the notions of 'we' and 'our,' in relation to definitions of culture and the Canadian state?
- How should the state organize itself in relation to public policies and programs dealing with diversity and pluralism, access and equity, and antiracism?
- Who really belongs in the mainstream of Canadian life?
- How shall we deal with our cultural, racial, linguistic, and religious differences, and with other social markers such as gender, sexual orientation, and class differences?
- Whose cultural knowledge, values, traditions, and histories should be recognized, and whose cultures given pre-eminence?
- How do the above issues impact on cultural production and aesthetic representations?

Cultural Appropriation

It is not surprising, then, that in many of the conference's sessions the issue of cultural appropriation was explored, debated, and agonized over. Controversies over 'cultural appropriation' have grown in recent years. The term refers to artists, curators, and writers incorporating into their cultural representations and productions (paintings, novels, plays, and so on), narratives, images, and artifacts derived from cultures of which they are not members.

In the appropriation process, cultural forms, expressions, and objects that have been developed by First Nations and people of colour are interpreted through the voices of White writers, publishers, artists, producers, and musicians. Williams describes the phenomenon of cultural appropriation metaphorically: When members of the dominant culture benefit materially from the production and dissemination of the history, traditions, and experiences of another cultural group, it is as if 'a literary party [is] being held in the house that's been in their family as far back as memory serves,' and the family is not included in the celebration (in Black and Morris, 1994: 20). Ayanna Black observes, 'The issue of appropriation has to do with access; it is rooted in the problem of access. For 300 years, we, women, we people of colour, have had no access to many institutions in this country' (ibid.).

Beth Brant made this point in a panel discussion (1991) by observing: 'I do not say that only Indians can write about Indians. But you can't steal my stories and call them your own. You can't steal my spirit and call it your own. This is the history of North America – stolen property, stolen lives, stolen dreams and stolen spirituality ... If your history is one of cultural domination you must be aware ... you have to tell the truth about your role, your history, your internalized domination and supremacy' (12).

Echoing a similar view, Lee Maracle (1992) observes that in order to challenge the existing colonial condition that characterizes Canadian literature, a new space must be created for the 'others' (15). This means that writers from the dominant culture must resist imagining that they can write on the behalf of 'others,' or that they should. 'It means that those who lay claim to a place in the dreamspace of creativity must come to understand the difference between honest stretching into the world of the imagination and pirating someone else's imagination' (15).

The production of images through the process of cultural appropriation has had lasting effects. For instance, the written and photographic depictions of Black people by White journalists (such as those which have filled the pages of *National Geographic* for generations) have long focused on the 'exotic,' the 'different,' and the 'alien' – on the natives in their 'local colour.' The misrepresentations, myths, and misconceptions resulting from cultural appropriation have imposed a sense of diminished humanity on people of colour. Such impositions reinforce notions of the intellectual and cultural inferiority of the 'other.'

Cultural appropriation is clearly seen in the appropriation of the cultural symbols and stories of First Nations peoples. White artists and writers often romanticize dying cultures. This expression of White paternalism then sends contradictory messages. For instance, writers and artists who claim to be 'saving' the legacies of doomed Indian cultures are often ignoring First Nations rights. W.P. Kinsella has won numerous literary prizes for his stories about First Nations people, but is seen in a less positive light by some. Drew Hayden Taylor (1995), a playwright who is an Ojibway, argues that Kinsella's characters 'don't sound like any Indian I ever heard' (17).

From a historic perspective, writing about, publishing, and profiting from another group's history and culture is closely tied to relations of property, power, and privilege. It is related to the histories, to the experience of erasure, and to the silencing of people of colour who have relationships to 'Third World' countries. For First Nations writers, it is tied to attempts to produce work in the colonial context of Canada.

In the symposium 'Whose Voice Is It, Anyway?' sponsored by *Books in Canada* (1991), a group of writers explored the issue of appropriation of voice. Daniel David Moses explained that 'native people should tell native stories.' Many native people feel that their stories, symbols, songs, and images belong to them and can only be given away by their owners (15).

Poet George Elliott Clarke (ibid.) raged against the dispossession of voice caused by ethnocentrism, which is reflected in First Nations writers being locked out of publishing houses and distribution networks, and in an absence of literary scholars and reviewers who understand and appreciate First Nations aesthetics. He concluded: 'We must seize the means of cultural propagation; we must fight to achieve the grants, the reviews, the public readings, the writer-in-residenceships, the media invitations, the university chairs ... all Canadians have tales to tell and poems to sing ... Whose literature is it, anyway?' (12–13).

In an aesthetic world dominated by Eurocentric values, images, and norms, people of colour are either absent from most cultural production or misrepresented by stereotypes and racial anomalies. Browning (1992) observed that 'any representation of ourselves and our cultural experiences done by an outsider would be from a comparatively superficial perspective, simply because he/she hasn't had the experience of surviving racial oppression – complete with all its complications, consequences, and contradictions' (33).

M.G. Vassanji (1991) responded to the allegation that resistance to cultural appropriation represents a form of censorship that threatens artistic creativity: 'How easy it is to cry "Censorship!" or "Art is universal!" and then sit back smugly – and safely ... There are many people whose stories have not been told while stories of those who dominated them have been stuffed down their throats *ad nauseum* ... It is when people have been colonized or worse, when their stories and even languages have long been suppressed, and are sold in the market-place by those belonging to dominant cultures that issues become charged' (16).

Writers like Vissanji have paid a heavy price for wanting to tell their own stories, for not fitting into the prevailing Eurocentric values and norms that govern traditional literary theory, and for not writing 'from the right location' (Mukherjee, 1994). Although his first novel, *The Gunny Sack* (1989), won the Commonwealth Prize for the African region, the book received little critical attention in Canada.

Literary Criticism as Biased Discourse

All literary criticism is ideological. Literary criticism is influenced by judgments and affected by particular sets of values and beliefs. When cultural critics offer a judgment of a text, they do so in some *social/ cultural and/or institutional context*.

The relevant context might include one or more of gender, race, and class, and differences in age, sexual orientation, and regional background. Literary authority tends to be accorded along lines of social and cultural dominance; those who engage in literary criticism are usually those with institutional, social, and cultural power. The interpretation of a text and the determination of its value depend on and are strongly influenced by 'the particular assumptions, expectations and interests with which we approach the work' (Hernstein Smith, 1995: 184).

Recent conceptions of literary evaluation underscore the centrality of the implicit assumptions a critic makes when judging a piece of work. These interpretations are likely to be interesting and useful to a particular audience to the extent that audience holds assumptions and perspectives similar to those of the literary reviewer. The appropriateness of a literary opinion for other people 'depends on the extent to which they share one's particular perspective, which is always a function of one's relevant characteristics' (ibid.: 184).

A literary critic who functions in the centre of the dominant culture feels safe in a cocoon of rigid adherence to the dual notions of 'objectivity' and 'neutrality.' So-called 'objective,' 'neutral' reviews and literary criticisms are explained on the basis that there exists a body of universal criteria and standards that can be applied to all literary (and art) analysis. But 'objectivity' and 'neutrality' are both contested categories.

The notion of 'objectivity' is indeed problematic. The difficulty for literary theory and criticism is that the notions of 'objectivity,' 'truth,' and 'universalism,' and similar traditional values held by literary critics, no longer provide the direction and meaning they once did. From the perspective of many writers who are not part of the mainstream dominant culture, these concepts are not absolute but should be interpreted 'relative to differing and competing vocabularies or paradigms' (Fish, 1994: 57). Critics who wed themselves to false notions of 'objectivity' and 'neutrality,' often end up displaying a dereliction of imagination. They fail to understand how racism structures (and limits) their own imagination. What is ignored is the fact that 'notions of literary quality are inevitably ideological, that we are as readers and critics resolutely situated' (Srivastava, 1991: 33).

In a presentation at the Writing Thru Race Conference, the writer and educator Arun Mukherjee examined the issue of literary criticism in relation to the double-standards that pervade the Canadian literary establishment. As a professor of Canadian literature with a particular focus on writers of colour, she has her students analyse reviews and articles dealing with some of these writers' texts. The purpose of this exercise is to help them identify the ways in which the literary establishment marginalizes and dismisses the work of First Nations writers and writers of colour. She points to the Eurocentric and racist nature of Canadian literary nationalism, which implies that the Canadian identity is defined in settler/colonial terms. Mukherjee believes there is a pressing need for secondary sources that respect and understand the contexts from which First Nations writers and writers of colour speak – the historical, religious, literary, and cultural traditions that inform a piece of work.

Through this analysis, Mukherjee's students discover that the work of First Nations writers and writers of colour is commonly labelled 'new,' 'hyphenated,' 'immigrant,' and 'ethnic'; rarely is there reference to the 'Canadianness' of the writing.

Similarly, M.G. Vassanji (1985) explains how the literary establishment marginalizes writers of colour by labelling them as immigrants: 'The term is ... used somewhat condescendingly to describe a transitional state of no vital importance, a stage of growing up which we all have to go through before maturity' (2). Vassanji continues that Canadian critics perceive that 'a writer demonstrates his maturity when he begins to talk of his "Canadian experience"' (ibid.: 3).

In another context, but expressing this same concern, Lee Maracle (1992) observes: 'Our words, our sense and use of language are not judged by the standards set by the poetry and stories we create. They are judged by the standards set by others' (13).

An example of the subtle way in which traditional literary criticism ignores the social context of writers of colour is found in a review in the *Toronto Star* of two recent books by bell hooks: 'hooks sometimes writes too ponderously for the general reader she is trying to reach in these books, she is thin-skinned about criticism of her work, and too ready to interpret negative comments as racist and sexist' (Martin, 1995). The reviewer comments that she admires the fact that hooks approaches race and gender from an intellectual rather than a confrontational posture. When we decode this reviewer's comments, however, her attempt to 'ghettoize' hooks's work as unsuitable for the *general reader*, the White audience, becomes apparent. By 'ghettoizing' an author's work in this way, we are reclassifying it; patronizing labels such as 'interesting' and 'a good example of minority art' are certain to follow. Writing that explores the writer's personal experiences with   racism is perceived as outside the boundaries of 'good literature.'

When issues such as race and gender are analysed, confrontational postures are seen as anti-intellectual. Another journalist, Crawford Kilian (1994), makes a similar critique of the quality of writing by writers who incorporate the subject of racism into their work: 'fighting racism is the job of a propagandist – not a free writer. A minority writer who must write only about the evils of racism is still a writer in chains.'

Reviewers such as these assume that resistance, protest, and dissent, in writing and in other art forms, are antithetical to intellectualism. Perhaps even more importantly, literary and other forms of criticism fail to imagine the significance of racism and diverse cultural experiences in the life of the writer and his or her work. Many White/Anglo literary critics have great difficulty accepting the centrality of cultural and racial identity in the work of any writer, and the imposed framework of 'otherness' that is so important to First Nations writers and writers of colour.

Nourbese Philip (1992) poses the following question to literary 'authorities' who reject the need or right of writers of colour to deal with the pain of racism in their writing: 'How do we lose the sense of being "othered" and how does Canada begin its m/othering of us who now live here, were born here, have given birth here – all under a darker sun?' (16).

Writing about this 'White gaze,' poet Meena Alexander (1987/8) says: 'To what extent I might ask myself if I were to take a theoretical distance from all this, was my sense of self-identity invaded by the gaze, by the look of the world to which I was the Other. But there was no way in which I could stand apart from that question. It was what I was and in many ways am, this perpetual reconstruction of identity.'

Zool Suleman (1991), a South Asian writer, provides an example of Eurocentrism in literary criticism. Suleman cites a television panel on the *Journal*, a CBC news magazine, that reviewed M.G. Vassanji's book *No New Land* (McClelland and Stewart). The panel consisted of three White reviewers: Browyn Drainie (Toronto), Susan Musgrave (Sydney, B.C.), and Rex Murphy (St John's). Clearly, the producer was sensitive to issues of gender and geography; yet that producer did not feel it necessary to take racial or cultural differences into account. The perspective of a South Asian writer/reviewer would have enriched the discussion, not because the reviewer would have necessarily been more positive, but rather he or she might have been more informed about the cultural reference points, and about the impact of racism on people of colour (in particular, South Asians) who are attempting to join Canadian society. Suleman suggests that the comments of two of the reviewers were coloured by a Eurocentric gaze, in that they attempted to explain the book's South Asian characters through a White, Anglo-European perspective.

Barriers to Cultural Industries Experienced by First Nations Writers and Writers of Colour

If, as suggested in the above analysis, notions of literary quality are influenced by social, cultural, and gender differences and by other social markers, these may be the crucial factors that prevent writers of colour and First Nations writers from accessing the publishing industry. This issue was identified and discussed in the Writing Thru Race Conference. Marwan Hassan (1994–5) asserts that while all writers are affected by problems in the production and distribution of their works, First Nations writers and writers of colour are further restrained by the social and economic inequalities and divisions that characterize society. Their racial and cultural identities affect how publishers view their work. Hassan analyses how market conditions rationalize publishers' decisions, and at the same time reflect the exclusion and discrimination experienced by people of colour in other arenas.

Marlene Nourbese Philip (1992) points out that a significant part of the publishing industry is not market-driven; rather, it is subsidized by a variety of mechanisms including government grants and loan guarantees. She argues that publishers who receive public support should show a greater commitment to those communities outside of the dominant culture – to what Graeme Gibson (1991) calls 'non-commercial minorities' (15).

The Women's Press provides an excellent illustration of minority exclusion from publishing. For the first sixteen years of its existence the Women's Press failed to publish the work of a single woman of colour. In 1988 this fact was publicly aired and became a source of contention within the organization. All of this was after three short stories for a proposed anthology had been rejected by the press's publishing and policy group after they had been accepted by the fiction manuscript committee. The reason cited for the rejection of the stories was that they were racist.

According to Nourbese Philip, the ensuing debate focused on two issues: first, whether the publishing and policy group had the right to reject material already accepted by the manuscript committee; and second, whether the stories were actually racist. What should have been a focus of attention – the lack of access by African, Native, and Asian women to publishing resources – was lost in the debate about 'whether White middle class women ought or ought not to be allowed, or should be able, to use the voice of traditionally oppressed groups!' (1992: 216). Eventually the Women's Press developed antiracist guidelines for submissions, which stated that the press 'will publish fiction and non-fiction work by women of colour on issues determined by their concerns' (ibid.).

Himani Bannerji (1993: xi) argues that the feminist presses and publications are 'bereft of our presence ... and even now, with the exception of the reorganized Women's Press, non-white women and men almost wholly rely on presses and publications within their own communities.' Throughout the conference, many participants shared Bannerji's view that the publishers and presses, including scholarly journals and cultural magazines, contribute to 'a situation of racism by omission' (ibid.). The problem of invisibility and inaudibility of writers of colour and First Nations writers leads to further entrenchment of stereotypes, and to the perpetuation of myths and misconceptions about those people.

Racist Discourse in the Media

As soon as the Writing Thru Race Conference was announced in the TWUC newsletter, a stream of media attacks began that lasted for several months and continued for weeks after the conference ended. Considering that fewer than two hundred people attended the conference, and that its budget was under $100,000, the media's almost obsessive coverage of the event was surprising to many. This coverage did much to heighten conflict and division, in that it helped construct and sustain the dichotomy between the 'excluded Whites' and the 'militant racial minorities.' As Scott McFarlane, a member of the conference planning committee, explained: 'The familiar conflation of political and aesthetic notions of representation in their articles is notably sensational and telling of both a state of crisis and the desire to sell newspapers' (1995: 28).

The largely negative coverage played on several themes. One of the most important of these was that the conference itself was an act of racial discrimination and reflected the tyranny of political correctness that had overtaken the country. Robert Fulford, a prominent media and literary critic, criticized a fellow journalist, Bronwyn Drainie, for pointing out that White journalists had become upset with the staging of the conference. He implied that she had fallen hopelessly into the politically correct camp, that she was mouthing 'skin-colour thinking,' which in his opinion had become the norm in Canada (*Globe and Mail*, see Drainie, 1994b). And Richard Gwyn (1994) in the *Toronto Star* noted that 'the conference is an example of racism practised by those who have suffered from it ... Something is going terrible wrong. All these noble intentions seem to be turning us into the hell of a "systematically racist society."'

Editorial writers also took up this theme. The *Toronto Star* (5 April 1994) stated that 'reverse discrimination does not end injustice, but rather feeds it.' On a related motif of reverse racism, Canadian Press (1994) suggested that restricting White writers from the conference was similar to the ban preventing Sikh and Jewish veterans from wearing religious headgear in Royal Canadian Legion halls.

Another theme played upon by the press was that policies such as multiculturalism and employment equity are examples of the hyperconsciousness about race and ethnicity that now characterizes Canadian society. For example, Richard Gwyn (1994) noted that 'we are at risk today of institutionalizing racism in Canada ... this often happens as a by-product of attempts to combat racism or to advantage the disadvantaged. But the effect of their actions can be to create a hyperconsciousness about race.'

Philip Marchand, the *Toronto Star*'s cultural critic, made a similar point when he commented: 'Whatever good effects the conference might have had for its participants, it is undeniably part of a recent trend toward intensifying racial and ethnic consciousness' (1994).

In addition, strong editorial positions were taken. The *Globe and Mail* (1994) argued: 'That these policies should sometimes lead to exclusionary events, such as the Vancouver Conference (will the next meeting be whites-only?), or mandated discrimination in hiring to further ethnic "balance" is simply government policy.'

Many writers took exception to the fact that there was public funding for this conference. In his usual exuberant manner, Pierre Berton suggested, 'Have a meeting! Have many meetings! But don't ask for taxpayers' money' (quoted in Ross, 1994).

An editorial in the *Toronto Star* (1994) wondered aloud whether public agencies such as the Canada Council, the Ontario Arts Council, British Columbia Cultural Services, and Vancouver City Council would fund an enterprise that, for example, banned Blacks or Browns.

A *Globe and Mail* editorial (1994) focused on the premise that multiculturalism is the core of the problem: 'As much as we share the revulsion to a publicly-funded racially exclusive conference ... it must be admitted this is entirely consistent with public policy ... governments spend many millions of dollars encouraging Canadians to "survive" with the help of hyphenations.'

Finally, a theme of some significance was that the conference was an example of apartheid, segregation, and the erosion of Canadian values, as well as a threat to Canadian culture and identity. Michael Valpy (1994) in the *Globe and Mail* described the conference as 'apartheid' and a manifestation of a 'cancer' threatening 'the continued existence of a Canadian cultural identity.' In his view, TWUC saw nothing in Canadian society 'except white or Anglo oppression.' The 'cancer' he alluded to 'mocks the ethos, values and social and political attitudes that, over years, have been painstakingly shaped into the rules by which Canadians govern themselves and the code by which they behave.'

In the *Toronto Star*, Philip Marchand (1994) made reference to Marshall McLuhan, who over thirty years ago predicted the rise of tribalism in our society because of the influence of the electronic media: 'Whether or not he was right about the cause, he was certainly right about the result.' And in the *Globe and Mail*, Robert Fulford (1994) took this very strong position: 'The no-white rule symbolizes a startling change in the way Canada handles issues of this kind ... We have apparently moved from the era of pluralism to the era of multiculturalism. The old liberal pluralism holds that each of us has rights as an individual: this is the idea that has animated social progress for generations. The new multiculturalism, on the other hand, focuses on the rights of groups, and sees each of us as the member of a racially designated cluster ... Now the Writers' Union of Canada wants to tell us that closed is open, limited is free, exclusion is inclusion, and private is public.'

The *Toronto Star* (1994) editorialized: 'What is more disturbing is that governments are about to be a party to an exercise that will stand the Charter of Rights on its head.'

The media also paid close attention to the public funding issues, especially the announcement that the federal ministry had withdrawn its funding at the last moment, forcing conference organizers to solicit money privately. It is noteworthy that the Writing Thru Race Conference attracted the attention of some of Toronto's most important and respected culture critics, including Fulford, Valpy, Marchand, and Gwyn. Moreover, both major Toronto newspapers took a strong editorial position on this issue and wrote about it more than once. Clearly, the decision to exclude non-Whites from all but the public events of the conference struck a major nerve in the media.

Conclusions

For First Nations writers and writers of colour, the Writing Thru Race Conference provided a space and place for developing individual and collective strategies for dealing with the racism that had long been embedded in their personal and professional lives. In the events leading up to the conference, the new and diverse voices of Canada demanded to be heard. The Writing Thru Race Conference also represented a significant shift in approaches to resisting and challenging racism in cultural production. In incorporating an exclusionary policy, designed to reflect and respond to the particular and pressing needs and interests of First Nations writers and writers of colour, the conference organizers were pursuing a deliberate strategy of moving away from multicultural inclusionary paradigms (McFarlane, 1995).

Contrary to the public discourse that resulted, a conference for a group of people who share a common body of interests and concerns is not a commitment to a lifetime of separation and exclusion from the mainstream culture. Nor does it represent the dismantling of Canadian culture or national identity. It is, rather, a manifestation of the need of every oppressed group to come together in a safe space where they can share their disappointments, pain, and anger; celebrate what they have created and accomplished; mobilize, energize, and empower one another; and explore, as individuals and collectivities, new strategies and tools for dismantling barriers and crossing boundaries.

The resistance to the conference and other similar initiatives on the part of the white writing and publishing industry reflects how threatened the literary élite is by the challenge to extend the definition of 'we' – that is, to expand the literary landscape to include those of different races, ethnicities, and other social markers.

The huge outcry from various constituencies – including the government, the media, and literary critics – against this conference and earlier initiatives suggests that the discourse of pluralism, inclusion, and equality has served as a facade to mask the power, position, and privilege of the dominant cultural community. Both individuals and cultural agencies resist change – in particular, change that threatens their own power base within a context of inclusiveness.

Ultimately, however, the conference was an act of affirmation and recognition, and an act of defiance and protest. For First Nations writers and writers of colour it was an affirmation and recognition of their identity as critical participants in what Lenore Keeshig-Tobias refers to as a 'cultural revolution' (see Griffin, 1994) that is redefining what it means to be Canadian, redefining what it means to be a Canadian writer, redefining the literary landscape of Canada. The conference was also an act of defiance against Eurocentric ideologies and exclusionary practices. It was an act of resistance to the notions of liberalism and pluralism that perpetuate White power and privilege within the arts.

Notes

1 Many of the observations and statements contained in this case study are based on interviews with writers of colour and other writers who played a key role in the evolution of the conference, and with those who organized and participated in the three-day event. For reasons of confidentiality the authors have had to refrain from identifying their sources unless their views have appeared in the published literature, or were used in public presentations, or unless permission was given by the respondent.

2 The conference objectives cited in the report were:

(1) To provide a context for writers of colour and other concerned writers to discuss 'race' and contemporary writing in the context of issues such as

colonization, appropriation, history, victimization, class, sexuality, first vs second languages, advocacy and subjectivity;

(2) To assist in the development of emerging writers of colour through small group workshops, interdisciplinary talks, panel sessions on practical and theoretical topics, and the sharing of information;

(3) To explore strategies that would allow writers of colour more access to various areas of the literary arts, including book and magazine publication, reviews, grants, and awards;

(4) To develop innovative terminologies and methodologies to foster a more sensitive and comprehensive critical and pedagogical awareness of 'racial' discourses, and racist assumptions in contemporary writing and theory;

(5) To devise means by which work by writers of colour could become vital components in the curriculum of public schools and academic institutions, especially in the area of Canadian literary studies;

(6) To recognize the contribution of First Nations writers and writers of colour to contemporary literature. (Hall, 1995)

3 Earlier, Callwood had been the subject of controversy when Marlene Nourbese Philip attempted to hand her a flyer as she was leaving a meeting of PEN. Callwood apparently said 'fuck off' to her. Nourbese Philip took this as a racist incident, and it generated considerable press coverage, including a cover story in *Maclean's*.

References

Alexander, Meena. 1987/8. 'The Poem's Second Life: Writing and Self Identity.' *Toronto South Asian Review*. Fall/Winter. 77–85.

Bannerji, Himani, ed. 1993. *Returning the Gaze: Essays on Racism, Feminism and Politics*. Toronto: Sister Vision Press.

Black, Ayanna, and Roberta Morris. 1994. 'More Black Talk: Race, Sex, Difference and Literal Methods.' *Fuse*. 15(6). 18–21.

Brant, Beth. 1991. Symposium: 'Whose Voice Is It, Anyway?' *Books in Canada*. January/February. 11–17.

Browning, Janisse. 1992. 'Self-Determination and Cultural Appropriation.' *Fuse*. 15(4). 31–5.

Canadian Press. 1994. 'Barring of White Writers Denounced: MP Likens It to Turban-Banning by Legion Halls.' *Vancouver Sun*. 4 June.

– 1994. '"Racist" Writers Hit: Workshop Bars Whites.' *Vancouver Province*. 5 June.

Cecill, Bet. 1994. 'Funding Cut for Writers' Conference Shows Ignorance of Racial Differences.' *Vancouver Sun*. 14 June.

Cernetig, Miro. 1994. 'The Race Controversy Fizzled.' *Globe and Mail*. 4 July.

Clarke, George Elliott. 1991. Symposium: 'Whose Voice Is It, Anyway?' *Books in Canada*. January/February. 11–17.

– 1994. 'After Word.' *Possibilitiis Literary Arts Magazine*. 1(2). 48.

Dabydeen, Cyril. 1994. 'Celebrating Difference.' *Books in Canada*. September.

Drainie, Bronwyn. 1994a. 'Controversial Writers' Meeting Is Both Meet and Right.' *Globe and Mail*. 16 April. E1.

– 1994b. 'Colour Me Politically Correct and Proud of It.' *Globe and Mail*. June 25. C1.

Fish, Stanley. 1994. *There's No Such Thing as Free Speech ... and It's a Good Thing too*. New York and Oxford: Oxford University Press.

Foster, Cecil. 1994. 'An Infusion of Colour.' *Quill & Quire*. September.

Fulford, Robert. 1994. 'George Orwell Call Your Office.' *Globe and Mail*. 30 March. C1.

Gibson, Graeme. 1991. Symposium: 'Whose Voice Is It, Anyway?' *Books in Canada*. January/February. 15.

Globe and Mail. 1994. Editorial. 'Writhing thru Race.' 9 April.

Griffin, Kevin. 1994. 'Minority Writers' Conference claims Revolutionary Success.' *Vancouver Sun*. 4 July. A2.

Gwyn, Richard. 1994. 'Good Intentions Pave Canada's Road to Racist Hell.' *Toronto Star*. 8 July.

Hall, Joyce. 1995. *Writing Thru Race Conference Final Report*. The Writers' Union of Canada.

Hassan, Marwan. 1994–5. 'Chain of Readers.' *Paragraph*. 16(3).

Hayden Taylor, Drew. 1995. *Toronto Star*. 28 January. J7.

Hernstein Smith, Barbara. 1995. 'Value/Evaluation.' In F. Lentricchia and T. McLaughlin, eds. *Critical Terms and Literary Study*. Chicago: University of Chicago Press.

Kilian, Crawford. 1994. 'Minority Writers Are Wasting Their Time.' *Vancouver Province*. 18 April.

Kostash, Myrna. 1994a. 'You Don't Check Your Colour at the Door.' *Globe and Mail*. 9 May.

– 1994b. *Saturday Night*. Letter to the editor, December. 19.

Lee, Jeff. 1994. 'Writers' Session Barring Whites Triggers Concerns.' *Vancouver Sun*. 7 April.

McFarlane, Scott. 1995. 'The Haunt of Race: Canada's Multiculturalism Act, the Politics of Incorporation and Writing Thru Race.' *Fuse*. 18(3) Spring. 18–31.

Maracle, Lee. 1992. 'The "Post-Colonial" Imagination.' *Fuse*. 16 Fall. 12–15.

Marchand, Philip. 1994. 'Politics the Real CanLit Power Fuel.' *Toronto Star*. 5 July.

Martin, Sandra. 1995. 'The Intellectual High Road.' *Toronto Star*. 17 January. C19

Miki, Roy. 1994. 'Why Are We Holding the Vancouver Conference.' *Globe and Mail*. 7 April.

Morrison, Toni. 1992. *Playing in the Dark: Whiteness and the Literary Imagination*. Boston, Mass.: Harvard University Press.

Moses, David. 1991. Symposium: 'Whose Voice Is It, Anyway?' *Books in Canada*. January/February.

Mukherjee, Arun. 1994–5 'Teaching Racial Minority Writing: Problems and Challenges.' *Paragraph: The Canadian Fiction Review*. 16(3) Winter/Spring.

Mukherjee, Bharati, and Clark Blaise. 1977. *Days and Nights in Calcutta*. Garden City, N.Y.: Doubleday.

Nourbese Philip, Marlene. 1992. *Frontiers: Essays and Writings on Racism and Culture*. Stratford, Ont.: Mercury Press.

Ross, Val. 1994. 'Shouting Match Mars Forum on Writers Union Conference.' *Globe and Mail*. 14 May.

Salutin, Rick. 1994. 'Islands in the Mainstream.' *Globe and Mail*. 8 April.

Srivastava, Aruna. 1993. 'Re-Imaging Racism: South Asian Women Writers.' In Himani Bannerji. ed. *Returning the Gaze: Essays on Racism, Feminism and Politics*. Toronto: Sister Vision Press. 103–21.

Suleman, Zool. 1991. 'Ventrililoquism and Vox: A Review of the *Journal's* Review of *No New Land*.' *Fuse*. Fall 19–24.

Toronto Star. 1994. Editorial. 'Excluding Whites.' 5 April.

Valpy, Michael. 1994. 'A Nasty Serving of Cultural Apartheid.' *Globe and Mail*. 8 April.

Vassanji, M. G. 1985. 'Introduction.' *A Meeting of Streams: South Asian Canadian Literature*. Toronto: TSAR.

– 1991. Symposium: 'Whose Voice is It, Anyway?' *Books in Canada*. January/February. 11–17.

'Whose Voice Is It, Anyway?' 1991. Symposium. *Books in Canada*. January/February. 11–24.

Williams, S. 1992. 'The Appropriation of Noise.' *Fuse*. 15(6).

5

The Black/Dance Music Station

Background

Prior Applications

African-Canadian music professionals have complained since the 1960s that mainstream radio is neglecting Black/dance music, particularly the music of local musicians. In October 1984, Robert Wood submitted a proposal for a Black/dance music radio station that would serve the needs of the African-Canadian community in Metropolitan Toronto. Wood was responding to a call from the Canadian Radio-Television and Telecommunications Commission (CRTC) for applications for a licence to establish a new FM station, 97.3 – the last frequency available in Toronto. Eighteen months later the CRTC, in Decision 86-232 released on 20 March 1986, announced that it had awarded that frequency to Redmon Communications, which had proposed a classical format.

The CRTC rejected the application for a Black/dance music format because it was not satisfied that such a station would actually increase minority talent. A determined Wood, with the assistance of engineer Mark Tilson, found a different frequency – 92.5 – that could be diverted to Toronto from Peterborough, and applied for it on 15 July 1987. The hearing for this application began on 1 February 1988 in Toronto; a short time later the CRTC, in Decision 88-293, denied Wood's application.

FM 92.5

On 31 July 1989 the CRTC issued a call for applications to operate FM 92.5. Except for frequencies used by the former CKO all-news format,

FM 92.5 was the last remaining frequency available in Toronto. This call was for the same frequency to which Decision 88-293 applied. Eleven applicants responded to the CRTC's call. Five of the applicants proposed a country music format, four proposed a Black or dance or rhythm and blues format, one proposed a mix of pop, folk, and jazz, and another proposed adult, contemporary programming. Two of the Black/dance music applicants – Milestone Communications, and J. Robert Wood – had the support of segments of Metropolitan Toronto's African-Canadian community. None of the other applications recognized the interests of African-Canadian communities to any significant degree, or made substantial provisions for African-Canadian participation in ownership, staffing, or on-air programming.

In making the application for FM 92.5, Wood was careful to respond directly to the concerns the CRTC had raised in Decision 88-293. Thus, his programming proposals for FM 92.5 included more programs devoted to diverse opinions, more news hours per week, and more hours per week devoted to the spoken word. As it related to a mandatory employment equity policy, the proposal increased the number of news and spoken word staff and made explicit provisions for six hours of enriched spoken word programs as type E, ethnic programming.

The Hearings

The CRTC held a series of hearings in Toronto. Industry associations, individuals, lobby groups, community-based agencies, consultants, and others intervened and made submissions in support of or opposition to particular music formats or individual applicants. Three of the nine commissioners, including the chairman, Keith Spicer, presided at the hearing. Following the hearings, the commission retired to make its decision. For large segments of the African-Canadian community, the critical question was whether the CRTC commissioners were going to once again deny the Black community access to mainstream media. If they did, they would again be sending a message to Black children that they had no place in Canada, and in doing so sowing 'the seeds of alienation and hostility,' contrary to the provisions of the Broadcasting Act (*Share*, 1990).

The Majority Decision

Days before the CRTC released its long-awaited decision, it approved the application of another station, CFGM, an AM country music station, to change its format. CFGM, in requesting the format change, had argued that country music was not profitable in the Toronto area. This change in programming left one other AM country station to serve Toronto.

The CRTC made its Decision 90-693 public on 8 August 1990, one week after Caribana, Canada's largest Caribbean festival, had rocked the streets of Toronto. In it, a badly split CRTC denied the African-Canadian community a Black/dance music radio station for the third consecutive time. Instead, it granted the FM 92.5 licence to Rawlco Communications, a Vancouver-based applicant that had proposed a country music format.

The CRTC argued that a Black or dance station, or one providing an eclectic mixture of pop, folk, and jazz, would have contributed to the diversity of radio services available to Toronto listeners (CRTC, August 1990). However, it also maintained that Decision 90-693 was in the public's interest: 'Given the complete absence from Toronto FM spectrum of both a country station and country music, a country music format contributed most to programming diversity, to the development of Canadian talent and to the Canadian broadcasting system as a whole.'

Although the CRTC placed certain conditions on Rawlco's licence, it stipulated no conditions with respect to the achievement of racial diversity within the programming structure of the station.

The Dissent

Keith Spicer, the CRTC's chairman at the time, was one of three commissioners who dissented strongly from the majority opinion. His starting point was that Decision 90-693 was ill advised for all Canadians and that it did nothing to add to national unity or to create a new Canadian identity (CRTC, 1990). In his view it represented a missed opportunity for the CRTC to recognize the equal dignity of all cultures and the right of all citizens to contribute to Canada as full-fledged Canadians (ibid.). He asserted that the CRTC's decision was wrong because it failed to give emerging communities a broadcasting voice. Moreover, Decision 90-693 would have the effect of excluding many other kinds of music from around the world that would have conveyed the traditions of peoples forming about one-third of Metro Toronto's population. Spicer also contended that the choice of a country music format for FM 92.5 would merely add to Toronto's audio spectrum another form of traditional

North American music – a type of music already massively represented by pop, rock, and easy listening stations.

In Spicer's dissenting opinion he stated that Decision 90-693 sent the wrong signal: that 'they' were unwelcome in Canadian broadcasting. He charged that Decision 90-693 would make it more difficult to achieve racial harmony through broadcasting, and that it would further marginalize groups that were already excluded from the broadcasting system. He proclaimed that the majority had failed to meet the commission's own policy objectives, Parliament's multiculturalism objectives, and the objectives of the Broadcasting Act.

Community Response

Decision 90-693 surprised large segments of Toronto's music, broadcast, and media communities. Opposition to Decision 90-693 was instantaneous and widespread. For example, in an editorial of 11 August 1990, the *Globe and Mail* stated: 'The CRTC hopes that an FM outlet in Toronto "will foster interest" in Canadian country artists – a case of putting the cart of supply before the horse of demand. At the same time the Commission has denied performers of dance music, including some whose music is better known internationally than in their country. It has abandoned a significant number of Torontonians to U.S. border stations that program dance music, and signalled, however unwilling, that the mainstream is not ready for music of particular interest to Black Torontonians and other urban youths.'

On 9 August 1990, Greg Quill of the *Toronto Star* posed the following question: 'This is the third time a dance music format has been proposed for Toronto listeners and denied. The first time the CRTC licensed an easy listening station. The second time it licensed classical. And the third time ignoring the desire of a large number of Torontonians, it licensed a country station. Is this logical?'

On 10 August 1990, the following appeared in a *Toronto Star* editorial:

In its role as guardian of our airwaves, The Canadian Radio-television and Telecommunications Commission is obliged to give a clear voice to the multicultural diversity that is Canada today. But the Commission blatantly turned its back on that mandate when it awarded the Metro area's last available FM license to a country music station – dashing the hopes for a station devoted to Black music ... And by rejecting dance music such as rhythm and blues, reggae, rap, calypso, salsa, and other Afro and Caribbean styles, the Commission displayed a woeful ignorance of the varied multicultural community that constitutes Metropolitan Toronto. It does not appear to understand that the once predominantly hogtown days are no more.

Said White People for Dance Music: 'Multiculturalism aside, the rights of the followers of black music have been ignored. Black music now forms a majority of the emerging music in North America. Aside from alternative music programming on late night commercial stations, university radio and Buffalo stations the Metro Toronto Community [sic] has no FM access to what is today mainstream music. The CRTC decision is reminiscent of the banning of rock and roll in the 1950s' (Ryckman, 1990).

Decision 90-693 incensed the *Toronto Sun*: 'Politically, it's unacceptable. How can the CRTC possibly maintain its integrity when its chairman, and two of its most expert commissioners on the Toronto hearings, disagree with the ultimate decision? ... The decision reeks in a social sense as well. Radio stations speak to communities in more intimate and immediate ways than other media. At their best they dispel rumours, quell unrest, dispense information, and as a consequence contribute to the overall harmony' (Payne, 1990).

The Black Music Association reasoned this way: 'This is a body blow to the people in this business and to those who enjoy the music. But it is especially a slap in the face to all the young Canadian artists who have been treated in a very cavalier fashion. This is a poor, inept, incongruous and repressive decision. The CRTC is not only blind and dumb, it is deaf ... There are obviously some people there who know what's going on but too many others who just do not care to learn. I do not think it is racism, but I think it is discrimination' (in DiManno, 1990).

The publisher of the magazine *Street Sound* complained: 'I'd rather spend my money here in Canada. But I have to advertise in Buffalo because there are no radio stations for this type of music here' (in ibid.).

Jason Deco Steele, a disc jockey and record producer, reflected: 'I went to the hearing here and saw these people who ended up making the decision. It's frightening. These people have no idea what music lovers want or need. They are so far removed from the streets. It's also a catastrophe for Canadian performers. The dance music artists here are being repressed. It's like swimming up Niagara Falls' (in ibid.).

Billy Bryans (1990), the Parachute Club's ex-drummer, accused the CRTC of 'forcing those who make and promote music to move to the U.S. or change occupations ... when it comes to real economic and political power, our so-called multiculturalism is a sham.' Howard McCurdy, then MP for a constituency in Windsor, called Decision 90-693 an 'act criminal to the multicultural ideal of Canada' (in *Contrast*, 1990). At least in the public domain, McCurdy seemed willing to label the decision as racist or having a racist impact, although some did describe the decision as 'discrimination.' However, the commentators almost unanimously urged the federal cabinet to review Decision 90-693 pursuant to section 28 of the Broadcasting Act. Four separate grounds were advanced in support of a review of Decision 90-693:

• The strength of the dissenting opinions.
• The decision's contradiction of CRTC's stated policy and of the goals of Canada's broadcasting system.
• The regressive nature of the decision.
• The message the decision sent to the affected communities. (Coalition, 1990)

Art Eggleton (1990), then mayor of Toronto, wrote to Marcel Masse, then communications minister: 'I believe that this decision was regrettable not only because of the unfortunate message to members of a vital community in our City, but [because] the people of our City, as a whole will miss out on the opportunity to be exposed to an important dimension of Toronto's cultural reality. Broadcast media are an important means of fostering understanding and appreciation of our City's cosmopolitan and diverse identity. Ultimately they should mirror the reality of Toronto. For these reasons I strongly urge the Cabinet to review the decision of the CRTC in this matter.'

Eggleton's views were echoed by numerous groups, including the Canadian Ethnocultural Council, the National Council of Jamaicans and Supportive Organizations, the League for Human Rights of B'nai B'rith Canada, Harambee, the Jane Finch Concerned Citizens Organization, and the Federation of Race Relations Organizations. The Urban Alliance on Race Relations (1990) wrote to Paul M. Tellier, Clerk of the Privy Council and Secretary to Cabinet:

The Canadian Charter of Rights clearly recognizes multiculturalism as one of the foundations of Canadian society. The Multiculturalism Act, Employment

Equity Act, and the new Broadcasting Act give substance to this statement. The Honourable Prime Minister and his Cabinet have spoken out time and again about the government's commitment to a new multiculturalism which does not ghettoize minorities, but ensures equal access to the country's institutions ... The licensing of a Dance Music station, by appealing to white and non-white listeners in all income groups, would have provided the wider society with an opportunity to better understand [*sic*] and accept the contributions of our non-white Toronto community. This would have contributed to a more unified society and better race relations in a city that is teetering on the edge of racial unrest.

Rabbi W. Gunther Plaut stated, in a reference to Native peoples, Blacks, and peoples of Asian background, 'It is my unshakable conviction that Canada will never reach its full potential until we draw all our citizens into the vortex of its opportunities – for their sake and even more for ours. For these reasons we are appealing the CRTC 90-963 to the federal Cabinet' (ibid.).

By the end of August 1990, a Coalition of Concerned Individuals had formed itself. Its members included distinguished people in the broader community. Its sole purpose was to appeal Decision 90-963. In its public statement the coalition stated:

The decision is wrong for Toronto and wrong for Canada. It must be changed. The federal Cabinet must review the CRTC decision. At this time, and at this place the decision is simply perverse. For all the talk about its commitment to multiculturalism, the CRTC has yet to show by its licensing decisions that it understands the need for minorities to directly access mainstream media instead of having their lives filtered through the presumptions of others. Once again, Black and other visible minority musicians continue to watch from the sidelines as others exploit their music ... Even from a strictly financial basis, the decision was wrong for Toronto. It makes no sense to refuse to license a Dance Music station, a format that is gaining popularity daily and a proven financial success for Buffalo stations broadcasting in Toronto. Instead the CRTC licensed a country station at a time when the last country station changed its format due to declining audiences. For these reasons, the Coalition is asking the federal government to exercise its discretion to refer the decision back to the CRTC for reconsideration. (Coalition, 1990)

In the meantime, the Dance Music Radio Committee (DMRC), originally hired to lobby on behalf of the dance music applicants, now turned its attention to lobbying for an appeal of Decision 90-693. The DMRC circulated a standardized letter, a petition, and more than 300,000 ready-to-mail postcards protesting Decision 90-963 (Dunford, 1990). The Dance Music Radio Committee organized the Dance Appeal, a group of locally based musicians who recorded a song called 'CRTC (Can't Repress The Cause).'[1] This same group also organized two separate 'Dance For Your Right To Dance' parties, held at the Spectrum nightclub in Toronto.

The Appeal

Five applicants appealed Decision 90-963, including Milestone Communications and J. Robert Wood, the two licensable dance applicants (Nunes, 1990). Milestone and Wood both challenged the CRTC's conclusion that a country music station was in Toronto's best interest, noting that a consulting group – Goldfarb Associates – had concluded that 'every research study done by the competing applicants showed that dance had more appeal than country in the total Toronto marketplace and especially among the group that had been found by the CRTC to be undeserved – under 35 year olds.' The petitioners argued that in licensing the country music station, the CRTC had failed to consider or had considered inadequately analyses carried out by its own staff as well as research commissioned by the competing applicants. Milestone and Wood also relied upon quantitative research submitted to the CRTC showing that dance music represented only 1.6 per cent of all music played on Toronto radio stations. By comparison, Canadian country music received not less than 30 per cent exposure on existing country stations, and on seventy-four country stations across Canada. Clearly, another country radio station would not contribute most to the development of Canadian talent. Other objections were that while dance music was absent from both the FM and AM spectrum and was a fledging industry, the country music industry in Canada was a mature one from coast to coast. Furthermore, country selections were played frequently on FM – for example, on CJEZ-FM, CHFI-FM, CJFM-FM, and CHUM-FM.

Milestone and Wood submitted that with respect to diversity, the commission had failed to consider factors other than music format in making its decision. In the petitioners' view, diversity also related to factors such as these: ownership, management, target audience, access for visible minority talent, representation of minority groups on the staff, and the composition of the board of directors and community advisory committee. The allegation was raised that Decision 90-693 breached section 3(d) of the Broadcasting Act in that the introduction of a dance music station, together with the provisions in the dance applications, would have ensured that differing views on matters of public concern would be aired.

The petitioners alleged that the commission failed to consider and give adequate weight to the principle that diverse groups in Canadian society deserve to have available on their airwaves a clear choice of different programming which recognizes their specific interests, needs, and concerns. According to the petitioners, this policy had not been followed, especially in light of the fact that the commission had on two separate occasions refused to license a dance format.

Having made these arguments and submitted them to the Cabinet, the petitioners' role in the process ended. Now it was up to Cabinet to decide whether to review Decision 90-693.

Cabinet's Decision

On 9 October 1990, Cabinet upheld Decision 90-693. Having done so, it indicated its sympathy with the desire many Toronto residents were expressing for greater diversity in musical formats and urged the CRTC to hold hearings as soon as possible for the allocation of the former CKO frequency, which had since become available. Cabinet apparently hoped that the CRTC would grant the former CKO frequency to a Black/dance music applicant (Information Services Canada, 9 October 1990). Once again, the fate of a Black/dance music radio station had been thrown back into the hands of the CRTC.

New Developments

FM 99.1, an all-news format station, had since gone off the air, so its frequency was available. On 12 December 1991 the CRTC called for applications.

Rawlco, Redmon Communications, and Martin Rosenthal of CFMX-FM all submitted applications. Rawlco's application was not based on any technical shortcomings associated with its newly acquired FM 92.5; rather, it claimed that FM 99.1 would capture an additional one million listeners from rural communities, who traditionally prefer country music.

Canada First Broadcasting objected to Rawlco's bid for CKO, describing it as a means for Rawlco to cure either its 'miscalculations or misrepresentations made in its bid for FM 92.5' (Canada First Broadcasting, 1992). Sher-Singh, a prominent Toronto lawyer, objected to Rawlco's attempt to enlarge its format through FM 99.1, pointing out that in the two years since Rawclo had won its bid for FM 92.5 it had spent not a single cent to fulfil any of its undertakings (Sher-Singh, 1992).

Milestone Communications, in its objection, argued that the very fact that Rawlco had applied for a replacement licence without at least first going on the air was an embarrassment to the fundamental principle of even *appearance* of due process. For the purposes of this hearing, Milestone was not so much concerned about the utilization of 99.1 as it was with the principle (Milestone Communications, 1992).

The Black Music Association of Canada (BMAC) objected to Rawlco's bid for FM 99.1 on the ground that it already possessed a viable commercial frequency, FM 92.5. More generally, the BMAC objected to the public hearing being used as 'a trade-in show for already licensed or established radio stations' (BMAC, 1992). Ralph Agard, appearing on behalf of Harambee, said that the CRTC, by limiting its call for applications for the former CKO frequency to existing Toronto FM stations, was further compounding the mistake. He observed: 'Two of the applicants were recently granted licenses and it may be presumed that they are upgrading their broadcasting abilities and capabilities since none of the other longstanding holders of licenses were interested in the CKO frequencies or contemplating a change. One of the applicants is definitely attempting to enter the Toronto market and enhance their share since their sound originates outside Metropolitan Toronto. Obviously the CKO frequency is so valuable that the recently licensed applicants are attracted' (Harambee, 1992).

On 6 August 1992, the CRTC rejected all three applications. The CRTC was unconvinced that Redmon Communications' technical difficulties were solely responsible for its financial difficulties or that a switch to FM 99.1 would solve the company's financial woes. It also decided that neither Rawlco nor Redmon would make the optimum use of CKO's frequency. The CRTC denied Rosenthal's application because it would not add to the diversity of FM radio in Toronto (CRTC, 1992).

Rather than open up the process to new broadcasters and a fresh set of applications, the CRTC decided *as an exception to its normal procedure* to initiate without delay an independent market study to assess the capacity of the Toronto market to support an additional radio service (ibid.).

The Market Study

The CRTC contracted NGL Consulting, an Ottawa consulting firm, to do the independent market assessment. According to NGL's study, a niche-oriented station that attracted targeted audiences might not reach commercial viability, although the Toronto market was broadly able to support a new, well-executed main-stream format. NGL cautioned that a new station might shift audiences from existing stations, would not likely attract new radio listeners, and would cause advertising fragmentation. It stressed that little audience and few advertising revenues were likely to be repatriated from American radio stations and that out-of-market tuning was not a major factor in Toronto because the radio advertising market structure did not easily accommodate niche radio. It found that no demographic group was underserved by Toronto radio stations. Finally, it speculated that a new radio station in the Toronto market could push the number of profitable stations below 50 per cent or even push overall profitability into a negative position. In summary, NGL characterized Toronto as being unable to sustain another radio station, in the sense that a new station might jeopardize the profitability of radio in Toronto. NGL urged the CRTC to determine carefully the impact of FM 92.5 before licensing another station.

FM 99.1 Application

On 6 June 1996 the CRTC issued Public Notice 1996-73, a call for proposals for the use of FM 99.1, the last remaining signal in the Toronto area.[2] It was therefore the last opportunity for a Black/dance music station to win a licence. Reportedly, there were five applicants for a Black/dance station.

In a letter dated 24 July 1996, the deputy heritage minister advised the CRTC that it might direct the commission to reserve the FM channels in several cities, including Montreal and Toronto, for the CBC's use. Reportedly, the CBC intended to convert its existing AM signals in Toronto to FM 99.1. Again the Black community responded to this announcement with outrage. On 29 August, the heritage ministry announced by letter that it was abandoning its intention to reserve FM 99.1 for the CBC. This announcement paved the way for the 1996 hearings to determine whether the CRTC would, for the fourth time, deny Toronto a Black/dance music radio station. In the end the CBC was the successful applicant. Once again the CRTC had denied Metropolitan Toronto a Black/dance music station.

Analysis

The Role of Economics in Decision Making

Radio frequencies are public property, and Parliament has given the CRTC the right to regulate the use of radio frequencies (Broadcasting Act, 1985).

The right to use a radio frequency carries with it the possibility of substantial profits. In 1989 the Toronto market represented 14 per cent of the country's broadcast revenues, or $111 million. In recent years the profit margins of Toronto stations have greatly exceeded the Canadian average. Clearly, Decision 90-693 had an enormous economic dimension.

As public property, radio stations are required to reflect diversity; indeed, this is an explicit objective of paragraphs 3(1)(f) and (i) of the Broadcasting Act (ibid.). A Black/dance radio station was an attempt to achieve this goal. By winning the right to a radio frequency, African-Canadian communities would have been able to share Canada's resources and wealth. For African-Canadian communities and artists, a radio frequency would have meant increased economic self-reliance. It would have provided jobs for Black music professionals, disc jockeys, recording engineers, publicists, managers, writers, and journalists. It would have helped Black communities gain access to lucrative advertising revenues, and it would have helped Black entrepreneurs enter the mainstream of the Canadian broadcasting marketplace. The CRTC's negative decisions prevented African-Canadian communities from using public property to generate wealth.

Purely from an economic perspective, the CRTC's Decision 90-693 was economically wasteful in at least four respects. First, Rawlco in its bid for FM 99.1 admitted that the audience for country music was larger in rural areas. It argued that a right to use FM 99.1 would increase its profit margin by more than 20 per cent. Arguably, then, Rawlco knew that the proposed format for FM 92.5 would not in fact be the optimum use for that frequency. Certainly, the CRTC was well aware that a country FM format was not financially viable in Toronto; after all, CFGM had demonstrated as much only weeks before Rawlco's application was approved. And since Rawlco's base is Vancouver, its start-up costs for FM 92.5 were arguably more than those of either Milestone or Wood. Second, Rawlco's promotional expenditures to attract listeners were wasteful, particularly when there was a built-in following for Black dance music in Toronto. Third, the significant time lag between CRTC's approval of FM 92.5 and its implementation represented lost opportunities, with significant opportunity costs. Finally, the process CRTC used in making its decision with respect to CKO frequencies was wasteful in fiscal terms. It was hardly necessary or justifiable to contract NGL to conduct an independent market study. NGL used no new data, and provided little new economic analysis and no answers not already known to the CRTC. Arguably, NGL had not been given the mandate to arrive at what turned out to be its major conclusion – that a new radio station in Toronto's market would divert advertising dollars from existing radio stations. In any case, NGL drew this conclusion without assessing the potential for generating new advertising dollars from small and medium-size businesses within 'ethnic' communities.

Relative to Wood and to Milestone, Rawlco had the advantage of a well-established reputation in Canadian broadcasting. Even so, when the CRTC chose Rawlco, it disregarded the regional economic goals of the Broadcasting Act and permitted further concentration of wealth in the broadcast industry.

Irregularities in Decision Making

The CRTC is a statutory commission with a mandate to guard the public interest in broadcasting. To this end, the CRTC has been given broad policy-making powers (although the CRTC is not automatically bound by the policies it creates, as section 7 of the Broadcasting Act makes clear). The CRTC cannot however deviate from its own policy when to do so would be contrary to the public's interest.

Several irregularities were evident in both the process and the substance of Decision 90-693. According to the CRTC's FM policy, radio must expand its content so as to provide new opportunities for the public to appreciate a wider spectrum of music and the spoken word. The commission's primary objective, according to the policy, is to make radio programming more diverse in both form and content. The purpose of encouraging diversity is to ensure that disparate groups in Canadian society have a clear and wide choice in music programming (CRTC, 1975).

Presumably, the CRTC's radio market policy is consistent with the public interest. It is difficult, then, to reconcile the commission's repeated rejections of Black/dance applications for Toronto with either its stated policy or the public interest. It is also difficult to understand how Decision 90-693 began to meet the policy objectives when prior to its release the CRTC approved the application of another station – CFGM – to abandon its country music format as no longer profitable. CFGM must have presented evidence to convince the commission that the format change was in the public interest. It follows that in granting the format change, the CRTC was agreeing with CFGM that a free-standing FM country music station was not financially viable in Toronto's market. Yet only weeks later, the CRTC made a decision in which it declared in effect that licensing a country music station (Rawlco's) was in the public interest. The CRTC's actions here seem unreasonable and contradictory.

The unreasonableness of this aspect of Decision 90-693 is even clearer when one considers the degree to which the Toronto public condemned it. While the 'public interest' is a nebulous concept, the various 'publics' in Toronto were almost unanimous in condemning the decision, which did not address the needs of disparate Canadians. Decision 90-693 did not broaden listeners' choices; rather, it ossified the mix that already existed, in contradiction to the CRTC's own policy.

Allegedly, two of the three commissioners who presided at the hearings for FM 92.5 dissented from the commission's eventual decision, and would have licensed a Black/dance music format for Toronto. It should also be noted that it is highly irregular that the recommendation of those conducting a hearing is not reflected in the final decision of a tribunal.

The CRTC admitted that the decision to appoint NGL to study the issues was irregular. The CRTC failed to give any compelling rationale for deviating from its normal course; however, it must have appointed NGL because it believed that a study of the issues would have some utility.

Yet apart from interviewing seven advertising representatives, NGL did no extensive new research; and while using the CRTC's own indicators, it made no conclusive findings. NGL failed to explore nontraditional sources of advertising dollars and failed to integrate diversity issues into its study design. Thus, from a technical and methodological perspective, NGL's study was flawed.

The CRTC's decision to follow NGL's tenuous findings seems to have contradicted its own policy, which is that its three indicators for a successful radio format are only guidelines, and can be set aside in the circumstances at hand. Moreover, even if market analysis shows that an additional station is viable, the commission is not bound to authorize an additional station; as well, the commission is not bound to refuse to consider an application if a market fails one or more of the individual tests (NGL, 1993).

There are at least three possible explanations why the CRTC decided to undertake a study in this case. The first is that the CRTC decision was based on technical factors; this, however, is highly unlikely, because the commission identified no such grounds. Besides, Decision 90-693 admitted that at least two of the submissions for a Black/dance music radio station were licensable. A second explanation is that the CRTC's decision was a political one. A third is that the CRTC needed an 'independent' assessment to use as a means to evade the racial issues associated with Decision 90-693. The CRTC, in other words, intended to use NGL's study to objectify its politics of avoidance – a highly irregular and counterproductive approach to awarding public property.

Another irregularity is apparent when we note that the CRTC attached conditions to Rawlco's licence, and that when Rawlco attempted to obtain the licence for FM 99.1 it had not fulfilled any of the conditions attached to its prior licence. Yet the CRTC, though it had the power to do so, failed to penalize Rawlco for not acting in accordance with those conditions.

Merits

Decision 90-693 was accompanied by written reasons. 'Based on all the evidence available to it, a majority of the Commission is satisfied that Rawlco's proposal for a Group III station is of superior quality and best meets the Commission's *long-standing criteria*' (our emphasis).

For the purposes of Decision 90-693, the CRTC attributed the 'superior quality' of Rawlco's application to the following:

- The large number of newscasts throughout the broadcast day – more than for any other country station. (No reference was made to what other applicants proposed.)
- The fifteen hours of enrichment programming a week.
- The provision for programming of special interest to children.
- The proposed level of foreground and mosaic programming, and Canadian musical content higher than that required by the commission.
- The earmarking of $800,000 for the development of Canadian musical talent. This included $317,000 for a country music festival, $275,000 for Canada Country Stars, and $138,000 for Toronto Country Stars.
- The staging of an annual country music festival in Toronto to showcase local artists at free outdoor concerts, at an annual cost of $317,000.

- Rawlco's extensive broadcasting experience, and its performance record in the industry.
- Rawlco's warranty that the new station would pose no undue technical harm to CHAY Limited. (CRTC, 1975)

The CRTC's reasoning here was of questionable soundness. For example, compare Rawlco's proposal with that of J. Robert Wood, whose application for a Black/dance music station provided for the following:

- High Canadian content. 30 per cent of all music played would be Canadian selections, with 15 per cent written and performed by Canadian racial minorities.
- $1 million of financial assistance for musicians to rent studio facilities for recording new music.
- 12 live to tape broadcasts each year.
- One hour each week devoted to new releases.
- Assistance to the Black Music Association for its Black music luncheon.
- A music director of African-Canadian background.
- The views of Toronto's minorities (20 per cent of the city's population) to be given air time.
- Air time provided for knowledgeable experts in business, science, and arts holding views other than those of the prevailing majority.
- Six hours of enriched spoken-word programming each week, the purpose being to reflect Canada's cultural diversity.
- An hour a week of programs relating to issues relevant to women.
- Teen confidential rap talk. One half-minute featured thirty times each week on the lifestyles, interests, and contributions of people from all ethnic groups and walks of life.
- Thirty-five community service announcements each week, including those for racial minority groups.
- 20 per cent racial minority men and women among all staff; 25 per cent in year three; and 30 per cent in year five, at both the staff and management levels.
- A visible minority training program, with $12,000 allocated to a scholarship fund for skills training for twelve students a year.
- A community advisory committee to monitor the station's policies.
- An employee stock purchase plan to increase minority ownership in the station. (Wood, 1989)

Wood's application also identified how a Black/dance music format would add diversity to Toronto's music scene:

The station will be the only station in Toronto to operate a Dance Music format. It will be the only station in Canada to emphasize a significant component of Black music. The station will be one of two to operate in Group IV format. The station will be the only station in Toronto to feature a weekly three hour program of Afro-Caribbean/Latin music. The station will be the only station in Toronto to emphasize Black music in daily foreground segments. The station will be the only station in Toronto with a commitment to play Canadian content in the Dance Music genre (25%, with a target of 30%). The station will be the only station in Toronto to fill the void between multi-lingual stations on the one hand and mainstream stations on the other. The station will be the only station in Toronto with a commitment to Type E (ethnic) spoken word programs (6 hours). The station will be the only stand-alone station in Toronto with no co-ownership links or affiliation with other radio or television stations in Canada.[3]

It is clear that at the very least, Wood's application was equal in quality to that of Rawlco. It is interesting to note that 'superior quality' was a contested category among the commissioners, some of whom agreed that the licence for FM 92.5 ought to have been given to the Black/dance format.

In its written reasons, the commission admitted that at least two of the dance applications were licensable. One can therefore conclude that the public interest would have been served if the commission had chosen to license a Black/dance format. It is possible that the CRTC thought that a new player on the broadcasting scene would not do as good a job as Rawlco, yet this concern was not raised in CRTC's written reasons.

When the CRTC licensed Rawlco's application, important questions as to the commission's commitment to its own policy principles and the legislative objectives were raised. The CRTC admitted that two of the dance applications were licensable, which leads one to believe that these two applications were free of 'technical' difficulties. Also, the commission could have granted a licence to one of the dance applicants but at the same time required it to increase the number of newscasts per day, or attached such terms and conditions as were appropriate. Many, including the dissenting commissioners, argued that the commission erred in not exercising its lawful powers in order to achieve one of its primary goals: diversification of radio programming.

In Decision 88-293, released years earlier, the CRTC stated its reason not to license a Black/dance music station as follows:

Given the ultimate effect that the above proposed musical discriminators, together with the Canadian content level of 20%, would have on the Applicant's musical programming, the Commission questions whether the proposed station would indeed be *capable of providing increased exposure to Canadian visible minority talent or of consistently offering a substantial degree of musical diversity.* Further the Commission questions the extent to which Wood's application would actually increase the diversity of opinions and news sources, as claimed by the applicant, or allow the expression of the views of the multicultural mosaic of Toronto, given that it proposed 11 hours and 57 minutes of spoken word of which only 2 hours and 5 minutes would be news. The Commission notes that these levels would be lower than any other FM station's currently licensed to serve Toronto. (cited in Wood, 1989: A10; author's italics)

Thus, in Decision 88-293 the commission accepted the need for a dance-music radio station for Toronto but also questioned the ability of the applicants to achieve the goal of increasing the profile of visible minority talent. From the commission's perspective, then, promoting and developing visible minority talent was a laudable broadcasting goal. Presumably, the commission acted in the public interest at that time when it rejected the dance applications. It was reasonable for Wood and others to conclude that the CRTC would license a dance music station once its concerns were addressed.

When the applicant responded to the CRTC's precise concerns, however, the CRTC redefined what it meant by diversity. No longer was diversity used to mean 'cultural and racial diversity.' Rather, CRTC shifted the meaning of 'diversity' to mean 'musical diversity.' In essence, the CRTC failed to acknowledge that musical genres are culturally determined. The genre of reggae, for example, is associated with Jamaica, opera with Europe, calypso with Trinidad, and so on.

Since musical genres are culturally determined, the CRTC's decision to license a country music station suggests the model it uses for accommodating the needs of other cultures. The view seems to be that multilingual stations are not legitimate because they are not mainstream. It may well be that the CRTC shared the view of a *Toronto Star* journalist that a mainstream radio station cannot be a 'Black radio station' (Antonia Zerbisias, 1996). The CRTC implicitly suggests that 'mainstream' means something other than multilingual, multiracial programming.

Decision 90-693 can also be criticized for another reason. The commission stated: 'A majority of the Commission is for the view that many of the plans proposed by the Black dance applicants, particularly with respect to musical programming, *may be accommodated by existing Toronto stations.*

At its disposal the CRTC had voluminous amounts of statistical information detailing what was being played by Toronto radio stations. This data showed that 'Black/dance music' was only 2 per cent of all selections on all radio stations in the region. By contrast, country music represented in excess of 25 per cent of existing radio station playlist. Given the data before the CRTC, its conclusion that Black/dance music might be better accommodated on existing stations was open to question. At best, the same could be said about country music. Yet the CRTC refused to acknowledge these inconsistencies, and baldly asserted that merit was the overriding consideration to its decision.

The Role of Politics

In granting licences, the CRTC is required to balance competing and sometimes conflicting interests, and must marry technical proficiency with politics. Several sections of the Broadcasting Act – sections 7, 15, and 28 – make it clear that there is an element of politics in broadcasting. Decision 90-693 is an example of a political decision rationalized on technical grounds. The political nature of Decision 90-693 has three dimensions: the politics of diversity, national and regional politics, and cultural politics and the politics of identity.

Politics of Diversity

Between the CRTC's second rejection of a Black/dance music station to serve Metropolitan Toronto and Decision 90-693, several politically significant events had occurred. First, Keith Spicer had submitted his report on the constitutional consultations, in which multiculturalism had been given some consideration. Second, the Meech Lake Accord had failed, with the result that the country was in a state of constitutional and political crisis. In this regard it is significant to this analysis that Decision 90-693 was made in Quebec, where issues of ethnicity were (and still are) being played out in that province's bid for separation. Third, the 'Black' community was becoming increasingly politicized in the wake of a number of heavily publicized incidents. For instance, days after the Rodney King verdict in Los Angeles, and the outcome of the Wade Lawson case,[4] there was an uprising in Toronto during which youths from all racial backgrounds protested social inequities, particularly in the justice system. They damaged and looted the property of many merchants in the downtown core. Several media organizations labelled this uprising as 'racial unrest.' Fourth, the Black community had been mobilized to lobby for its own music station – in other words, the issue had been politicized. At the same time, African-Canadian entrepreneurs had indicated that they intended to submit an application for FM 92.5. This had a number of practical effects. While there was consensus in the community as to the need for a Black/dance radio station, there now existed choice as to which application would be supported. The politics of race had entered into the equation at the community level. Finally, the CRTC had granted Rawlco a licence to operate a station in the Ottawa region.

Spicer had agreed with the view that 'cultural minorities do not want multicultural programming ghettoized or confined to special ethnic television and radio services. They want the multicultural mosaic of Canada reflected in both the English-language and French-language programming of mainstream, conventional broadcasters' (Task Force on Broadcasting, cited in Wood, 1989: B13).

When faced with a decision about whether to license a Black/dance music radio station, the majority of CRTC commissioners apparently focused on the word 'Black' rather than 'dance.' Dance music radio stations currently operate in both Quebec and British Columbia, and Wood's application made it clear that neither in Quebec nor in Vancouver was the application for a 'dance' music station tied to a racially specific group. Even so, the commission felt that it was being asked to specifically license a 'Black' dance music station. Most of the commissioners felt that licensing a 'Black' radio station would set a dangerous precedent. That is, in the future the CRTC might be faced with the possibility of future applicants applying for a Chinese or Arab or Indian station. This raised the possibility that too many mainstream stations would eventually become ethnically segmented.

Implicit in this reasoning is that a 'mainstream' radio station cannot be 'Black' – that a mainstream radio station cannot be 'ethnic' or multiracial, but must remain purely 'traditional.' Fragmenting the market along ethnic lines, so the argument goes, does not assist national unity but maintains divisiveness and promotes racial segregation. In the view of most of the commissioners, the current multicultural model,

CHIN Radio, was sufficient to accommodate culturally specific programming.

Some of the commissioners may have felt that licensing a Black/dance station in Toronto might exacerbate racial tensions in Quebec. This point is particularly important, since throughout the national unity consultations minorities within Quebec were openly challenging racism within Quebec's francophone communities. The decision to deny a Black/dance station in Toronto was made soon after the failed Meech Lake Accord. In this respect, it can be suggested that the commission was influenced by the national political climate in reaching its decision.

The CRTC's failure to address the issue of 'Black music' was understood by many as another example of how racism was allowed to continue unabated. Competing definitions of 'Black music' were in play throughout the controversy over the CRTC's refusal to license a Black/dance station. In a brief (20 May 1992), the BMAC suggested that regardless of what you label the urban music/dance format, it takes its roots and central core from Black music both rhythmically and melodically.

Yet the CRTC in its Decision 92-543 stated that Black music included 'Black ... rhythm and blues, Black reggae, calypso and salsa, soul, funk, hip hop, Hi NRG, rap, house, world beat, Afro and Latin Caribbean styles and Lambada' (CRTC, 1992).

Despite this imprecision, there was general agreement that Black music is at the core of much popular music. Daniel Caulderon argued that much of today's popular music, including blues and rock and roll, has its roots in Black music. Yet Black music itself has little access to Toronto's radio waves. Thus, the term 'Black' was symbolically important in the quest for a dance music station. For one thing, it served to highlight the authenticity of the music that would be played on the station. Moreover, many of Canada's Black racial minorities are active in this musical genre.

Besides the vexing issues of the correct definition of Black music, the CRTC was faced with another political reality: While Wood's application was licensable, Wood himself is White. Moreover, only 9 per cent of the shares of Wood's company would have been owned by people of colour. Their participation represented 22.5 per cent of the shares held by outside investors – just over $1 million of the $4.5 million raised to establish the radio station. Milestone Communications, on the other hand, was led by Denham Jolly, a prominent Black businessman. Milestone's application was also technically licensable, and it was supported by a larger percentage of investors of colour. The CRTC was therefore faced with a dilemma: How could the CRTC license a 'Black' dance music station to a White man in whose company only 9 per cent of the shares would be held by people of colour? On the other hand, how could CRTC license Milestone's application when FM 92.5 had been discovered and rerouted to Toronto by Wood? Granting a licence to Wood might in itself raise allegations of racism. On the other hand, granting a licence to Milestone might result in allegations of favouritism and unfairness. The CRTC may well have thought it was in a no-win situation.

Awarding the licence to Rawlco raised no issues of race, since Rawlco itself was not minority owned or controlled. In a decision fuelled by the politics of avoidance, the CRTC rejected all Black/dance music applications, and then rationalized its decision on technical grounds that could easily be defended. The CRTC could point to 'objective' factors to demonstrate the validity of its choice. A rationalized technical, or 'pseudotechnical,' decision would help insulate the CRTC from any political backlash. It was a way to defer to Cabinet a difficult political question.

It is in this sense that Decision 90-693 was a double-edged sword. On the one hand, the CRTC reinforced the status quo when it awarded the licence to Rawclo. In so doing it sent a strong message to people of colour that it was not ready to make the tough trade-offs that were required to address diversity and its politics. On the other hand, the commission failed to provide any guidance on the manner in which diversity would be operationalized at the level of programming (apart from the multicultural, linguistic model characteristic of CHIN radio). The CRTC's avoidance of the politics of diversity set the stage for Cabinet's treatment of the issue. Once the issue reached Cabinet, the relative importance of diversity to regional politics would be decided.

Regional Politics

Cabinet was probably faced with a conundrum. The CRTC operates at arm's length of government, and it is important in our political system that political intervention into the operations of administrative units be avoided. Cabinet needed to resolve the matter without suggesting to the public that racial minorities were being given 'special treatment.' Cabinet could have set aside the CRTC's decision, or it could have directed the CRTC to rehear the dance application. However, in doing either the government might have suffered serious political consequences.

We speculate that Cabinet had little legal basis for concluding that the

CRTC's decision was unreasonable, especially since the decision was couched in technical terms. In other words, Cabinet could only intervene in this matter on political grounds. Thus, while Cabinet may have recognized the CRTC's consistent practice of denying Metropolitan Toronto's African-Canadian communities the opportunity to hear dance music, its options for resolving the problem were, we believe, somewhat limited. Furthermore, Cabinet's decision could not deal with the pattern being described here, but only with the circumstances surrounding Decision 90-693. In all probability, Cabinet was placed in a no-win type of situation, in that failing to review the CRTC's decision might lead to allegations of racism, but reviewing it might lead to counterclaims of reverse discrimination, undemocratic practices, and so on.

When the appeal was finally debated in Cabinet, Rawlco lobbied hard. Its strategy was to play on Western alienation. It argued that Cabinet ought to uphold the CRTC's decision because it was important that a Western-based group gain access to the nation's largest radio market.

At this time the Progressive Conservatives were in trouble in Western Canada. Cabinet had two broad choices: it could opt for diversity and hope to weather out the backlash, or it could cater to Western Canada in the hope that doing so would rejuvenate the party there. Fortunately for Cabinet, the circumstances were such that it did not have to address this political question, because CKO's frequencies had become available. From Cabinet's perspective, intervention was unwarranted because there was still the possibility for a Black/dance music station. Accordingly, Cabinet upheld the decision, noting while it did so that Black/dance applicants were now in a position to apply for the available CKO frequency.

Cultural Appropriation of Black Music

Secular Black music has long been appropriated by White musicians. The appropriation of Black music such as rag, jazz, be-bop, funk, rhythm and blues, blues, reggae, gospel, soul, rap, and dub poetry has always been central to the evolution of popular music. Black music has a structure, flow, rhythm, and internal consistency altogether different from European music. Many of Black music's 'tools' – syncopation, polyrhythm, the reliance on 'groove' and feel, the prominence of bass and drums, the use of call-and-answer patterns, the use of suspended chords and chord progressions, and so on – are rarely encountered in European music forms.

The cultural encounter between European and African music can be traced back to the early half of the nineteenth century, to the interaction between the religious and folk music of poor rural Whites and the African-derived spiritual and choral music of Blacks. From the very beginning, the appropriation, consumption, and production of Black music by White entertainers has been the site of complex power relations linking both Black and White musicians to the entertainment industry. These relations turned on the contradictions inherent in Whites' use of Black musical forms, which had been forged out of the experience of racial oppression, as sources of meaning and pleasure. There is a fundamental tension between White musicians and consumers, who struggle for more responsive and articulate modes of cultural expression, and Black musicians, who struggle against Whites' cultural and economic power to redefine their music. This redefinition takes place when White musicians transform Black forms into something else without reference to their Black roots.

The result has been a unique cultural dialectic between White appropriation and Black innovation that has long been central to the evolution of popular music. This dialectic can be witnessed in the intermittent counter-rebellions of Black musicians against the usurpation of Black forms such as bebop and new wave jazz.

In contemporary Toronto and in the Canadian music scene, there is widespread collaboration between musicians from all racial groups. No genre of music is restricted to any one racial group. In Toronto, for instance, there is much cross-racial collaboration at all levels of reggae and dance music production. It follows that the problem is not that Whites are appropriating and transforming Black music, but that the new music's Black roots are being erased. Many White people would be surprised to learn that Elvis Presley's hit 'Hound Dog' was written and first popularized by a Black woman, Big Mama Thornton. Elvis and his music live on in the collective memory of Whites, yet Little Richard, some of whose work Elvis borrowed, has been forgotten. In the Canadian context, while some radio stations celebrated the music of Parachute Club, the name Mojah meant little to the Canadian public. While the White reggae artists 'Snow' reached international status, the Black youths in Toronto's Jane-Finch neighbourhood, which is predominately Black, from whom 'Snow' learned to DJ, are unknown to the Canadian public.

The appropriation of Black musical forms is not often discussed in the mainstream media. The people who appropriate Black music benefit financially; their Black counterparts often struggle for recognition. When the CRTC decided not license a Black radio station it not only stifled free speech, but also suppressed truth and denied Canadians the opportunity to learn about how cross-cultural interactions in the arts have shaped their identity.

Identity

Radio is more portable than other broadcast media. One only needs to look at people walking along a street, travelling on the TTC, or standing outside a school to understand the importance of radio in the everyday lives of Canadians. It is clearly one of the most accessible media. The Broadcasting Act acknowledges in paragraph 3(1)(b) that radio is critical for developing and maintaining a collective national identity. For African Canadians, then, the quest for a radio station was a quest for control, or perhaps more accurately for a means to balance the everyday images of Black people as disseminated by and in the media. It was an attempt to diversify – albeit in some minute way – the ownership of the broadcasting industry. The Fowler Commission on Broadcasting stated: 'Canadian broadcasting would not be doing its job if it did not strive to permit all Canadians from one ocean to the other to know themselves better; if it did not permit each of the two Canadian national cultures to express itself; if every ethnic group and every region in the country could not recognize itself through the broadcasting system and could not be known by every ethnic group of every other region; if it did not provide something special for all Canadians – artists, politicians, teachers, farmers, workers, students, or housewives' (cited in Wood, 1989).

People speak to their own communities and others through the medium of radio. The media, of which the broadcast industry is part, are a vital transmitter of society's cultural standards, myths, values, and images. In theory, the media provide for the free flow and exchange of ideas, opinions, and information. As such, they are a cornerstone of democratic society and a vital tool for producing and perpetuating its ideals. In a liberal democracy, media institutions are expected to reflect alternative points of view, to remain neutral and objective, and to provide free and equitable access to all groups.

In reality, however, while espousing democratic values of fairness, equality, and freedom of expression, the media reinforce and reproduce racism in a number of ways: through negative stereotyping and ethnocentric judgments, by marginalizing people of colour and rendering them invisible, and by racializing issues such as crime and immigration (Henry et al., 1995).

For many people the mass media are a crucial source of information, beliefs, and values. Because of the marginalization of racial minority communities from mainstream society, many White people rely almost entirely on the media for their information about minorities and their communities. The relationship between the white community and these groups is largely filtered through the perceptions, assumptions, and values of media professionals. These professionals are predominantly White (Fleras and Elliot, 1992).

The effects of Decision 90-693 can be understood in relation to the importance of broadcasting in forming collective and national identities. The granting of a licence to operate a Black/dance music radio station would have signalled that the CRTC recognized and was committed to the equal dignity and value of all cultures; and that it recognized and welcomed diversity. Such a decision would have affirmed the right of all citizens to contribute to this country as full-fledged Canadians (CRTC, 1992). A radio licence would have given access to those who currently have no access to the radio waves; it would have given a voice to those communities which traditionally have been marginalized and silenced; it would have secured the right of all consumers to receive broadcasting services that reflect their needs and interests. All radio and television programs must eventually be paid for by consumers. Therefore, all consumers have an equal right to participate in the national identity question using the broadcast media as a vehicle.

The CRTC's decisions have made it more difficult than ever for people of colour to contribute to the development of a cohesive national identity. Identity is formed through a continuing dialogue and struggle with others; this process is by nature complex and conflictual. Underlying this quest for the 'self' are different and sometimes conflicting values, beliefs, and needs – not only between different communities but also within individuals themselves (Rutherford, 1990). Struggles to achieve a reconciliation between individual needs and the collective needs of diverse communities, along with the identity needs of a national culture, are *ongoing* struggles. They are basic to a postmodern society. They also reflect the tensions that arise from mainstream cultural production.

Few would dispute that people of colour are often portrayed negatively in the media. The stereotypical images and racist discourses encountered on radio and television and in the print media help form and maintain the collective identity that is imposed on racial minorities – an identity that bears little resemblance to the self-definitions of those affected. The scripts offered by the dominant culture are limited in vision, knowledge, and understanding of the 'others.' It is within this context that the application for a Black/dance music station has been an issue with profound consequences. For many people of colour, no shared national identity will ever be developed until stereotypes are shed and misunderstandings are lifted vis-à-vis the collective identity of minority groups.

Implicit in the attempts to obtain a Black/dance music station was the realization that much of modern society and political life turns on questions of recognition. In our liberal tradition we see recognition largely as a matter of acknowledging individuals and their identities. That is, people have the right to be acknowledged publicly for what they really are (Appiah, 1994: 149).

In a society where racism is widespread, and where racist ideology and discourse label a person of colour as 'other,' one form of restoring a sense of collective well-being to a minority community is to find ways of recognizing and supporting the talents and contributions that exist within it. This leads to cultural work and aesthetic creativity by artists of colour, which in turn provides a vehicle for resisting stereotypes, deprecating images, and racist discourse. As Appiah puts it:

These old restrictions suggested life-scripts for the bearers of these identities, but they were negative ones. In order to construct a life with dignity, it seems natural to take the collective identity and construct positive life-scripts instead. An African-American after the Black Power movement takes the old script of self-hatred, the script in which he or she is a nigger, and works, in community with others, to construct a series of positive Black life-scripts. In these life-scripts, being a Negro is recorded as being Black, and this requires, among other things, refusing to assimilate to white norms of speech and behaviour. (1994: 161)

When people of colour demand that they not be limited by demeaning stereotypes and racist discourse, the dominant community typically responds with indignation, hostility, and denial. White Canadians cannot 'imagine' racism. They cannot accept that racism shapes Canadian culture. Instead, they draw upon the critiques of multiculturalism to defend the status quo. They hide behind the wall of liberalism to diminish the legitimacy of the claims of racial minorities as collective communities.

In some respects, liberalism cannot accommodate what the members of marginalized communities really aspire to, which is cultural survival. The failure to establish a Black/dance music station reflects the dominant culture's unwillingness (as represented by the CRTC) to affirm that members of minority communities have identities with distinctive traditions and values, as well as important aesthetic traditions and cultural practices to contribute to all Canadians. Recognition of one's collective identity requires social acknowledgment of that collective identity and a demonstration of respect for it.

The application for a Black/dance music station set into play the historic tensions that have always existed in this country between national, regional, and local identities. In Decision 90-693, Spicer and the majority agreed that the decision should reflect positively on the question of national identity. However, Spicer clearly wanted, and did not get, a decision that would send the political message of inclusivity to ethno-racial groups across Canada. His theory was that the political goal of national unity must incorporate the reality of Canada's ethno-racial diversity, not only in symbolic terms but in other ways as well. To that end, he was prepared to license a dance music radio station to serve Toronto, despite the definitional controversy regarding what constitutes 'Black music.'

Conclusion

The majority in the CRTC's Decision 90-693 failed to realize that what was required above all was an admission that we are very far away from our ultimate goal as a multicultural society, which is, to embrace at their true value all of Canada's different cultures within the construct of a national identity. The decision to reject the Black/dance radio station was based on the notion that Canadian culture solely reflects European achievements and contributions – a notion that wrongly excludes or dismisses the presence and contributions of the 'others.'

Notes

1 Singers on the track, written by Rupert Gayle, Richard Rodwell, and Eria Fachion, included B. Kool, Michee Mee, Maestro Fresh Wes, Lorraine Segato, Lillian Allen, Berry Harris, Leroy Sibbles, and Lorraine Scott.
2 FM 92.5 had been the last remaining frequency for the Toronto. But when CKO was forced to rescind its licence, FM 99.1 became the last remaining frequency in Toronto.

3 Wood did give an undertaking not to interfere with CHAY's frequency. Appendix A of Wood's application was an agreement between Wood and CHAY respecting interference with CHAY's frequency. Paragraph 1(b) of that agreement read: 'CHAY hereby waives any objections to the allocation of channel 223B to Toronto, subject to compensation set forth in clause 3 and the limitation of interference set forth in clause 4.'

Clause 4 reads: 'In the event the area of interference of the proposed station exceeds the boundary indicated by the broken line in the map Attachment "A", Wood shall take the necessary steps at his expense to remedy the problem, by reducing the power or making such other technical adjustments as may be required to reduce the area of interference to the boundary so indicated. Any dispute therein shall be arbitrated by a qualified broadcasting engineer named jointly by the broadcasting engineer consultants employed by Wood & CHAY.'
4 Lawson was a Black youth shot by police officers in Toronto in 1988.

References

Appiah, Anthony. 1994. 'Identity, Authenticity, Survival: Multicultural Societies and Social Reproduction.' In Amy Gutman, ed. *Multiculturalism: Examining the Politics of Recognition*. Princeton, N.J.: Princeton University Press.

BMAC (Black Music Association of Canada). 1992. Brief to the CRTC. 20 May. See transcript of the proceeding. 309.

Broadcasting Act. R.S.C. 1985. Section 3(1)(b),

Bryans, B. 1990. 'CRTC Unqualified to Rule on Media Control.' *Toronto Star*. 17 August. A22.

Canada. 1990. News Release. 'Cabinet Upholds CRTC Country Music Decision.' 9 October. Information Services, Ottawa.

Canada First Broadcasting. 1992. Brief to the CRTC. 20 May. See transcript of the proceeding. 382.

Canadian Radio-Television and Telecommunications Commission. 1975. FM Radio Market Policy.

– 1989. In J. Robert Wood application to CRTC. 12 December.

– 1990. Decision CRTC 90-693. Ottawa: August. 2.

– 1992. Decision 92-543. 6 August. 6.

Caulderon, D. 1990. BMAC Presentation, CRTC Public Hearing. Transcript of the proceeding. 20 May. 305.

Coalition of Concerned Individuals. 1990. Letter to Clerk of the Privy Council. 22 August.

Contrast. 1990. 'McCurdy Attacks CRTC Rejection of Toronto Black FM License Bid.' 16 August.

DiManno, R. 1990. 'Give Us Soca, Salsa, Not Hurtin' Music.' *Toronto Star.* 10 August. A7.

Dunford, G. 1990. 'Did You Know?' *Toronto Sun.* 21 September 6.

Eggleton, A. 1990. A letter to Cabinet. In *Contrast.* 27 September.

Fleras, Augie, and Jean Elliot. 1992. *The Nations Within: Aboriginal–State Relations in Canada, the United States and New Zealand.* Toronto: Oxford University Press.

Fowler Report on Broadcasting. Cited in Wood, B15.

Globe and Mail. 1990. Editorial: 'A License Denied to Dance Music.' 11 August.

Harambee. 1992. Brief to the CRTC. 20 May. See transcript of the proceeding. 329.

Henry, Frances, Carol Tator, Winston Mattis, and Tim Rees. 1995. *The Colour of Democracy: Racism in Canadian Society.* Toronto: Harcourt Brace.

Milestone Communications. 1992. Brief to the CRTC. 20 May. See transcript of the proceeding. 369–70.

NGL. 1993. Market Potential for New Radio Broadcasting Service in Toronto: Final Report. 16 March.

Nunes, J. 1990. 'Voices of Protest: More Groups Appeal CRTC Decision on Dance Music Station.' *Globe and Mail.* 24 August.

Payne, R. 1990. 'A Twang of Trouble at CRTC.' *Toronto Sun.* 12 August. 28.

Quill, Greg. 1990. 'Black Music Loses Bid for Spot on Metro FM.' *Toronto Star.* 9 August. A24.

Rutherford, Jonathan, ed. 1990. *Identity: Community Culture and Difference.* London: Lawrence and Wishart.

Ryckman, A. 1990. 'Black Music Followers Ignored.' *Contrast.* 30 August. 5.

Share. 1990. Editorial: 'Will CRTC Recognize Us?' 28 June. 7.

Sher-Singh, T. 1992. Brief to the CRTC. 20 May. See transcript of the proceeding. 344–7.

Toronto Star. 1990. 'Why Black Music Lost Out.' 9 August. A21.

– 1990. Editorial: 'Music for Everyone.' 10 August. A18.

Urban Alliance on Race Relations. 1990. Letter to Paul M. Tellier, Clerk of the Privy Council. 21 August.

Wood, J.R. 1989. Application to CRTC, 12 December. Toronto.

Zerbisias, Antonia. 1996. 'Why Can't We Hear Toronto on Toronto Radio?' *Toronto Star.* 10 August.

6

Miss Saigon

Introduction

On 26 May 1993, *Miss Saigon*, a modern-day version of Puccini's opera *Madama Butterfly*, opened in Toronto at the Princess of Wales Theatre. The state-of-the-art theatre was built especially to house the musical at a cost of over $30 million. Over 300,000 Asian Canadians live in Toronto. About one hundred protesters, mainly Asian-Canadian artists and activists, turned out on opening night to protest the musical.

The musical's story takes place in the closing days of the Vietnam War. Thus, it is situated in the context of a civil war that had long divided the country into two opposing forces: North Vietnam, backed by the Soviet Union and China, and South Vietnam, backed by the United States and Britain.

The story opens in Saigon in April 1975. The Viet Cong have begun to capture provinces in the South and are advancing toward the last American stronghold, Saigon. An innocent young Vietnamese orphan girl named Kim has been forced to flee her destroyed village. To survive she becomes a bar girl in an after-hours club frequented by American marines and South Vietnamese officers and civilians. The women who work in the club are all prostitutes. Kim meets a White American soldier, Chris, who is intrigued by Kim's innocence and promises to take her to America with him. The relationship ends abruptly when the war ends and he returns to America. Kim, pregnant, is left alone to raise the child. She believes, however, that Chris will come back for her. Several years later, Chris returns with his wife, searching for Kim. Unaware that she has had a child, he finds her working in a bar in Bangkok. When

Kim discovers that Chris is married, she commits suicide so that her son will be free to go to America with his father.

Miss Saigon ran for two years and was a commercial success. However, it also became 'a flashpoint in the long-standing debate about politics and culture whose key words are racism, sexism, political correctness, censorship and artistic freedom' (Fung, 1993/94).

Events

After the play opened on Broadway and well before its Toronto premiere, a group of Asian women from diverse cultural communities came together to consider what actions they could take once the production opened in Toronto. Many of those who attended the first meetings were advocates working within their communities. One of the reasons these women chose to organize themselves into a collective was their disillusionment with the feminist movement. From their perspective that movement was expressing little concern about the play's racism and sexism. One respondent observed that White feminists do not understand and cannot think from an Asian perspective.[1]

Several of the women in the group were artists struggling to find ways to gain better access for their cultural products, and to respond to the cultural appropriation of their experiences. Members of the group shared the view that Asian women, like Black women, were doubly oppressed: as women and as persons of colour. For those who were lesbian, the oppression was even more profound. These Asian-Canadian artists felt a compelling need to challenge the negative images created and circulated by White Anglo writers, producers, critics, reviewers, and others – images deeply embedded in North American culture.

The group believed that the time had come to systematically contest the racist images that are so pervasive in the popular culture (which includes films, theatre, and the electronic and print media). As Asian-Canadian women they felt trapped by the limiting and ubiquitous stereotypes, for example, that they were 'exotic,' 'dragon queens,' or 'suffering, self-sacrificing, passive, acquiescent victims.' In the same vein, Asian males were too often seen as brutal killers, ruthless businessmen, or karate street fighters. This led to the following question: 'What are the images we never see of ourselves?'

The name of the collective, Asian ReVisions, was taken from a film festival and highlighted the felt need of Asian Canadians to take control of their own identities – that is, to 'revision' the movies, musicals, and television programs that distort, misrepresent, and misinterpret what is learned about their culture. The name also suggests a desire to revision the society in which Asians live, but from which they are largely marginalized and excluded. In a collective interview, many members of the group expressed the view that much of what is known about Asian history 'has been told to us by others ... As activists we needed a vision of what direction change should go.' They decided to follow the model of protest provided by the Coalition Against Show Boat. Thus they would hold demonstrations against *Miss Saigon* to coincide with the time of its opening. They established public education as their primary goal.

Educational and advocacy efforts focused on these themes: the misrepresentation of Asian cultures; the distortions and omissions of what passes as history (framed from a Eurocentric perspective); the replaying of denigrating stereotypes; and the sexism and racism that have been embedded in representations of Asians in both film and theatre for the last hundred years.

By opening night the group had expanded into a coalition representing more than twenty different community and racial minority groups. Support for the protest came from many different groups and organizations, including the Congress of Black Women of Canada, the National Action Committee on the Status of Women, and members of the Black community who had been involved in the protest against *Show Boat*.

On opening night the coalition distributed flyers outlining their objections to the musical to guests as they entered the theatre. Among the issues addressed in the flyers were these: the stereotyping of Asian women as compliant sexual objects; the distorted, Eurocentric view of Vietnamese culture; the misrepresentations of history; and the negative image of Vietnamese people as reflected in the two central male Vietnamese characters. In the musical, the Engineer, a Eurasian who owns the club in which Kim is employed, is portrayed as a scheming, unscrupulous pimp; and Thuy, Kim's fiancé from her village, is a brutal Vietnamese soldier who is meant to incarnate despotism and communism. Kim ultimately kills him when he threatens to 'erase' her son.

Members of Asian ReVisions contested the cultural and racial assumptions and biases reflected in every aspect of the play: 'We were tired of being the backdrop to a Western story.' 'We were concerned about the lack of historical context.' 'We were especially disturbed by the linking of commercialization to the real tragedies experienced by

Vietnamese such as child prostitution and the issue of colonialism, issues which are not really examined in this play.'

The coalition prepared this public statement: 'We should recognize how dehumanizing portrayals of Asian people – as "gooks," "chinks," "japs," or in the case of Asian women as "oriental flowers," "geisha," "lotus blossoms" – have been used to fuel military and sex based exploits in Asia' (*Nikkei Voice*, 1993).

Miss Saigon helped the Asian community put racist discourse 'on the table.' The controversy the musical inspired helped identify traditional values and prejudices embedded in mass culture, demonstrate how these codes and conventions named the Asian community, and challenge the practices of cultural industries and promoters.

The *Miss Saigon* Protest and the Schools

The protest against *Miss Saigon* helped inspire some of the city's school boards to create new policies. When the Toronto Board of Education bought tickets for students to see *Miss Saigon*, Asian ReVisions decided to intensify its efforts to reach students. The coalition took its concerns and its action plan to the Toronto Board of Education and the Race and Ethnic Relations Committee of the City of Toronto. As a result of this intervention, and concerns about another musical, *Show Boat*, the board decided to develop a policy limiting school tours to both the productions to grades eleven to thirteen. Also, the teachers were required to do pre- and post-educational sessions with the students, the point of these being to address the issues raised by both *Miss Saigon* and *Show Boat*.

The Toronto board created a resource kit for teachers to use with their students before and after seeing *Miss Saigon*. This kit included an article exploring how teachers could best deal with complex, politically controversial issues in the school curriculum and in the classroom; a detailed plot synopsis; a historical timeline for the Vietnam War; and articles written by Asian writers and members of Asian ReVisions. The board was careful to include topics that had been omitted from the production. These topics included, but were not limited to, the following: American imperialism; American draft resisters and the protest movement against the war; the consequences of ethnocentrism and cultural ignorance; the lessons of the Vietnam War; the impact of stereotyping Asians, then and now; the experience and legacy of Amerasian children born in Vietnam and abandoned by their American fathers; and the sexual exploitation of children in Asia.

At the end of each module in the resource kit was a list of questions addressing issues of racism, sexism, and classism (see chapter appendix). These questions were linked to many of the concerns that had fuelled the protest against *Miss Saigon*. Thus, through the intervention of the Toronto Board of Education and Asian ReVisions, *Miss Saigon* became a learning tool for examining the issues of stereotypical representation and the exclusion of Asian people in the arts.

Analysis

Racist Discourse: Misrepresentation

Power, and its uses and misuses, was at the core of the protest over *Miss Saigon*. Power takes different forms and manifests itself in different ways. Here, one type of power was the power of Mirvish Corporation to produce a play that created and disseminated images and narratives that distorted, ignored, and misrepresented the historical memories and experiences of those who were most deeply affected. Another type was the power these images had to maintain a culturally stratified society. Yet another was expressed in the racist discourse and images of Asian people, which blended together to form the central thrust of this play. Still another was the institutional power of the police, who were always at the theatre in large numbers with vans and horses, even when there were only a few protesters. Lastly, there was the power of the media. As one of our respondents expressed it: 'Mostly the print and electronic media acted as if it was their role to promote the show.' She maintained that after one month of production, the *Globe and Mail* censured the *Toronto Star* and the *Toronto Sun* for not being more critical of the demonstrations. Clearly, some of the media perceived any kind of dissent as a violation of 'artistic freedom.'

But for members of the Asian-Canadian community, artistic licence in musicals such as *Miss Saigon* translates into freedom for cultural producers to reinforce racial and sexual stereotypes and discourse. It has been suggested that the racism and sexism found in this play are situated within the American musical form itself, which has 'proven an effective medium for refurbishing stereotypes and presenting compellingly simple accounts of cross-cultural relations' (Maclear, 1993: 17). American theatre after the turn of the century was fascinated with 'oriental' themes. *The King and I, South Pacific, Sayonara, Teahouse of the August Moon,* and many other productions were set in 'exotic' Asia. In these early cultural productions all Asian characters were played by Caucasians in make-up.[2]

Maclear contends that musical productions commonly rely on 'sugar-coated cliches' to explain complex historical, political, and social realities. In its musicals as in its films, the entertainment industry largely avoids critical issues. Instead it falls back on telling 'love' stories. For many, the strength of *Miss Saigon* and *Madama Butterfly* is indeed the tragic love story. In each work, a young Asian woman commits suicide following her doomed romance with an American serviceman.

However, lurking beneath the overt textual themes is the hidden narrative: the superiority of Western culture and Western values. Phil Cohen notes that the hidden narrative in cultural productions mobilizes and expresses a 'minefield of vested interests' (quoted in Roman, 1993). Against these, the 'romantic' tragedy of *Miss Saigon* replays a favourite fantasy and theme in Western cultural idioms: the submissive Oriental woman, 'the porcelain doll, awakened to passionate life' by the strong, heroic, white North American male. The central narrative of movies and musicals about the 'Orient' is this: 'The conquering hero brings her (the Asian female) to the door of his superior civilization by making her bear his child, but he returns to the West, and marries a woman of his kind. The Asian female than commits suicide, stepping down in favour of his wife and enabling her child to pass through the door' (Lowe, 1993).

A member of Asian ReVisions commented: 'The White man is always rescuing the poor woman of colour, belying the social context and the history.' But the key and contested questions are, Whose history is this? Whose voice and perspective is privileged and dominant? And whose experiences and stories have been ignored, marginalized, or sanitized? The real stories of women like Kim are never revealed in these plays. If they were, comments one respondent, there would be 'nothing to sing or dance about.'

One of the ways, then, that racism manifests itself in cultural production is by dismissing the histories of the cultures and societies it is subjugating (Jordan and Weedon, 1995). The glorification of Western White history focuses on 'his story,' the story of largely White Anglo men – their struggles and their victories. These narratives are preserved and replayed in cultural productions. In the same way, the events in *Miss Saigon* are portrayed through a White, male, Eurocentric gaze that shapes the content, meaning, and mode of presentation.

In *Miss Saigon*, as in many of the other cultural productions discussed in this book, it is the White people who *act*, and who are the primary subject; it is the people of colour who are acted *upon*. In this process, the victims of colonialism and racism are 'out of the game.' In this context, they can never be the subject of the history; rather, they bear the burden of history as an object (ibid.).

Setting the play within the 'Orient' provides the subtext of *Miss Saigon*. Doing so serves to perpetuate powerful racist myths and stereotypes. Within the European construction of 'Orientalism,' the 'Orient' serves as a vehicle for expressing the superiority of Eurocentric values, beliefs, assumptions, and norms. The 'Orient' and the 'Oriental' are, as cultural and literary critic Edward Said suggests, 'almost a European invention, and [have] been since antiquity a place of romance, exotic beings, haunting memories and landscapes, remarkable experiences ... The Orient is not only adjacent to Europe: it is also the place of Europe's greatest and richest and oldest colonies, the source of its civilizations and languages, its cultural contestant, and one of its deepest and most recurring images of the Other ... Orientalism expresses and represents that part culturally and even ideologically as a mode of discourse with supporting institutions, vocabulary, scholarship, imagery, doctrines, even colonial bureaucracies and colonial styles' (1978: 1–2)

Orientalism is inseparable from racist myths and stereotypes: 'Orientals were rarely seen or looked at; they were seen through, analyzed not as citizens, or people, but as problems to be solved or confined or – as the colonial powers openly coveted their territory – taken over' (ibid.: 207).

The term 'Oriental' is loaded with stigmatizing meanings. The concept is built on a system of categorization. It orders the world through a discourse in which the Orient is imagined as the 'Other' – the antithesis of the West. It depicts the 'other' as both a place and a people.

This essentializes Asian culture and identity and supports the racist discourse that leads to a construction of Asians as a homogeneous, monolithic group or culture. *Miss Saigon* and other musicals draw upon Orientalism; to avoid historical specificity, *Miss Saigon* offers a conventional East/West 'love' story and plays it out against a 'Third World' backdrop.

Imperialism is often obscured in discourse emanating from Western mainstream cultural institutions such as literature, media, education, and film. The cultural premises of the victors virtually eliminate the narrative of the vanquished: 'Since "we" are civilised and "they" are not, the mass death and suffering inflicted by soldiers in a righteous cause merits understanding ... In the U.S. narrative on the war, with few exceptions, the very form of telling deprives the Vietnamese of moral reciprocity – indeed, of human identity' (Landau, 1993: 97).

Because it lacked a strong narrative, and was empty of substantive and challenging social and political issues, and because its historical context was in fact totally nonhistorical, *Miss Saigon* had to rely on the usual glitzy trappings of mega-musicals, which here included a full-sized helicopter.

Racist Images and Identity

Marginalization, misrepresentation, and the use of racial differences to support racist values and beliefs have played a central role in North American popular culture (Said, 1978). The impact on audiences of plays like *Miss Saigon* is to reinforce stereotypes and eroticize racial identity. Protesting against a show like *Miss Saigon* is a way of challenging this kind of misrepresentation.

The pervasive stereotyping of Asian women in Western culture leads to contradictions and distortions. Such negative views can influence the self-image of women from these ethno-racial backgrounds and deeply affect how they see themselves, especially in societies where sex and women are so 'grossly commodified' (Yee, 1993). There is a tension between the ubiquitous images of Asian women as submissive, exotic, and sexually available 'china dolls,' and the somewhat less common but still conventional image of Asian women as 'dragon ladies' who use their 'exotic' sexuality to manipulate men (ibid.: 23). But both kinds of portrayal rely on limiting and demeaning stereotypes.

The stereotype of Asian women in Western cultures is linked to the history of the American military presence in Asia following the Second World War – to the Vietnam War and the presence of military bases in the Philippines. The huge contingents of American soldiers in these and other Asian countries led to the creation of 'rest and recreation' areas where soldiers were able to fulfil their sexual fantasies by buying Asian women and girls as prostitutes and mail-order brides (ibid.: 22). In more recent years, these same stereotypical images of Asian women, combined with poverty and economic underdevelopment, have created huge sex markets in many Asian countries, which Japanese and Western tourists visit for the express purpose of sexual exploitation. Prostitution has exploded in the Philippines, Thailand, South Korea, Taiwan, Vietnam, and other Asian nations (Neumann, 1984).

The acute sensitivity about racial stereotypes felt by those who protested this and other cultural productions derives from what has been labelled the 'burden' of representation (Stam, 1993) and the 'burden of degradation' (Jordan and Weedon, 1995). These stereotypical representations reinforce the existing negative images of Asian people and other people of colour – images that are pervasive in the dominant culture.

Socially empowered groups do not need to be overly concerned with negative images of themselves, as they have the power to challenge and resist them. On the other hand, historically marginalized groups are generally less able to control their representations and therefore have far less power to escape being harmed by them. By their very nature – their incessant repetition, simplistic generalizations, and denial of individuality – stereotypes provide the ideological framework in which racism thrives. For Asians and Blacks, each stereotype becomes, within the dynamics of domination, supercharged and encrusted with meaning. These images enter into the continuum of racist ideology and create a form of societal typecasting that is difficult to escape. For example, 'the criminalization of Vietnamese youth, the sexual marketing of Asian women, and the vilification of an Asian business threat are standard features of contemporary North American public discourse and institutional practice' (Fung, 1993/4: 8).

This discourse and institutional practices encourage the fragmentation of society into 'us' and 'them.' Power relations are rooted in a White/minority axis. Institutionalized whiteness confers upon Whites, both individually and collectively, cultural as well as economic and political power (Grossberg, 1993).

The protest against *Miss Saigon* was fueled, then, by a growing assertion of Asian-Canadian identity and by the resistance within diverse Asian-Canadian communities to these kinds of representations of Asians.

Protesters connected the play's distortions and racist subtext to many recent Hollywood films, in which Asians are generally portrayed as menacing and unscrupulous villains – as the 'other.' For example, Francis Ford Coppola's *Apocalypse Now*, considered by most North American cultural critics a film 'classic,' reduces the Vietnamese people to stereotypes of 'Oriental viciousness.' The film *Rising Sun* repeats this theme by portraying the Japanese as ruthless, brutal, and deceitful. Other films that represent Asians as the threatening 'other,' as a force of evil struggling to overwhelm and destroy Western culture and civilization, include *The Deer Hunter, Platoon, Full Metal Jacket*, and the *Rambo* series.

For Hollywood film-makers, Southeast Asia represents a 'primary site of a national nightmare' where Americans are under constant threat from menacing 'gooks,' and where Asians are 'the source of fear, danger and death' (Carby, 1993: 239).

These images become historical and cultural reference points for Western culture (Said, 1993). In each of these productions, the American invaders are portrayed with sensitivity, sympathy, and understanding, while the Vietnamese (and other Asians) move across the screen as monsters, as puppets of no importance, or as childlike figures to be treated with patronizing sentimentality.

Richard Fung observes that these cultural productions inevitably focus on the White American, who is generally portrayed as a heroic soldier or a liberal patriot. In these stories it is always the Americans who are front and centre, who are the victors or the tragic heroes. The 'foreigners' (from the Western perspective) are reduced to a threatening/ titillating backdrop; or they are a device for highlighting the valour, anger, or compassion of the Americans (1993/4: 8). The Vietnamese (or other Asians) are dehumanized, and are used to perpetuate American ideology and to provide local colour to the production. The only sympathetic Vietnamese characters in *Miss Saigon* are those for whom America represents deliverance – for example, Kim, who surrenders her body, her child, and ultimately her life.

Maclear (1993) reflects Asian ReVisions's position when he contends that these kinds of stereotypes are neither neutral nor benign; on the contrary, they are extremely harmful. Entertainment and mainstream representations spill over into the everyday lives of people of colour and play a role in mediating the relationship between different cultural communities. They affect how Asians are viewed by other groups, and how those groups relate and respond to Asians. To emphasize this point, he cites data collected by the New York–based Committee Against Anti-Asian Violence, which shows that racially motivated crimes against Asians in New York City have risen 680 per cent since 1985 – the greatest increase for any ethnic group.

Resistance

For many of those involved in the protest against *Miss Saigon*, and for members of Asian ReVisions, the process of resistance was a very empowering one. It was the first public political protest organized by a pan-Asian group. There had been a number of other campaigns, such as the protest organized by Chinese Canadians in the early 1980s against the racist CTV documentary on *W5,* and the struggle by Japanese Canadians for redress, but these earlier actions had been formed around the concerns of a specific community.

The resistance against *Miss Saigon* empowered artists and cultural activists in their efforts to challenge hegemonic traditions and practices. Two key objectives were to question the validity of the dominant cultural tradition, and to create alternative and oppositional cultural traditions. The ultimate aim was to increase access and equity for Asians and, by extension, for other people of colour in order that all groups might be actively involved in cultural production, consumption, and legitimation. For many members of the coalition and for others in the community, the protest against *Miss Saigon* was not merely about the racism in one theatrical production; it was about the *cultural* racism they faced in their daily lives.

On the rare occasions when people of colour do appear in cultural productions and the media, they are expected to be grateful for being tokens. But as Richard Fung (1993/4) points out, while productions like *Miss Saigon* and *Show Boat* provide work for artists of colour, they need to be able to gain stage experience and make money 'without having to perform such neo-colonial fantasies.' What is required, Fung adds, is 'a commitment to bring forward more complex images of Asians, and therefore, to change the face and terms of cultural production in this country.'

The Asians who were involved in the protest believed it was necessary to give political and cultural expression to their struggle to break the racist and sexist barriers of silence that had been imposed upon them. There were really only two possible approaches to *Miss Saigon.* One was the passive approach, with its assumption that given the popularity of the play, it couldn't be that bad, and 'anyway, it's not advisable to create a fuss because people would resent us.' The other was 'to say that we have had enough of this [racism], and try to create a change in perception, through public education, leafleting and (yes) protests' (Sumi, 1993: 9).

Asian ReVisions was highly critical of the mainstream culture for its unwillingness to recognize the seriousness and validity of their concerns: 'The dominant culture needs to learn that Canada has always been a country populated by people of colour: We can't go back home. Who are they trying to send us back home? We belong here.'

From a similar perspective, Yee maintains that this is precisely why collective solutions are required – that is, why communities must organize on a broad basis to build a society that is not based on exclusion, exploitation, and division. The struggle for Asian communities and other people of colour is to find their own voices and stake their own place in Canada: 'We have not been silent, just silenced or not listened to. That is why we must speak for ourselves, and why questions like political and cultural appropriation are so important' (1993: 36).

However, as in the case of *Show Boat*, the demonstrations against *Miss Saigon* were dismissed by the producers and the media, both asserting that the protests were a serious threat to artistic freedom. When the Asian-American community protested against the play during its run on Broadway, it faced similar harsh criticism from the mainstream media. The Asian-American community responded to the accusations of censorship with a pamphlet that stated in part: 'The Asian-American community supports the true concept of "artistic freedom" but ... it quite simply refuses to continue to sit in the back of the proverbial "artistic bus"' (Maclear, 1993: 31).

The Production and Ownership of Cultural Production or Culture as Consumer Product

Miss Saigon, like other cultural products, cannot be removed from the context of economics and profit. Cultural industries are the fastest-growing economic sector in Canada. In 1993–4 the Council for Business and the Arts in Canada, in its annual survey of performing arts organizations, polled seventy major dance, music, opera, and theatre organizations in Ontario. It reported that total income generated from ticket sales, admissions, and sales of arts-related products equalled $76,925,582.

Traditional values are reflected in Canada's dominant culture and are embedded in its system of governance, official languages, system of property ownership, concepts of law and order, and world of art and cultural representations. Among the values embedded in these systems are individualism, freedom of choice, freedom of expression, objectification, consumerism, capitalism, and so on. Unquestionably, a cultural product or production is a commodity. The value of a product is measured in terms of its market price or marketability. This is the foundation of the economic organization of our society. Thus, the economic system, driven by the profit motive, which determines mass production and mass consumption, is reflected in the products it produces. And 'every commodity reproduces the ideology of the system that produced it' (Fiske, 1989: 14).

For any product to succeed in a market-oriented society it must capitalize on consumer tastes; but in a hegemonic society the consumer is assumed to be identified with the dominant culture and the social differences of potential audiences are ignored. Popular entertainment forms are designed to emphasize and reinforce traditional beliefs and the ideological assumptions of the dominant culture audience. Thus, from the perspective of the producer/promoter, cultural productions like *Miss Saigon* need not dwell on how the 'others' view the product as long as they are not seen as consumers.

Miss Saigon and *Show Boat* both demonstrated the social and economic power of producers to control public discourse with respect to these cultural productions. Both Mirvish and Livent Productions invested millions of dollars in promoting these musicals. The *Globe and Mail* and the *Toronto Star* each ran daily (often full-page) advertisements. Radio and television promotions also were aired daily. City TV aired a half-hour American Express–paid promotion for *Miss Saigon* in the same hour it covered and dismissed the protests on opening night (Maclear, 1993). At the same time, the protests organized by Asian ReVisions (and the Coalition Against Show Boat) were met with strong criticism by the mainstream media and mainstream cultural critics. The media's interest coincided with the interest of the producers, which was to increase revenues and stifle dissent. The media deflected attention away from the real concerns of the protesters – that is, racial misrepresentation and stereotyping – and framed the discussion solely in terms of artistic licence and creative freedom, and in so doing dismissed the protests as simply an expression of censorship and political correctness.

As a result of all of this, the coalition shifted its educational, outreach, and advocacy activities. Recognizing how important it was to 'recover' the politics of dissent by working through more sympathetic media, it gave interviews to and prepared resource materials for the media in the Chinese-Canadian, Japanese-Canadian, and Korean-Canadian communities (McFarlane, 1993/4: 12–13). It also targeted other ethno-specific newspapers and the alternative media.

The reality that cultural products are consumer-driven commodities is also reflected in how the entertainment value of the productions is determined. The tastes of the presumed audience influence the processes through which cultural producers select particular cultural forms. Culture depends on an audience; it follows that the producer of popular entertainment will in all likelihood try to shape the cultural product to please the audience. Both *Miss Saigon* and *Show Boat* were created to amuse predominantly White theatre-goers, who approached both shows as entertainment.

But as Maclear (1993) asks: 'Entertainment for what and at whose expense?'

For much of the Asian community, *Miss Saigon* was not entertainment. At a demonstration against *Miss Saigon* in New York in 1991, a protester said: '*Miss Saigon* turns our screams into songs, and our pain into pleasure, and our thousand year old heritage into brothels, and our bodies into exotic sex toys, and our lives and our deaths, ultimately into nothing. This is the *Miss Saigon* fantasy. It is not our reality' (Maclear, 1993).

Members of the coalition protesting *Miss Saigon* encountered hostility and resentment when they tried to hand out their pamphlets to theatre patrons. One protester observed: 'I was struck by the overwhelming aggression directed at us ... Our efforts to freely express dissent were viciously attacked by theatre patrons who chose to throw the leaflet back in our faces. Odd behaviour for those who expound "freedom of expression"' (Maclear, 1993).

As a result, the audience left the production with their stereotypes intact, having learned nothing about the underlying issues the Vietnam War, or the problems of sexual exploitation and child prostitution, or the plight of Amerasian children, or the values, norms, traditions, and aspirations of Vietnamese people. For them, Vietnam was simply an exotic backdrop for articulating American values.

The high-tech glitz, sugar-coated clichés, and sexually titillating scenes of scantily dressed prostitutes all served to erase the history of American imperialism and the tragedy of two million Vietnamese dead. As Kyo Maclear observed: 'You could come out of *Miss Saigon* thinking that Agent Orange, napalm and My Lai were "Oriental" cocktails' (1993: 32).

Conclusions

Miss Saigon provided the catalyst for Asian Canadians to take collective action to change racist cultural idioms. Asian artists combined their voices with those of community activists from diverse groups. Thus, an important outcome of the protest campaign was that a number of Asian-Canadian groups formed alliances for the first time. Collectively they spoke out against cultural racism, in the emancipatory interests of their collective identity as Asian Canadians.

Appendix: Excerpts from the Toronto Board of Education Package, 1994

The comprehensive set of questions that students were asked to consider provides a helpful summary of many of the critical unaddressed issues that were raised by this cultural production. Listed below are the questions by subject area:

Stereotyping

a. Cultural productions such as *Madame Chrysanthemum* (Victorian novel); *Madama Butterfly* (opera); *Sayonara, South Pacific, Flower Drum Song* and *Miss Saigon* (musicals) all include an Asian woman as a main character. Identify similarities in the storylines and the ways the Asian women are depicted.
b. How are Asian men and Asian women portrayed in *Miss Saigon*?
c. What are some of the stereotypes popular culture and the media use in portraying Asian women and Asian men?
d. What impact might such stereotypes have on the lives of Asian people?
e. How do negative stereotypes harm the group being stereotyped?
f. How do positive stereotypes harm the group perpetuating the stereotypes?
g. How might the casting of Asians in sterotypic roles create a double bind for them?

Power

h. How do decisions get made about what productions are mounted in large commercial theatres? When the production involves the portrayal of oppressed groups, should producers take into account the sensibilities of these groups? If not, why not?
i. What role does the media play in determining survival of a theatrical production?
j. How might community groups without status and economic power oppose stereotypical representations in the media and popular culture?

k. *Miss Saigon* is said to be historically accurate. Is it?
l. Whose history is depicted, and from whose perspective?

Education

m. What criteria should be used in selecting dramatic productions suitable for school visits?
n. What kind of blanket policy should the Toronto Board develop to deal with the possible school visits to controversial productions such as *Miss Saigon*?

U.S. Imperialism

o. How has the media and popular culture such as the films *Apocalypse Now, The Deer Hunter*, and *Platoon* represented the roles of Americans as compared to the Vietnamese in the context of the Vietnam war?
p. In the play *Miss Saigon* and during the Vietnam war, offensive racist language such as 'gooks' and 'chinks' were used to describe the Vietnamese. How did the training of the U.S. soldiers contribute to the use of such language?
q. How were the racist attitudes of the U.S. soldiers played out during the war in their treatment of the Vietnamese?
r. Miss Saigon is a metaphor for East/West relations. Explain. In what ways has Asia and the 'Third World' been exploited in the West? How is the relationship between East and West presented through the characters in the play?
s. How do the characters Kim, in the song 'I'll give my life for you,' and the Engineer, in 'The American Dream,' through the lyrics convey their perceptions of the superiority of life in the U.S.A.?
t. How did the U.S. and Canada benefit economically from the Vietnam War?
u. How did politicians justify Canada's involvement in the war industry? And, what were the counter arguments?

Industrialization of Sex: Exploitation of Women and Children

v. How have the distorted stereotypical perceptions that some Westerners have of Asian women contributed to the exploitation of poor women in Asian countries?

w. How did the presence of U.S. troops in Asian countries contribute to the increase of prostitution and the exploitation of women and children in those countries?

x. How is the industrialization of sex played out in *Miss Saigon*?

y. *Miss Saigon* has been called a 'love story.' Is it? What arguments can be made for or against that position?

Notes

1 A focus interview was held with members of Asian ReVisions. Any unreferenced quotations appearing in the text are taken from this interview.

2 Similarly, Black characters were traditionally played by White performers in blackface.

References

Asian ReVisions. 1993. 'Mission Statement by Coalition.' *Nikkei Voice*. 7(5). June.

Carby, H. 1993. 'Encoding White Resentment: Grand Canyon, A Narrative for Our Time.' In C. McCarthy and W. Crichlow, eds. *Race, Identity, and Representation in Education*. New York: Routledge.

Fiske, John. 1989. *Reading the Popular Culture*. Boston. Unwin Hyman.

Fung, Richard. 1993/4. 'Call in the Troops: Miss Saigon Undergoes Analysis.' *Fuse*. 17 Winter.

Grossberg, Lawrence. 1993. 'Cultural Studies and/in New Worlds.' In C. McCarthy and W. Crichlow, eds. *Race, Identity, and Representation in Education*. New York: Routledge.

Jordan, Glenn, and Chris Weedon. 1995. *Cultural Politics: Class, Gender, Race and the Postmodern World*. Oxford, U.K., and Cambridge, Mass.: Blackwell.

Landau, Saul. 1993. 'What Link Does Jane Austen Have with the War in Vietnam?' Review of *Culture and Imperialism* by Edward Said. *Race and Class*. 35(2). 97, 98.

Lowe, Keith. 1993. 'East Meets West Meets Stereotype.' *Toronto Star*. 19 August.

McFarlane, Scott. 1993/94. 'The Rising Sun in the Media.' *Fuse*. 17 Winter. 12–13.

Maclear, Kyo. 1993. 'Miss Saigon: Sex, Lies and Stereotypes.' *Nikkei Voice*. 7(8). September.

Malinowski, B., in Nourbese Philip. 1993. 'That Was Then – This Is Now.' *Border/Lines. Race and Representation*. 29/30. 18.

Neumann, A. Lin. 1984. 'Scandal in Manila: The X-Rated Business Trip.' *Ms.* February. 99–102.

Pieterse, J. 1992. *White on Black: Images of Africa and Black in Western Popular Culture.* Stratford, Ont.: Mercury Press.

Roman, Leslie. 1993. 'White Is a Colour! White Defensiveness, Postmodernism and Anti-Racist Pedagogy.' In C. McCarthy and W. Crichlow, eds. *Race, Identity, and Representation in Education.* New York: Routledge.

Said, Edward. 1978. *Orientalism.* New York: Pantheon.

– 1983. *The World, The Text, and the Critic.* Cambridge, Mass.: Harvard University Press.

– 1993. *Culture and Imperialism.* New York: Knopf.

Stam, Robert. 1993. 'From Stereotype to Discourse.' *Cine-Action.* 23 Fall. 12–29.

Sumi, Glenn. 1993. 'Sites of Struggle: Metamorphosizing the Gaze.' *Nikkei Voice.* 7(9). August.

Toronto Board of Education. 1994. *An Information Package on Miss Saigon.*

Yee, May. 1993. 'Finding the Way Home Through Issues of Gender, Race and Class.' In Himani Bannerji, ed. *Returning the Gaze: Essays on Racism, Feminism and Politics.* Toronto: Sister Vision Press.

7

Show Boat

Background

The Ford Centre for the Performing Arts precipitated a wave of protest, polarization, and conflict when it decided to open in the fall of 1993 with the musical *Show Boat*. The new, publicly funded centre would be opening its doors by producing a sixty-six-year-old American play with a long history of racist associations. This, even though North York, where the theatre is located, is one of the most racially diverse municipalities in Canada and has a large population of African Canadians.[1]

This case study explores the racial politics in the cultural production of *Show Boat* at two levels. On one level, we will analyse the production's images and discourse, and deconstruct its stereotypes, language, and literary structure to uncover the hidden meanings and messages encoded in it. On another level, we will examine the controversy itself, and analyse how it was received, responded to, and understood by different groups. This analytic process will reveal how relations of dominance, marginalization, and exclusion are developed and maintained by the élite producers of culture. This case study of *Show Boat* will provide a concrete example of new forms of resistance being utilized by ethno-racial groups, who are increasingly demanding the right to control images and representations of themselves.

The Plot of *Show Boat*

The play is based on a 1926 novel by Edna Ferber. *Show Boat* chronicles the lives of the Hawkes, a White, southern family, and the performers who work on their steamboat, the *Cotton Blossom*, a floating theatre that travels up the Mississippi River over four decades, entertaining White audiences in the American South and Midwest. The story begins during the post-Emancipation period, the 1880s, and continues into the first decades of the twentieth century. Captain Andy Hawkes and his wife Parthy are the owners of the *Cotton Blossom*. Their daughter Magnolia falls in love with Gaylord Ravenal, a riverboat gambler who joins the show boat troupe as an actor. A subplot deals with one of the actresses aboard the boat, Julie Laverne, who is of mixed race but light-skinned enough to pass for White. Julie is married to a White man, Steve.

Early in the first scene, while the boat is moored in Natchez, Mississippi, there is an altercation between Pete, the engineer of the *Cotton Blossom*, and Steve. The struggle is over Julie, whom Pete has attempted to seduce with unwanted gifts. After the fight, motivated by revenge, Pete reports to the sheriff that there is a case of miscegenation on the *Cotton Blossom*. At that time, miscegnation was a criminal offence in Mississippi. Before the sheriff arrives to arrest Julie and Steve, Steve cuts Julie's hand and sucks her blood. In this way the couple is spared arrest, since Steve, having ingested Black blood, would henceforth be considered partly Black. However, they must leave the boat, since Whites and Blacks are not permitted to live together.

Magnolia eventually begins to perform on the boat. Gaylord Ravenal, a gambler who has been warned to leave town by the sheriff, seeks passage on the *Cotton Blossom*. Ravenal becomes a member of the cast, with Magnolia as his leading lady. A romance develops between the two, and they have one child, Kim. Eventually they leave the boat and move to Chicago, where they live on the proceeds from Ravenal's gambling.

Over the next decade Gaylord and Magnolia run into hard times, and Ravenal abandons Magnolia and their daughter. Magnolia is forced to seek work at a club, where the featured singer is Julie. While backstage, Julie overhears Magnolia auditioning for the manager and sacrifices her own job to give Magnolia a chance to work. Magnolia meets Julie once more, at a whorehouse, when Magnolia goes to return money borrowed by her husband.

Magnolia becomes a famous musical comedy star, singing (as Ferber writes in the novel) 'American coon songs.' Twenty years later, Magnolia and Ravenal are reunited on the *Cotton Blossom*. Realizing they are still in love, they 'live happily ever after.'

Production History

The musical premiered in Washington, D.C., in November 1927. It was revised and restaged many times in the United States, Britain, and Canada. Also, three films were made based on the original novel. Each new version of *Show Boat* was different in some ways from the earlier ones, but all retained the stereotype that had Blacks happily singing and dancing. Only the character Joe, played most famously by Paul Robeson, laments his plight in the famous song 'Ole Man River.' While he moves White audiences with his music, his character retains the stereotype of the lazy, good-natured 'negro' who displays no rage or resistance to his plight. All the other Black characters are equally passive.

In the first production, two Black roles, Julie and Queenie, were played by White performers in blackface. Tess Gardella, who played the part of Queenie, was billed as 'Aunt Jemima.' The show was a great success and ran for 572 performances. The opening lines of the song 'Ole Man River' were 'Niggers all work on the Mississippi / Niggers all work while the White folks play.'

The following year *Show Boat* was staged at the Theatre Royal, Drury Lane, in London, with Paul Robeson as Joe. Robeson played the role again in the Broadway revival three years later, and still later in the film versions.

Show Boat was first filmed in 1929 by Universal. In 1936, for the first film remake, Universal brought together many of the original Broadway cast, plus Robeson. This version has been described as *exceedingly* offensive (Rickards, 1993a). Queenie is played by Hattie McDaniel as a 'rolling-eyed head-tied plantation darky.' The Black men are depicted as lazy boozers. In this version the opening lines of 'Ole Man River' have been sanitized to 'Darkies all work ...' Also, the word 'nigger' doesn't appear in the dialogue, although 'coon' does. The film includes a scene in which the White cast – in 'blackface' and with banjos in hand – breaks into a song called 'Galivantin' Around.' Rickards argues that no one, including Kern and Hammerstein, the songwriters for the musical version, could have been unaware of the blatant racism of this number.

In 1947 there was another Broadway revival. In this production, once again, a White woman was given the role of Julie. The first lines of 'Ole Man River' were revised to 'Colored folk work ...'

In the film version of 1951, 'Ole Man River' is sanitized to 'We all work ...' Ethan Mordden, a historian of musicals, calls it 'sadly inauthentic ... the epic vulgarized.'

In 1954, *Show Boat* was performed as an opera. In 1966, a stage production was mounted at the Lincoln Center in New York. There was a complete reworking by Robert Russell Bennett, who had orchestrated the 1927 production, but the production was not a success. The Black chorus was omitted. When it played at the O'Keefe Centre, *Toronto Star* critic Ralph Thomas complained that it 'dismisses the drama almost entirely and plays the show more as a costume concert, where everything is sung straight to the audience and the music is all that matters' (in Rickards, 1993a).

In 1971, *Show Boat* was revived at the Adelphi in London, England, where it ran for two years. Its success may be attributed in part to the popular British-born jazz singer Cleo Laine, who played the part of Julie. She was the first Black to play the role. In 1983 there was another revival on Broadway, and in 1990 *Show Boat* was again performed in London, England.

Events

In March 1991, impresario Garth Drabinsky of Live Entertainment Productions (Livent) announced his intention to produce *Show Boat*. It was not until eighteen months later that the decision reached the attention of the Black community. Drabinsky had seen a production in London in 1990, and thinking that there might be problems with the play he had consulted a few prominent American Blacks, including Harry Belafonte, James Earl Jones, and Vernon Jordan. One of the subjects discussed was the offensive language and negative stereotypes in the original production.

In October 1992, Drabinsky met with a group of prominent Blacks in Toronto. The meeting was orchestrated by Lincoln Alexander, the former federal cabinet minister and lieutenant-governor of Ontario. Also present at this gathering were Dennis Strong, a management consultant and former president of the Black Business and Professional Association, who later was hired by Drabinsky on a contract; Sheldon Taylor, a historian and community worker; Robert Payne, a columnist with the *Toronto Sun*; Lloyd Perry, former head of Ontario's Office of the Official Guardian; Anthony Sherwood, an actor; and Howard Mathew. Not present were any members of the leading advocacy groups for Blacks in Toronto, or of the Black Action Defense Committee (BADC), or of the numerous community associations and groups within the city's Black communities.

Most of those at the meeting were people whose opinions were generally sought after by the White mainstream community. In fact, as Cecil Foster points out, Alexander was known for his role in castigating Caribbean immigrants who complained about the lack of opportunity in

Canada. Foster quoted Lincoln Alexander as saying: 'Fortunately for me, I was born here and I know how the Canadian system works ... It's only Toronto where you can get away with this *whining*' (Foster, 1993c: 51).

In response to the question about how the Black community was likely to react to *Show Boat*, some of the participants pointed out how difficult it was to anticipate how the community would respond, given the significant social, economic, political, and cultural differences characterizing this diverse community. However, members of the group warned Drabinsky that *Show Boat* could be 'treacherous ground if you mishandle it' (ibid.). At the conclusion of the meeting all the participants refused to sign a form that Livent had prepared in advance endorsing the show.

In the fall of 1992, Livent asked the North York City Council for a permit to place its box office on the North York School Board's property, which adjoined the North York Performing Arts Theatre property. (The box office was a construction in wood of an actual show boat.) The motion passed.

In January 1993, after reading *Show Boat* in its original text, a North York Board of Education trustee, Stephnie Payne, an African Canadian, became deeply troubled that *Show Boat* was going to be the Ford Centre's very first production. She began speaking to other people in the Black community, and found that many of them shared her concerns. She decided to bring forward a motion to the North York Board of Education in February 1993, coinciding with Black History month. The motion related to Livent's established practice of bringing in students from boards of education to see performances of its productions. For other musicals, such as *Joseph and the Amazing Technicolour Dreamcoat* and *Phantom of the Opera*, Livent typically prepared and distributed educational kits (including videos and other resource materials) for teachers to use in the classroom to prepare children for the productions. Previous experience led Livent to anticipate that approximately 200,000 students from different school boards in Ontario would attend *Show Boat*. Even after discounting of student tickets, this would provide a significant source of revenue for Livent.

In her motion, Payne was asking the board not to allow students, under the auspices of the board and at taxpayers' expense, to attend the musical. After hearing about the motion, Drabinsky called an urgent meeting with Payne. She met with him and brought with her eight members of the African-Canadian community and one member of the Jewish community. The group included novelist Austin Clarke, schoolteacher Courtney Doldron, Morley Wolfe of B'nai Brith, teacher Lennox Farrell, and Rick Gosling and Al Mercury from the North York Mayor's Committee on Race and Ethnic Relations. All were in agreement that there might be negative consequences if the Ford Centre opened with this show. Drabinsky defended his choice, arguing that as a Jew he empathized strongly with their concerns about the language in Ferber's text. Moreover, as a Jew they could not consider him a racist. He pointed out that Blacks and Jews had worked together in the civil rights movement and that some Jews had been murdered in that struggle (Foster, 1993c).

Some members of the group were uneasy that Drabinsky was attempting to focus the discussion on Black/Jewish relations. One member responded that their concerns had nothing to do with Black/Jewish relations and suggested that this was a 'fight against human dignity and that what you're doing is not right.' There was strong consensus among the group that the show should not be staged, and that if Livent insisted on producing the musical, it should be the 1927 version – unsanitized and uncensored. In this way the audience. would understand why the Black community was so offended. They tried to explain what the Black community found so troubling about the play, and they discussed the images in the advertisements that were already appearing in the media, commenting that 'the poster you are putting out depicts an African slave in bareback, while genteel folks are waving their hats. Isn't that a negative depiction of Blacks?' (Foster, 1993c: 52).

It was also pointed out to Drabinsky that the ads included an image of the Confederate flag, which is also the flag of the Ku Klux Klan and the Heritage Front. These posters were later changed.[2]

One further issue on the table at this meeting was the role of the media. The participants at the meeting asked that Livent not go to the media and air the controversy, and Drabinsky agreed to this request. The group left the meeting with the impression that Drabinsky had heard but not listened to what had been said (ibid.). Shortly thereafter, Drabinsky appeared on *The Ed Needham Show,* where he denounced the *Show Boat* protesters.

Anticipating that the motion would be presented at the North York Board of Education, television station CTV contacted Payne and conducted a twenty-minute interview with her. She was asked why there was a need for this motion and what her exact problems were with *Show Boat.* Payne talked about the racism in the original text upon which the musical was based, and also in the two prior versions of the musical.

The interviewer asked what had transpired at the meeting with Livent, and Payne indicated that part of the discussion had focused on racism and anti-Semitism and how in the past both groups had worked together to fight oppression. The interview conducted that day was never aired.

On 24 February the motion came forward, and the board decided to defer its decision until after Livent had been given a chance to present its case to a more broadly based group of Black community members (Foster, 1993c).

The next day, CTV's Peter Murphy called Payne to arrange another interview. Murphy brought a crew to shoot pictures of Payne and other colleagues watching the 1951 version of *Show Boat*. The interviewer again brought up the subject of Black/Jewish relations, and Payne talked about the struggles against racism that had been part of the Jewish and Black experience in North America. Payne offered that she had always been there fighting on the front lines for justice for people who have been oppressed, and that 'what really hurt is to see that musicals, plays, and movies that portray people of African ancestry in a negative way is always done by a White male and usually a Jewish person.' This comment was the only part of the lengthy interview that reached the airwaves, two weeks later on 7 March 1993.

Members of the Jewish community rose immediately to protest Payne's remarks, and words of outrage and indignation flowed from the city's mainstream media. Two days later, Stephnie Payne issued a public apology for her statement.

About one week later, singer Salome Bey organized a meeting at the North York Board of Education. She began her remarks by suggesting that in her view, the production should not be stopped. She noted that her personal goal was to lay the groundwork for Blacks to write, produce, and finance their own shows so that they would not have to be concerned about how others portrayed them (Foster, 1993c). She went on to suggest that it was important to consider the fact that Black artists needed employment and that this musical would provide work for about thirty Black actors, although she herself would not be auditioning for a role. She also pointed out that there could be a serious backlash from White producers if this protest were to succeed. There was a good deal of antagonism toward Bey's position, and her remarks generated a negative response among many of the participants in that meeting.

One week later, a group of concerned parents, teachers, lawyers, and other members of the Black community met at Brookview Middle

School in North York to discuss what could be done about *Show Boat*. That evening the Coalition to Stop Show Boat was formed. Jeff Henry, a York University professor and former chair of the Department of Theatre Arts, and Angela Lee, general manager of the Canadian Black Artists' Network, were selected by consensus as co-chairs, and a steering committee was established. Later, Lee would resign and be replaced by Roger Rowe.

The coalition meetings were difficult, as there was no formal structure and no funding. At each meeting money was collected to help defray costs. There were contentious issues to deal with, as well as significant differences among members of the coalition with respect to ideology, politics, and strategies. These differences were a reflection of the diverse nature of the community. In a sense, there were struggles at two distinct levels. First there was the internal struggle of a community group trying to organize and mobilize members of the larger community, interact with other groups and communities, develop priorities, create an agenda, determine goals and objectives, establish timelines, and seek support. At the other level there was the larger struggle relating to what the coalition and the Black community would ask for, how they would deal with the different institutions such as the media, how they would appeal to the conscience of the mainstream community, and so on.

The coalition's first decision was to organize a two-hour protest outside the theatre every Saturday from April to October. Its second major decision was to make deputations to several school boards in Metropolitan Toronto, which it proceeded to do through May and June. The group's concerns about bringing students to *Show Boat* were shared by other groups such as the Anti-Racist Multicultural Educators' Network of Ontario. This group, whose members all worked in public education, protested the choice of musical, rejected the educational value of bringing students to it, and vigorously opposed the development of educational materials based on a racist text. In a letter to Ontario's education minister, the chair of the network said: 'Creating the opportunity for the school going community to be entertained at the expense of some of its members is not the best strategy for helping eliminate racism. To argue that seeing Show Boat would itself be a lesson in racism is to argue that one learns best about radiation by being exposed to it. Likewise, the central impetus for the show is entertainment and economic gain. It was never intended to be educational ... Any educational package accompanying it would therefore be at best inadequate and inappropriate' (Ijaz, 1993).

Arguing from a similar position, another community organization, the Black Educators' Working Group (1993), stated in a letter to Premier Bob Rae that 'it is inappropriate for the producers of Show Boat to use the educational system of Ontario to make a dollar over the objection of the Black community and at the expense of the self-esteem of Black children and youth.'

In the months following the opening, several boards of education considered what action to take with respect to *Show Boat*. Some school boards in Metro, after lengthy debate and consultation, decided not to sponsor official school tours for students to see the play. Others developed other strategies.

For example, the Toronto Board of Education established a Show Boat Advisory Group, which included eleven members selected from the Curriculum Division, the Equal Opportunity Office, the Equity Studies Centre, and the Elementary and Secondary Principals' Associations. The committee was charged with formulating recommendations regarding the suitability of the play for elementary and secondary students. Members of the committee attended a performance of *Show Boat*. They then held several meetings to thrash out a policy for the board. Having seen the production, all of the committee members were in agreement that the show was not an appropriate educational vehicle. In their view the play contained racist depictions, and taken alone the production would do nothing to enhance the self-esteem of Black students. However, there was a significant division in the group as to whether students should be permitted to attend as part of a school-sponsored curricular activity. There was intense discussion over a range of issues, including these: racism and anti-Semitism, sexism, stereotyping, the role of the media, censorship, artistic integrity, cultural appropriation, authentic versus sanitized productions, curricular relevance as a basis for attending *Show Boat*, the relationship between depicting and propagating racism, community reactions, the Toronto board's image as a leader in antiracism, and the adequacy of teacher training.

Some members of the committee felt that the show was so offensive and its stereotyping so pervasive that no students should be allowed to go. Others agreed that the show was racist at number of complex levels that younger students would be unable to comprehend either cognitively or emotionally as well as beyond the cognitive abilities of students who lacked the tools to analyse the subtle kinds of racism that were embedded in the production. However, they argued that the board should not ban *all* students: with effective teaching support, there could be some positive outcomes for students in the senior division of second-ary schools.

After several meetings the committee recommended to the board that attendance be limited to students in grades eleven to thirteen. Also, teachers were to accompany students to the show. Beforehand, the teachers would have to contact the Equity Studies Centre or the Equal Opportunity Office and arrange for appropriate resource support. Teachers would also be required to submit to their respective principals written curricular/pedagogical lesson plans consistent with the board's antiracism goals. The policy recommendation was passed by the board.

The board developed its own teaching materials, which carefully detailed the many socio-political issues raised by the production. Implicit in the board's action was the belief that the issue of censorship was irrelevant to the discussion. Explained Pat Case, equity adviser with the Toronto Board of Education: 'Boards of education have always been in the business of determining what children will learn and what they will not learn – always. You do it every day in your role as a teacher, determining the appropriateness of particular learning materials ... in the case of *Show Boat*, we are making a decision whether the material is appropriate for children' (1994: interview).

At the North York Board of Education the decision to review the issue of students attending *Show Boat* came about largely as the result of community pressure. At the three board meetings, parents' delegations, community organizations, and other concerned members of the community presented submissions arguing that the play was racist. According to one trustee, there were as many as seventy-five of these submissions. There were also many letters and phone calls to trustees and some members of council. There were also delegations from Livent, from members of the artistic community, and from others who believed that North York students should be allowed to see *Show Boat*.

A committee of five board officials was struck to study the issue. Using a systematic review process, the committee conferred with antira-cism educational experts; consulted internal staff; identified and exam-ined the relevant sources; reviewed the literature; read Edna Ferber's original text; worked with a human rights lawyer; reviewed the board's own policies; and reassessed board guidelines on the use of controver-sial materials in the curriculum. Following this extensive process, the committee attended a performance of *Show Boat* and recorded their observations on a prepared form.

The chair of the committee, Diane Dalton, said that two of the committee's main concerns were the impact of this play on students and its value as a learning experience. According to Dalton, the committee considered it the role and responsibility of the educational system to find an appropriate balance between two conflicting rights: the right to free expression, and the right of individual students not to be harmed as a result of attending this performance. The members asked themselves whether this particular vehicle was appropriate for teaching antiracism. Among all the educational resources out there, was *Show Boat* an effective learning tool?

The committee concluded that the play could have a negative impact on how students felt about themselves (Moloney, 1994). This was communicated to the school principals in a brief memo written by the director of education, Veronica Lacey, who also stated that the play was not a suitable field trip for elementary and secondary school students.

On 15 April, Livent called another meeting of the Black community. Dennis Strong had been hired on contract by Livent as a liaison with the Black community. Hal Prince, the director of *Show Boat*, flew in from New York to attend. At the meeting there were about seventy people, of whom fifty were Black. They were not all opposed to *Show Boat*. The meeting was chaired by David Crombie. The coalition co-chair, Jeff Henry, had asked Crombie to speak first, because at that point the media was not reporting anything about the coalition, and given all the controversy, the coalition members were very anxious to communicate to the public precisely who they were and what their purpose was. They were particularly concerned about the rumours that were circulating regarding the possibility of violence and allegations that the coalition was anti-Semitic.

The coalition's mission statement, read by Henry, stated the following:

The Coalition to Stop Show Boat is composed of diverse individuals, groups and organizations opposed to all forms of negative discrimination such as racism and anti-semitism etc. It intends to do all that is legally and politically required to stop the musical production based on Edna Ferber's anti-Black novel, *Show Boat* that is scheduled to inaugurate the opening of the publicly-funded North York Centre for the Performing Arts.

The Coalition to Stop Show Boat intends to use a variety of strategies to achieve its objectives. The Coalition will organize public demonstrations, public lectures, and dialogue as well as write articles and letters on this issue. To reach these objectives, the Coalition will facilitate the sponsoring of artistic-cultural, religious, political and other activities with community organizations and institutions.

The Coalition to Stop Show Boat will rely on the technical, social organizational and other resources of individual members, groups, organizations and institutions that share our views about the insensitivity of inaugurating the North York Performing Arts Centre with a musical based on a racist novel. We believe that the mounting of this production transcends the concerns of the Black community and has become an issue of 'human decency.' The Coalition also depends on the goodwill, financial support and work of all other individuals, groups, sectors, organizations and institutions who have an interest in this issue, and are willing to take responsibility for making a truly just and therefore peaceful society in the city of North York and in the rest of Canada.

Lincoln Alexander spoke next and asked Drabinsky if he was going to clean up the play. Drabinsky agreed that he would. Hal Prince expressed his view that it was not possible to remove the negative stereotypes from the play and suggested that there were certain things in the play that the community would have to recognize and accept. Prince also stated that the production would remain faithful to the story and to the history of the period. At this point Alexander cut him off, noting that 'what you are going to have is not a lot of stereotyping but just a little bit of stereotyping' (Henry, 1994). The meeting in the end accomplished very little. A great chasm remained between the two opposing positions.

Later that same day, 15 April, the United Way of Metropolitan Toronto held a meeting to determine whether it should proceed with its plans to hold a fund-raiser using *Show Boat*. Several volunteer organizations had undertaken to sponsor performances of *Show Boat* for fund-raising purposes. The United Way had planned to join with the Canadian National Institute for the Blind to reserve the theatre for an evening performance as a fund-raiser. The partners were to sell seats at a premium price, and the proceeds – estimated at about $100,000 – were to be shared by the two partners.

When the controversy over the play first arose, the board of the United Way considered withdrawing but decided that the play was not racist but rather, 'about racism.' This decision to proceed with the fund-raiser caused a wave of protest from United Way volunteers and staff, from the organization's own antiracism consultants, and from members of diverse communities. Given the nature of the controversy and its potential impact on the organization's credibility in terms of its antiracism work, the board delegated the decision about whether to continue with the event to the executive committee, which supported the board's initial decision to go ahead with the fund-raiser. In protest, nineteen of the twenty-two members of the Black and Caribbean Fund-raising Committee of the United Way resigned. According to the chair of the Anti-Racism Committee, one of the real problems with the *Show Boat* issue was that the organization was choosing to proceed with its plans without consulting the committee and despite staff advice to stay clear of the production. This led to significant morale problems, particularly among those staff involved in implementing United Way's antiracism policies. Adrian Johnson, the chair of the committee, observed: 'I resigned from the Committee because I thought that I would not be able to effect change in the organization. Anti-racism was not valued ... *Show Boat* created a lot of distrust of the organization and its motives.'

Another organization, the Canadian Friends of the Hebrew University, now withdrew its commitment to a fund-raising event using *Show Boat*. About a year before *Show Boat* became an issue, a group of individuals from the Black community had begun meeting with the Social Action Committee of this Jewish organization with the goal of promoting a better understanding between the two communities. The two groups had been meeting on a regular basis to discuss an array of issues and concerns pertinent to both communities. When the controversy over *Show Boat* began to grow more tense, the two groups decided to organize a workshop to explore this subject and other potentially divisive issues. Following this process, the Social Action Committee met with its organization's board and urged it to not to sponsor an evening at *Show Boat* as a fund-raiser. The board withdrew.

In September 1993, as the Saturday protests continued, the coalition members felt it necessary to extend their efforts into other arenas. Efforts to gain support from the provincial government – in particular, the Ontario Anti-Racism Secretariat – had failed. Later it was alleged to the coalition that the premier, Bob Rae, had instructed the secretariat to stay out of the debate on *Show Boat*.

On 2 September 1993 the coalition formally requested the Ontario Human Rights Commission (OHRC) to intervene under section 29 of the Ontario Human Rights Code. The group was asking the OHRC to inquire into the dispute by meeting with various parties, to report the findings of that investigation, and to issue a public declaration that the advertising and presentation of *Show Boat* systematically discriminated against the African-Canadian community in Toronto. The main ground of the application was that the decision to produce *Show Boat* had poisoned the cultural, social, and economic environment for many African Canadians. The coalition alleged that the musical's denigrating images, when so publicly reinforced and supported, inhibited and prejudiced the African-Canadian community's right to enjoyment of not only the cultural life of Toronto, but also the economic and social life available to White Torontonians. The OHRC met with the parties to the dispute but refused to issue the public declaration requested (Rowe, 1995).

Also in September 1993, the coalition made a public deputation to the Metropolitan Toronto Police Services Board, requesting that the Hate Crime Unit of the Toronto police investigate the racist novel *Show Boat*. They hoped to demonstrate that the novel upon which the play was based was a gross misrepresentation of history and that the decision to produce the musical had created a hostile environment for members of the African-Canadian community. The Hate Crime Unit decided that *Show Boat* was not hate literature and therefore did not fall under the mandate of the Criminal Code. On 17 October 1993, *Show Boat* opened.

In 1994, Livent announced its intention to sue the Ontario government for $20 million in damages. The suit was based on an allegation that the Anti-Racism Secretariat had funded the Coalition to Stop Show Boat and several other Black organizations. The suit claimed that Livent had lost box office revenue, and that public funds had been used to censor a theatre production. These allegations originally appeared in Thomas Walkom's book on the NDP government in Ontario (1994). Members of the coalition categorically deny that they received any government money in support of their protest activities. While the Ontario Anti-Racism Secretariat did fund Black and other ethno-cultural organizations, it did not provide any funding to the Coalition to Stop Show Boat, nor were any of its grants used to challenge the production.

The publicity given to this lawsuit led one media commentator to write: 'If Live Entertainment's allegations are valid, there existed the extraordinary situation of the money of Canadian citizens being spent by a small group of *unelected zealots* [emphasis ours] on activities that could and did harm and hinder those very same citizens' (Coren, 1995).

The Site for Show Boat

Show Boat was staged in a new theatre that had been built with public funds: $31 million from land deals attached to the site, and about $5 million that had been redirected from the Yonge Street Streetscape fund, a project supported by contributions from private developers (Colin Taylor, 1993). Livent, chaired by Garth Drabinsky, was awarded an exclusive contract to manage this important new cultural institution. (There had been no tendering process.)

The decision to inaugurate the arts centre with a production of *Show Boat* was to prove extremely problematic. North York is one of the most multicultural and racially diverse areas in the Toronto region. According to the 1991 Census, almost half of North Yorkers identify themselves as racial minorities; this includes over 44,000 Blacks. Many African-Canadians are of Caribbean origin; together, they represent the largest racial minority group in the municipality. The Black community in North York continues to make significant social, economic, and social contributions to the life of their city.

North York Council's decision to build a major new public arts facility was in itself a forward-looking initiative. However, as Colin Taylor, artistic director of Theatre WUM, pointed out (1993), to open the arts centre with a cultural production that a significant number of North York's people could not enjoy was seen by many African-Canadians as 'a grotesque failure of human empathy.' As well, it was seen by this community as an abrogation of responsible leadership on the part of North York politicians. Mel Lastman, the mayor of North York, and the North York Council, seemed indifferent to the pain felt by many of their African-Canadian constituents, and unmoved by the tensions that erupted as a consequence of their powerful institutional backing of *Show Boat*.

It is somewhat ironic that in proposing to the municipal council that a performing arts centre be built in North York, the city's Development and Economic Growth Committee commented: 'It is not an elitist facility. It will not be planned as a monument in its own plaza detached from the urban fabric. It will be connected with street life and offer such a variety of performances as to culturally connect with the everyday lives of North Yorkers' (cited in Anderson, 1993).

The vision of that committee was far from realized. The centre's choice for its very first production had implications that reached far beyond the City of North York, which had been known affectionately as 'the City with a Heart.' The ensuing controversy provides a powerful example of the contradictions, conflicts, and deep divisions that mark cultural production within a multicultural society.

Analysis

'Showboat': A Postmodern Racist Discourse

Racist discourse can be understood, regardless of its specific content, as having 'the effect of establishing, sustaining and reinforcing oppressive power relations' (Wetherell and Potter, 1992: 70). It is discourse that justifies, maintains, and legitimates those practices which maintain the power and dominance of a particular group – that favours in-groups and denigrates out-groups. In the following discussion we examine the discourse in the production as well as the discourse of the producers. We contend that racist discourse operates at two levels in *Show Boat*. On one level, there is the overt racist language, images, and narratives embedded within the cultural production itself. The plot and subplots, the portrayals of Black characters, the distortions and misrepresentations of the history of the period, and the language and images incorporated in both the text and the music all serve to organize and communicate a set of meanings and messages that reinforce racism. At another level, we contend that racist discourse was used by Livent, the media, and others to deny, resist, and discredit the protesters and *their* message. Within the framework of 'liberalism,' dominant cultural institutions employ a number of discursive strategies to stifle debate, silence dissenters, and reinforce existing cultural practices.

Stereotyping and Misrepresentation in the Performance of 'Show Boat'

The issue of representation was of critical importance in the debate over *Show Boat*. These were some of the key questions: Does a cultural production such as *Show Boat* accurately reflect or represent the reality of the world it is depicting? Does the content of the musical (which includes its language, images, narrative, and characterizations) ring true today for those who identify themselves as African Canadians? Does the play reinforce historic and current negative perceptions, assumptions, and stereotypes?

While few expect total realism in the theatre, minorities have developed a 'hair-trigger sensitivity about racial stereotypes that derives to some extent from what has been called the 'burden of representation'

(Stam, 1993) and the 'degradation of representation' (Jordan and Weedon, 1995). The importance of stereotyping and misrepresentation to people of colour and other socially powerless groups needs to be understood in relation to two things: the social location of minorities within the dominant culture; and the continuum of a prejudiced social ideology, discriminatory social policies, and racist practices that form the social reality of disempowered groups.

Those who are outside the mainstream of society are acutely sensitive to distorted representations of themselves. In large part this is because, as members of historically marginalized groups, they have long been powerless to control the production of their own representations. A significant segment of the Black community perceived that the stereotypical portrayals of Blacks in *Show Boat* were linked to the biased, negative attitudes, assumptions, and behaviours that African Canadians encounter in their everyday life and their interactions in the workplace, the educational system, the media, the legal and justice system, and other social institutions and systems.

Stereotypes are based on simplification and generalization and on the denial of individual variability. Although they have no basis in reality, stereotypes have a very real social impact, creating a system of social typecasting. The targets of stereotyping are 'assigned' set roles and patterns from which escape is difficult. Stereotypes become part of the psychological and cultural fabric of mainstream society (Pieterse, 1992).

A central feature of stereotypes is that they reflect shared beliefs; this point is crucial, as it stresses the *social* importance of the process (Taylor, 1981). One of the effects of prejudice directed at groups is that those groups are systematically created as 'others.' 'Otherness' is charged with meaning and value. Boundaries and mechanisms of inclusion and exclusion are developed which in turn enhance in-group solidarity. Images of 'others' do not circulate because of their truthfulness, but rather because they reflect the interests of the image-makers and the spectators/consumers.

Since the late nineteenth century, the dominant culture has held two conflicting images of Blacks. On the one hand, Blacks have been perceived as menacing, uncivilized, uncontrollable savages, as oversexed, untruthful, and manipulative, as a primitive people who belong to a 'race' that must be controlled. This perception did much to rationalize systems of oppression, including slavery.

The counterimage of Blacks has been that they are childlike, simpleminded, and obedient, that they like to sing and dance and are content to spend their lives serving White people. These comforting images of Blacks allow White audiences to avoid responsibility for racism.

Minstrel shows incorporating Black characters, which first became popular in the late nineteenth century, were always performed by White actors in blackface. In the same way, Black characters in films were always portrayed by Whites in make-up. The most famous 'blackface' film, *The Jazz Singer* (1927) with Al Jolson, was seen by nearly 26 million people. Later, when Blacks were actually allowed to appear in cultural productions, they were limited to humiliating roles, and were often compelled to tell 'coon' jokes, acting the fool, grinning and tapping away. Attention was drawn to those physical traits marking Blacks as different; their hair texture, lip size, and other facial features were depicted as unnatural. Black entertainers gained employment but at a significant cost to their own cultural and racial identity, to their self-esteem, and to their collective image in the African-American community.

From the perspective of those who opposed *Show Boat*, the world depicted in the novel and in the many theatrical productions and films based on it was one that included Blacks, but essentially as ethnic markers for the entertainment and pleasure of Whites (Nourbese Philip, 1993). The Black characters exist outside the central narrative. They are there to serve the interests and needs of Whites. They are compliant and submissive. Their brief appearances provide a 'colourful' backdrop.

The original text, written by Ferber, incorporates any number of double-images of Blacks.

A simple ignorant soul, the black man, and a somewhat savage ... (30)

... all around him now were his helpers, black men like himself, with rolling eyes and great lips all too ready to gash into grins ... (30)

Captain Andy liked and trusted them [Jo and Queenie]. They were as faithful to him as their vagaries would permit. (122)

One drop of nigger blood makes you a nigger in these parts ... (145)

I kind of smell a nigger in the woodpile here in more ways than one. (148)

Eight months of flies and niggers and dirty mud-tracking loafers is enough for me, Captain Hawkes. I'm thankful to get back for a few weeks where I can live like a decent white woman. (239)

Long before white-aproned Jo, breakfast bell in hand, emerged head first from the little doorway beneath the stage back of the orchestra pit, like an amiable black python from its lair ...

The Negroes lolled in the shade of their cabins and loafed at the water's edge (383).

'Show Boat' Maintains the Racist Myths of Popular Culture

Edna Ferber did not invent these stereotypes; she was, in all likelihood, influenced by the dominant social and political ideology of the period. At the time she wrote *Show Boat*, and at the time the musical debuted, theories of white supremacy were being treated as highly credible and were being legitimized by pseudoscientific methods of inquiry. The concept of race was socially constructed on the assumption that visible phenotypical differences reflected mental and moral differences. Notions of White superiority and Black inferiority were firmly entrenched in the social, political, and economic discourses of Ferber's day. *Show Boat* reflected the popular discourse of that era.

A 1986 film, *Ethnic Notions*, documents the history of racism in film and other forms of cultural production, and also demonstrates the many ways that popular culture has reinforced certain messages about Black people. The mammy figure, an image so pervasive in American cultural production, is one example of the stereotyping that pervades *Show Boat*: Queenie is a very clear example of the type. The smiling image of Aunt Jemima that has appeared on the box of pancake mix for over one hundred years is another example of the mammy/servant figure.

Like Aunt Jemima, Queenie is presented as loyal to her White masters. In many of the productions she too wore a bandanna to cover her hair (to mask her desirability). The mammy figure is strong in relation to her own family or community; this is to highlight the weakness of the male. For Sandi Ross, a Black actor who has performed the role of Queenie in three different productions of *Show Boat*, playing the dignified mammy servant part was a very difficult experience: 'The language in *Show Boat* is just appalling. It's a stereotype language for that time, full of "dis" and "dat."' She asks rhetorically: 'Did anybody ever speak like that?' (Hanlon, 1993).

For the same reason, Salome Bey rejected an offer to audition for the part of Queenie in the Livent production. She also did not like the way the musical portrayed Blacks: 'It was an artistic decision. Those are not the roles I like to play' (in Kate Taylor, 1993b). She believed that both the 1926 novel and the 1951 film version portray Blacks in unflattering terms, and added that the way Blacks are portrayed in the work is difficult to explain to children growing up in a multicultural society.

The character Joe also represents a familiar stereotype. In some respects he is not unlike Rastus, who still appears on boxes of Cream of Wheat. There is an implicit negative association between Uncle Ben and Uncle Tom, who is a deeply offensive image in the minds of Black people. Like the smiling, grandfatherly Black man who has been pictured on the box of rice for more than half a century, Joe is presented in the novel and in many stage and film productions as passive, docile, and weak.

In his mature years, after he left the United States, Paul Robeson looked back on his stage and film career with a good deal of pain. He had found the stereotypical roles humiliating to play. He once described *Show Boat* to author Rebecca West as 'that pathetic melodrama'; and to a British reporter he suggested that he hated the lyrics to 'Ole Man River.' As he wrote in 1958 in his autobiography, *Here I Stand*:

In the early days of my career as an actor, I shared what was then the prevailing attitude of Negro performers – that the content and form of a play or film was of little or no importance to us. What mattered was the opportunity, which came so seldom to our folks, of having a part – any part – to play on the stage or in the movies; and for a Negro actor to be offered a starring role – well, that was a stroke of fortune indeed! Later I came to understand that the Negro artist had a responsibility to his people who rightfully resented the traditional stereotyped portrayals of Negros on stage and screen. So I made a decision: If the Hollywood and Broadway producers did not choose to offer me worthy roles, then I would choose not to accept any other kind of offer. (31)

These images, although created decades ago, have been woven into popular culture. As Craig Neville, a Washington advertising analyst, states: 'These are symbols that are so ingrained in the society and culture that most people do not even notice them any more ... these symbols promote stereotypes' (in Graham, 1993: B5). In the same article, sociologist Gaynelle Grant comments: 'The very nature of advertising is to alter how we look at ourselves and things in our environment ... and advertising that perpetrates negativity – like Blacks as smiling, simple-minded servants – affects the way our culture regards Black people.'

Pieterse (1992) argues that for the last 150 years and continuing today, cultural production has represented Blacks based on five dominant stereotypes: (1) Uncle Toms, who are passive and dignified, and who stoically accept their fate and serve their masters well; (2) 'coons,' who are funny, and not very bright, but who can sing and dance; (3) mulattoes, who are tragic figures because they are not White; (4) mammies, who are sexless archmothers; and(5) bucks, who are superstuds, bestial and uncontrolled. In the case of *Show Boat*, it can be argued that the first four dominant stereotypes were a part of the original text and reappeared in the many productions of the play.

Despite Livent's attempt to 'sanitize' its version of the play, the story was still of a White family and the performers who work with them, and the Blacks still served as an entertaining backdrop. Moreover, Black one-dimensional caricatures still found their way into the production, although more subtly and (perhaps to many White theatre-goers) more invisibly.

The original ads for the musical showed White people dressed in their finery standing on a dock while Black men pushed a bale of cotton. Singing Black labourers opened the show with 'Ole Man River,' and a mammy character cooked and sang in the servant's kitchen; these reinforced images that were already deeply rooted in North American culture. Throughout the play, White characters were always front and centre on stage and in the narrative. As one viewer explained: 'White characters sing and dance and fall in and out of love. The Black characters sing and dance. The White characters sing and dance, get married and have babies, suffer painful separations and tearful reunions. The Black characters sing and dance. The White characters succeed and fail, hate and love, are evil and kind. The Black characters sing and dance. The White characters sing and dance and forgive and forget and Black Joe sings "Ole Man River"' (Blenman, 1996).

In this context, the only Black character who has any role in this story is Julie, who is half-White. She appears in only four of the nine scenes in the Act I. She appears again in Act II, sings one song, and then disappears before the act is half over. She is not seen again for the rest of the play.

Racism 'Sanitized'?

Garth Drabinsky, in the meetings with members of the Black community discussed earlier, admitted that negative and offensive stereotypes existed in the novel. He repeatedly tried to make the point that it was 'unfair' to judge the musical by the novel, or even other productions;

and that significant changes would be made to this production. The notion of a purified and bias-free *Show Boat*, a 'Born again Musical,' failed to satisfy many members of the African-Canadian community: 'The new mythical Show Boat is formed from the perceptions and beliefs of Whites, and remains in a world where joy and suffering, good and evil, superiority and inferiority, dance hand in hand, where there are human rights and freedom – but no justice and equality – and where the producer's and promoters' vision of racism is ironic rather than tragic' (Harris, 1993: 7–8).

Champions of *Show Boat*, including Livent, throughout the production's history have argued that *Show Boat* is *about* racism, and that it broke new ground in dealing with the subject of miscegenation. This view suggests a very limited understanding of the nature of racism. Racism is evaluated by how many times the word 'nigger' is used. At the same time, racist ideology is buried within commonsense beliefs, assumptions, and stereotypical images that play all around us (Essed, 1991; Goldberg, 1993) and that are seamlessly woven into the play. This everyday, unconscious familiarity with racist representations makes it difficult for White people to identify the more subtle manifestations of racism that are embedded in many cultural productions, including the 'sanitized' version of *Show Boat*.

Pat Case, co-ordinator at the Toronto Board of Education's Department of Equal Opportunity, provided in an interview this metaphorical analysis of how cultural racism was operating in this 'sanitized' version of *Show Boat*: 'I thought that generally speaking the racism expressed in *Show Boat* was like the stealth bomber. Up to now, we've been able to develop all kinds of antennae to detect high-flying racism just as much as radar detects high-flying war planes. The trouble with *Show Boat* is that like the stealth bomber, they've figured out a way to get below people's detection – below the radar. That's what *Show Boat* does: it flies in below the level of our received antennae, the stuff that people normally don't use to analyse racism.'

What Livent failed to understand was that the issue for the protesters went well beyond a matter of simply cleaning up the negative stereotypes and removing the overtly offensive language and images so that the images and language would not disturb the liberal instincts of a 1990s audience. The opposition to *Show Boat* was based on a number of stains in the work that no scrubbing could erase. Underlying the obvious problems of the play were deeply racist assumptions about the nature of Black people and their rightful place in American society. The fact that characters like Joe are lifted from their earlier state of ignorance, laziness, and primitiveness and are now dignified in their resignation and is an affront of a different kind. There were many reasons why Livent's efforts to recreate *Show Boat* did not provide much reassurance to the African-Canadian community. Here are a few: the absence of a historically accurate context; the symbolic importance of inaugurating a public arts centre, partially paid for by African-Canadian North York taxpayers, with this particular production; the lack of concern for the past and present discrimination that afflicts Blacks in their everyday lives; and the absence of any kind of acknowledgment of the pain *Show Boat* caused the Black community. As co-chair of the coalition, Jeff Henry commented: '*Show Boat* has resonated in the Black community. It is the symbol of systemic and cultural racism. It symbolizes what we suffer in our daily lives, no matter what we have achieved in this society, no matter who we are. When we step out publicly, we face certain things that keep reminding us we are Black people unless we put a sign on our chest that says, I am a doctor, a lawyer, a professor' (Foster, 1993c: 54).

Representation and the Role of Audience

For the largely White audiences, the glitz and glamour of *Show Boat* – the high quality of the acting, the lavish sets, beautiful costumes, and spirited dancing, the familiar and stirring music, and the power of the spectacle – all served to render the racist images, characterizations, plot, and subplots invisible.

In a sense, we are a culture of spectacle consumption (Mitchell, 1988). Throughout the nineteenth and twentieth centuries, non-Europeans often found themselves being placed on exhibit or made the exotic objects of European curiosity. *Show Boat* achieves the same end. By placing Black people on exhibition to be observed by Whites, *Show Boat* as spectacle feeds White curiosity about racism, but in a very superficial and circumscribed way. The audience remains fixed in its own sociocultural location. What viewers see and hear is not reality itself, but reality *refracted through* the images, preconceptions, and attitudes that are part of their frame of reference. Each individual spectator's gaze on the 'other' is influenced by familiar narratives, allusions, and stereotypes that are part of his or her cultural experience (Corbey, 1995).

Toni Morrison describes a process, common in North American cultural production, whereby attention is deflected away from 'the racial object to the White subject; from the described to the describers and the imaginers; from the serving to the served' (1992: 90). The White gaze represents the White perspective and the White preconceived notions that define the social roles – but not necessarily 'true' roles – of Blacks. Handler refers to this as 'the congruence between one's outer position, or the role one played, and one's inner or true self' (1986: 3).

The stereotypes and caricatures, which are based on distortions of the truth constructed by Whites about Blacks, are used to 'entertain' White audiences. Blacks are used as objects. The objectification of Blacks in *Show Boat* is evident in the way they hang around on stage: they are inactive, inanimate props and are being used to tell a story that is supposed to be historically 'authentic.' By their everyday familiarity with these stereotypical images, the White audience is lulled into a subtle, unconscious, unquestioned acceptance of the subservience of Blacks. Blacks, like women, appear as fleeting images in the spectacle, whose images, thoughts, feelings, ideas, and words are shaped by others (White writers, White composers and lyricists, White producers, and White directors). Stam describes this as a process in which Black souls are transformed into White men's cultural artifacts (1993: 18).

While the constant revising of *Show Boat* over the last sixty-odd years has been viewed as an ethical issue by its producers, the objective of the revisions has been essentially to ensure that the racial sensibilities of the period are not offended. As Angela Lee (1993) points out: 'The problem with the revisions always has been and always will be, that the racial sensibilities being considered are those of the white audience. Because *Show Boat* has always elicited controversy whenever it has been performed, producers, directors and writers have consistently sought to revise the material in ways that would allow white audiences to view themselves with little discomfort.'

Richard Fung (1994) concurs with the notion that *Show Boat* was a product of White writers for White audiences. He adds: 'When I say White audiences I mean both literally and in terms of audience address.' A demonstration of this is the way in which the theme of miscegenation or interracial love is handled in the play, as well as in many other theatrical productions and films, including *Miss Saigon*. That is, they always had to kill off 'one or both of the protagonists so that the miscegenation could actually never come to fruition – a child could never be born.' Fung suggests that there is a kind of liberal framework in both productions that creates sympathy on the part of the audience for the story's victims.

Duberman (1989), in his biography of Paul Robeson, commented thus on the mixed reception of the 1927 production of *Show Boat*:

> Despite the mixed critical reception, the public made *Show Boat* a huge hit – and moneymaker. That is, the white public. Many blacks who saw the show came away distinctly less enthusiastic. The European correspondent for the New York Amsterdam News, J.A. Rogers, reported in an indignant column (reprinted in the *Pittsburgh Courier*) that he had talked to 'fully some thirty Negroes of intelligence or self-respect' who expressed 'their disapproval of the play,' and he had 'also heard many harsh things said against Robeson for lending his talent and popularity towards making it a success.' If anyone were to call him a 'nigger,' Rogers quoted one informant as saying, 'he'd be the first to get offended, and there he is singing "nigger, nigger" before all those white people.' (114–15)

Paul Robeson's son, Paul Robeson Jr, who was an archivist for his father's papers, and a highly regarded lecturer on American society and its history, was interviewed by Cecil Foster (1993a) about his views on the decision to launch a production of *Show Boat* and the controversy that followed in Toronto. Robeson was opposed to the use of his father's name in defence of the musical, as producing the musical would only serve 'to perpetuate and buttress a culture which has inherent built-in racist undertones.' He also pointed to the fact that the racism woven into the play so troubled his father that he changed the original 1927 lyrics of 'Ole Man River,' which had originally been: 'Niggers all work on the Mississippi / Niggers all work while the white folks play / ... I gets weary and scared of dying / And ole man river just keep rolling along.'

By reworking these lyrics and rejecting the stereotypes of the popular culture, Robeson turned the song into a message of defiance and resistance. The new words were: 'There's an ol' man called the Mississippi / That ol' man I don't like to be / What does he care if the world's got troubles / What does he care if the land ain't free / I keeps laughing instead of crying / I must keep fighting until I'm dying / And ol' man river, he just keeps rolling along.'

One might pose this question: Why didn't Livent choose to use these lyrics? Instead, the producers returned to the lyrics based on the original version, keeping only the change to 'coloured folk' from 'niggers.' Did Robeson's revised words reflect not resignation but a resistance too threatening and intimidating for the 'imagined' audience?

'Show Boat' Reflects Contested Notions of Truth and History

As the controversy over *Show Boat* escalated, the issues of historical rep-resentation, authenticity, and truth were raised by both sides. Drabinsky and many others challenged the protesters by arguing that the play reflected an authentic and important period of American history, and that those who were opposing it were trying to revise or ignore history. But for the coalition and others, the central questions were these: Whose history was being narrated in this story, and from what perspective? And what does 'authentic' history really mean? Uncovering the history of margin-alized people who have been denied their history is a difficult task.

In Eurocentric conceptions of history, White people commonly appear as subjects, people of colour as objects. White people *make* history, while people of colour remain on the sidelines (Weedon and Jordan, 1995). Handler suggests that the term 'authentic' is a form of discourse about others that 'proves to be a working-out of one's own myths' (1986: 2).

Despite Ferber's disclaimer in the introduction to her novel that *Show Boat* is *'neither history nor biography, but fiction'* (author's italics), Livent and other critics of the protest continued to insist that it reflected the his-tory of the period and that the protesters were, in fact, trying to close down an opportunity for viewers to participate in a historical learning experience. However, *Show Boat*'s 'authentic' history lesson is wrapped into a fiction; it contains racism cloaked in all those commonsense images, stereotypes, and caricatures that are embedded in popular discourse.

Show Boat ignores powerful social realities. While the theme of misce-genation is dealt with in the first scene, the play is devoid of any of the social history that relates to the African-American experience. No Black character challenges the status quo. Blacks continue singing and danc-ing, and remain passive and dignified in their acceptance of their fate.

It is clear to us, therefore, from the debate around the play-as-authen-tic-history, that notions of 'truth' and 'reality' are social constructs indic-ative of a particular perspective at a given point in time. The actual experiences and events that relate to African Americans living in the South during and after the Reconstruction were not reflected or even hinted at in the Toronto production or any that preceded it.

While *Show Boat* was sailing up and down the Mississippi (1887 to 1927), Blacks living in the South continued to experience every form of political, economic, and social exploitation. In the aftermath of the Civil War, a social revolution was taking place in the Southern states. Planta-tion slavery had involved a complex system of racial domination. After its demise, a new system of labour, social, racial, and political relations had to be built (Foner, 1983). The passage of the Reconstruction Acts by the federal government in 1867 heightened the instability of the immediate post–Civil War period. The South was faced with the reality of defeat and was also being forced to acquiesce to the authority of the federal government, which many perceived to be an outside power.

This period was characterized by general economic and political instability and by worsening racial tensions. White southerners feared labour competition from Blacks, and the potential for mixing of the races and miscegenation. Whites were being threatened with a radical change in their position of power, privilege, and domination. They also feared rebellion and perhaps retribution by Blacks (Nourbese Philip, 1993).

These anxieties fuelled existing racist attitudes. Whites needed a mechanism for keeping Blacks 'in their place.' The perpetuation and circulation of negatives images and stereotypes helped ensure that White racial supremacy was maintained. Life for Blacks became increasingly difficult despite their status as a freed people. Institutionalized racism was pervasive. Because the federal government did not impose land redistribution, which would have provided Blacks with an economic base for consolidating their political and civil rights, unemployment and poverty continued to haunt their lives. Northerners believed that 'Negroes' needed no further assistance than the ballot and were unwilling to provide social and economic assistance.

After the Civil War, Blacks feared that despite the fact that they were 'freemen,' they would not gain political or economic rights. They were afraid of not gaining the right to the land they were promised, of not finding employment. Perhaps most of all, they were afraid for their lives. This period saw the rise of reactionary movements such as the Ku Klux Klan and kindred groups, which functioned as terrorist organizations. Blacks who tried to assert their newly won freedoms found themselves the target of systematic terror and violence. Mob actions and lynchings were commonplace.

By the late 1880s it was generally conceded that the attempt to make the South constitutionally, socially, and politically part of the nation again had failed. The post-Reconstruction period was characterized by the total repression of the Blacks through 'Jim Crow' laws, and by the beginning of a vast migration of Southern 'Negroes' to the North, where they hoped to find the freedoms that had been denied them in the South (Franklin, 1994; Rable, 1984; Foner, 1983).

This is the period covered by *Show Boat* – a period characterized by racial oppression, conflict, and violence. In a climate of racial hysteria, old stereotypes were adapted to the new politics. Images of Blacks during the post-Reconstruction harken back to the good old days when 'all darkies were happy,' singing and dancing, and resigned to their place in the natural order. The most famous example of the virulent cultural racism of the period is D.W. Griffith's *Birth of a Nation* (1915), one of the most racist movies ever produced in the United States. Yet this movie was also widely popular. It was produced during the worst period of violence against African Americans in the history of the South and served to metaphorically lynch the Black presence (Rogin, 1996). Despite these forces, the post-Reconstruction was also characterized by the political and social mobilization of the Black community. This period raised Blacks' aspirations and expectations and allowed them space to create institutions that helped them survive the repressions that continued to characterize their lives. There are many examples from this time of individual and collective forms of resistance against subjugation and discrimination (Foner, 1983).

Dozens of organizations, including the National Association for the Advancement of Colored People (NAACP), and Marcus Garvey's Universal Negro Improvement Association (UNIA), were established to fight for equal rights and social change. 'Black resistance reached a feverish pitch' during these forty years. In Tulsa, Oklahoma, resistance was so widespread that city officials ordered the bombing of the African-American community. UNIA had seventy-four branches in Louisiana alone (Richmond, 1993).

It has been argued that the entertainment industry has conducted a 'siege on the past – systematically excising knowledge of the consequences of the historical exploitation of African Americans' (DeMott, 1995). Superficial and misleading renderings of the American past, in film and other forms of cultural production, obscure the outlines of racial conflict and redefine Black grievances for the purpose of diminishing their importance.

The Construction of a Racist Discourse: Livent's Response to the Protest

The very successful opening of *Show Boat* in New York without protest from the African-American community, and the many positive reviews in the American and Canadian media, served to reinforce Livent's central message before, during, and after the Canadian production: that

Show Boat was not a racist production, and that the coalition represented a very small, misguided fringe group interested mainly in furthering its own political agenda.

In an effort to discredit and dismiss the criticism and protest of the Canadian production of *Show Boat*, Livent repeatedly pointed to the lack of protest by African Americans to the many productions of the play in the United States, including the present, Livent version.

What Livent and others failed to consider were the significant historical and socio-cultural differences between African Canadians and African Americans that might account for their differing responses to issues of cultural racism.

Many of those most involved in the protest were immigrants from the Caribbean who had come to Canada in the past thirty years. Their cultural background is vastly different from that of most African Americans, with whom they share little except skin colour. They came from postcolonial societies in which they were the majority population, but in which they had suffered under colonial rule. Immigrants from Jamaica, Trinidad, Barbados, and other Caribbean countries bring with them an acute sense of how significant it is to lose one's culture and history or have it devalued. Moreover, Blacks in Canada do not live in segregated ghettos, as do many African Americans, nor do they experience complete social, cultural, and political isolation from mainstream society, as do many African Americans. Although African Canadians are also the objects of racial discrimination, the society they live in is not entirely compartmentalized with respect to race.

These differences strongly influence how the two communities are likely to respond to the mounting of a cultural production in the public arena. Not only are African Canadians aware of such cultural activities, but they become particularly concerned and engaged when these cultural events attempt to represent some aspect of Black life or culture. African Canadians read the same newspapers as Whites, and watch the same television news, and in general are as well informed about White culture as participating members of Canadian society. This is in contrast to the situation in the United States, where what happens in the White world is rarely acknowledged by significant numbers of Black Americans, who are almost totally marginalized from the dominant culture. African Americans are concerned about bread-and-butter issues such as employment, education, and housing; they are less engaged by cultural events that take place within the dominant mainstream, which are largely directed at White audiences.

One striking example of the difference between the two communities is Caribana, a street festival and parade organized by members of the Caribbean community and strongly patterned after the famous Carnival in Trinidad. This is one of the most significant cultural events of the year in Toronto and attracts nearly one million people. This celebration of Black Caribbean music and culture also attracts substantial numbers of White Canadians and members of other ethno-racial communities. It is quite unlikely that a city's largest festival – one that attracts Whites from the mainstream as well as members of other ethno-racial communities in significant numbers – would take place in the United States.[3]

A local production of *Show Boat* was running in Akron, Ohio, at about the same time as in Toronto. A director of a Black cultural centre in that city noted at the time: 'The Carousel [theatre] isn't of interest to 99 per cent of African Americans here.' A director of the Urban League pointed out that 'if we were major contributors or major participants in the theatre world in Akron, I wouldn't be sitting here today saying I had never heard of *Show Boat*.' He added that the theatre world belongs to the mainly White élite and is irrelevant to most American Blacks (Gombu, 1993).

Livent used a number of other discursive strategies in an attempt discredit the protest. On 12 May 1993, Drabinsky in a written submission to the North York Board of Trustees described those involved in the protest as 'using *Show Boat* as a platform to promote their own agenda and causes which have nothing whatsoever to do with this show.' He describes the concerns of the African-Canadian community as 'shouted slogans, mob rule and wild accusations which have no substance behind them.'

Livent also tried to emphasize and reinforce the divisions within the Black community by raising doubts about its solidarity on this issue. To this purpose, Livent lined up endorsements of the play from several Blacks, in both the United States and Canada, including the well-known actor James Earl Jones, whose voice was used in all the radio promotions. At first, Livent retained the African-American scholar Henry Louis Gates to develop educational packages for the schools.

The theme that the Black community was divided was reinforced by a remark by the mayor of North York, Mel Lastman. In an effort to defend Livent's decision to open the Ford Centre with *Show Boat*, Lastman commented that Black opposition to the play was somewhat scattered and disorganized (Slinger, 1993b).

Several months after the production opened, on 2 February 1994,

Drabinsky delivered a widely excerpted speech to the Empire Club at the Royal York Hotel (Drabinsky, 1994). It was videotaped and replayed several times on Rogers Cable Television. Drabinsky said in the presentation that he regretted that 'public discourse' on matters like racism tends to 'disintegrate into a confusing and bewildering babble of meaninglessness and recrimination.' He described his opponents using phrases like 'radical segments' out to advance 'their own agendas ... self-appointed community "leaders" ... pedants ... exploiting the empathy of our tolerant society ... confused individuals ... irrational juxtapositions ... strange obsessions ... hurl epithets ... nefarious misconception ... simple lack of knowledge ... cynical disregard for truth ... irresponsible and bigoted ... corrosive torrent ... vile and repugnant anti-Semitic rhetoric ... ponderous machinations of the politically ambitious ... willing to pass off meretricious slogans for real debate' (in Salutin, 1994). In this same speech, he related the activities of the coalition to the German Nazi regime's burning of books (*Canadian Jewish News*, 1994).

Construction of Racist Discourse by the Media

The media played an extremely important role in the controversy surrounding *Show Boat*. No other cultural event in the history of this city, or possibly even the country, produced as much media coverage as did this single production. Racist discourse in the print and electronic media relating to the controversy and the protest played a significant role in reinforcing certain messages.

Monitoring of the three major Toronto dailies found that the *Toronto Star* devoted forty-two articles to the subject of *Show Boat*, the *Globe and Mail* twenty-three, and the *Toronto Sun* sixty (excluding letters to the editor). In all, 125 news articles, features, reviews, and editorials were written on this subject in the mainstream press. This figure is probably low, since our monitoring may not have caught every single article. Also, this figure excludes the extensive coverage generated by *Show Boat* in mainstream magazines such as *Maclean's*, and in alternative newspapers such as *Eye Weekly*. Regarding the community press and the ethnic press, most of the coverage was in Toronto and in Ontario generally, but the media across the country also covered the events. It can be safely assumed, then, that the print media in this country published at least two hundred articles on this single event. (This survey does not begin to address the extensive coverage on television and radio.)

By all criteria, *Show Boat* was a newsworthy item, and the media interest was largely fuelled by the protest against the production and by the charges of racism directed at the play. The story expanded to become much more than a relatively minor cultural item because it pressed one of the hottest buttons in contemporary multicultural Canada – that of racism. Its newsworthiness was also enhanced by the formation of the Coalition Against Showboat, which demonstrated regularly in front of the theatre. The appearance of chanting, placard-waving, Black protesters every Saturday, and at the previews and opening of the play, called for a significant police presence. The appearance of dozens of heavily armed police on horseback to guard the theatre during the previews and on the opening night sent a powerful signal to the media. Protestors plus police raised the possibility of overt conflict and even violence, which made the media even more vigilant.

The media coverage related to the production focused on controversy, conflict, and discord. Many of the journalists ignored the substantive concerns about the racist content of the musical and instead highlighted the tensions between the Jewish and Black communities, the staging of demonstrations by mainly Black protesters, and the presence of the police. All of these are potent symbols raising at the very least the *possibility* of conflict. The media were ever on the alert in case the peaceful demonstrations turned violent.

Since the media play a crucial role in structuring the social and cultural reality within which people live, it is not surprising that most people who receive their information from the media quickly became aware of the controversy. The production rapidly became part of the public discourse, and many phone-in radio shows devoted programs to a discussion of the alleged racist nature of the play. The electronic media in particular structured the discussion around the issue of censorship. Many broadcasters maintained that since the coalition wanted to stop *Show Boat*, they were indulging in censorship, which could not be tolerated in a liberal democratic society.

A closer examination of the media coverage of *Show Boat* reveals that most of the articles published were straight news stories without a particular point of view. The rest of the articles – mainly features and editorials – expressed an opinion, usually in favour of the production. Many of these articles stated that there was no racism in the production and that the protesters were at the very least 'uninformed,' or in a more extreme response, 'lunatics.' A limited number of articles took the opposite position, arguing that the protest had merit and should be supported. The following table shows the breakdown for two of the dailies.[4]

	Neutral	Supportive	Unsupportive
Toronto Star	25	10	9
Globe and Mail	15	5	6

It is important to note who wrote the feature stories. Of the nine relatively positive articles published in the *Toronto Star*, only two were written by staff writers; the remainder were written either by freelancers or by community members contributing unsolicited articles. The two staff writers who took a positive stance on the issue were Joey Slinger and Michele Landsberg, two well-known proponents of progressive journalism. The seven 'outside' contributors included, among others, the present authors, Henry and Tator (28 May 1993); Jeff Henry (15 November 1994); Angela Lee (1993); and Sol Littman (22 June 1993), director of the Simon Wiesenthal Centre. (Jeff Henry and Angela Lee were co-chairs of the Coalition to Stop Show Boat.)

In the *Globe and Mail*, two positive articles were written by staff writer Michael Valpy. Freelance journalist Cecil Foster contributed an article (19 October 1993). Rick Salutin wrote sympathetically about the issues driving the protest against *Show Boat* in the context of broader cultural issues (19 March 1993 and 11 March 1994). Of the six negative articles, three were written by the paper's editor, William Thorsell (17 April 1993, 16 October 1993, and 28 September 1996).

Most of the pieces supportive of the protest were written by outsiders; this had the effect of undermining the issue's legitimacy. The newspapers can state in their defence that they opened the forum to the community voices; but it is also true that the articles written by Angela Lee and Jeff Henry – little-known members of the community, who had no public profile – carried little weight with readers when set against those of well-known commentators like William Thorsell and the *Star*'s art critic, Christopher Hume.

Analyses that critically examine written (and verbal) media texts reveal many linguistic and structural techniques for conveying specific messages to the audience (van Dijk, 1991). Such analyses consider headlines, placement in the newspaper, use of photos, use of specific adjectives and metaphors, and various grammatical devices such as heavy reliance on the passive voice. An examination of the articles identified as negative – that is, those written by journalists who took the position that there was nothing wrong with *Show Boat* and that the protesters were misguided – reveals some strong and often punitive language.

For example, much was written about the small number of protestors. References to 'forty' or so protesters or to the 'handful' were frequently made in order to dismiss the importance of the protest.[5] By consistently focusing on the 'small' numbers, the media intended to convey that this was not a widespread or serious protest. They carefully avoided any reference to the dozens of organizations within the African-Canadian community and other communities who had given the coalition their support.

Commentators blindly followed the lead of Livent, which claimed (without ever producing any evidence) that the protesters represented only a very small minority in the Black community. According to this view, the coalition was not only misguided but also vastly unrepresentative of majority Black opinion. For example, an editorial in the *Toronto Sun* (1993) commented: 'There isn't much room to pretend this is a major protest. What it is really is an excuse to agitate and get attention.' Yet even a cursory glance at the ethnic press – at *Share*, *Pride*, or *Metro Word* – or attendance at any one of the many meetings held by protesters, would have revealed enormous community support for the protest. It was support that crossed differences of socio-economic class, place of origin, and age. Even Joey Slinger (1993b) noted that 'Blacks of all political shades and all economic classes feel deeply about it and what they feel most deeply has to do with respect.'

The words used to describe the protesters also had negative connotations. They were referred to as 'unelected zealots' (Coren, 1995) and the 'politically correct gang that wants to censor Show Boat' (Berton, 1993). In the *Toronto Sun* they were described as 'the professional screamers' and 'the goofies who are screaming racism' (Fotheringham, 1993). In the same piece, the writer called the coalition 'the grandly named,' and asks its members to 'read some history.' He described the protesters as witless and suggested that 'if the protestors had the wit' they would have ventured into the theatre; yet at the same time he described them as 'instant experts who make a living out of protesting.' In same paper, Peter Worthington (1993) contended that 'the activists (to use a polite term) engaged in trying to stir up the community and create racism for their own political and/or power seeking ends, don't care what the facts are. They want confrontation.'

The theme of power is a central one in the media discourse, as if the desire for power was an aberrant form of behaviour. William Thorsell, the editor-in-chief of the *Globe and Mail*, wrote: 'The apparent issue is race – the allegation by some Black people in Toronto that Show Boat demeans them. But the real issue is power. Show Boat is just a vehicle to advance the campaign of some blacks in Toronto for more power in the life of the city, in particular the City of North York' (1993b).

The statements issued by the coalition protesters were described as 'ludicrous' claims that *Show Boat* was racist (Coren, 1995). The *Globe and Mail* found the 'protesters' rhetoric annoying' (Kate Taylor, 1993d) and their accusation that the show promoted cultural genocide 'of course ridiculous.' The protesters' message was an attempt to 'rewrite history,' according to William Littler of the *Toronto Star* (1993), who failed to realize that *Show Boat* did not present accurate history. Also in the *Star*, Pierre Berton characterized the message of the protesters as a 'silly argument ... led by a small group of activists' (1993). He added that 'to say [*Show Boat*] is racist is dangerous nonsense' and noted, somewhat parenthetically, that 'a great deal of fuss has been made about the use of the word "nigger."'

Writers tried to trivialize the issues. Some tried to joke about it. Example: 'To ban the musical and to be blind, oops, to be optically challenged ...' (Adilman, 1993a). Peter Krivel in the *Toronto Star* (1993) described the North York Board of Trustees meeting as a 'shouting match' using terms such as 'raucous' and 'emotion packed.' In discussing the North York Board of Education's decision to ban field trips to the play, a *Toronto Sun* feature writer noted that it had taken a 'timid stand' (Chong, 1994). The same writer described an article written by a foremost supporter of the protest as 'a tirade.'

The *Toronto Star* of 17 April 1993, in an otherwise moderate editorial, described the *Show Boat* controversy as 'the uproar which began last month.'

An example of trivialization was a piece by Lorrie Goldstein in the *Toronto Sun* that attempted to be tongue in cheek. The writer claimed that now that the *Show Boat* controversy had ended, race relations in the city were improving. He cited as evidence carefully selected sets of very negative propositions, which he alleged said the same things, taken from two newspapers: the Black community's *Share* and the newsletter of the Heritage Front. Goldstein ended his article this way: 'Isn't it nice to see some black people and some white people seeing eye to eye?' (1993).

In the same newspaper, another writer not only trivialized the issues but also insulted one of the leading protesters by noting that 'Stephnie Payne is missing considerably more than just a vowel in her first name.' She continued by asking, 'Is Payne a nasty mean-spirited woman or is she simply dumb as a post?' (Barnard, 1993) The same article concluded facetiously by stating, 'Remember, anyone referring to Broadway as the "great white way" ... will be put to sleep immediately.'

Some writers injected an element of fear and danger in their reportage – for example, one described the protesters as 'becoming increasingly aggressive' (Paltiel, 1993). This sentiment was strongly reinforced by Raynier Maharaj, in the *Toronto Sun*, who lamented that no effort was being made to 'stop this race war in the making' (11 January 1994). In another article, headlined 'Show Boat Cauldron Boils Anew,' events at a calypso festival were described in terms of 'the racial hostility plaguing the Show Boat musical' (25 May 1993). In an interesting twist, H.J. Kirchhoff of the *Globe and Mail* actually agreed that *Show Boat* is racist, as well as probably sexist, but gave it a four-star rating anyway. In answering the question 'Is racism appropriate for the 1990s?' he commented, 'I think so ... at least as much as any other 65 year old piece of theatre' (1993). In response to such attitudes, Marlene Nourbese Philip (1993) observes that the age of these oppressive ideologies and systems is a poor reason for dismissing their significance, and simply demonstrates how deeply embedded they are in our culture and how difficult it is to eradicate them.

It is important to note that the media's strong stand in support of the production may have been influenced by the fact that several media organizations – in particular the three Toronto newspapers – had a vested interest in the production. All three papers received substantial revenues from the advertisements for *Show Boat*, which appeared daily over a period of several months. (See Chapter 8 for further discussion of this.)

One of the *Toronto Star*'s own columnists, Joey Slinger, pointed to this conflict of interest: 'Live Entertainment Corporation of Canada is among the Star's half-dozen biggest advertisers' (1993c). On 2 October 1993, the *Star* art critic, Christopher Hume, waxed eloquent over the production in his column and was cited in the *advertising* (authors' italics) section of the newspaper. Several radio and television networks also ran frequent ads for the play.

Censorship

In the strategies used by Livent Productions as well as those discursive strategies the media used in managing the events surrounding the production, one common theme was pervasive: the demands of the protesters were characterized as a threat to cherished liberal values, as censorship, and as an overdose of political correctness.

The African-Canadian community's view that selecting *Show Boat* for a publicly funded institution was detrimental to the community was interpreted by Livent and much of the media as a threat to freedom of expression. The protesters were seen as undermining one of the fundamental values of a democratic society. Editorials and columns were published in the *Toronto Star*, the *Globe and Mail*, and the *Toronto Sun* decrying the Black community's position on *Show Boat* and suggesting that what was being called for was the rewriting of history and the stifling of creative expression.

But as V.W. Farrell (1993), chair of the African Heritage Educators' Network (AHEN), observed: '"Artistic license" does not include the exacerbation of human dignity. Historic oppression is perpetuated by dominant groups, who establish criteria for artistic merit without regard to the sensibilities of the oppressed. The question arises: who defines *us*?'

Marlene Nourbese Philip (1992) commented that the quantum leap from racism to censorship was 'neither random nor unexpected.' The issue of censorship is central to the dominant cultures of liberal democracies like Canada. In these cultures, she observed: 'Censorship becomes a significant and talismanic cultural icon around which all debates about the "individual freedom of man" swirl' (270).

The Coalition to Stop Show Boat argued that to call for a play to be boycotted is not to condone censorship. Rather, it is to ask whether it is socially responsible, as well as morally right, to inaugurate a publicly funded building, in one of the most racially diverse cities in the world, with a work that demeans a segment of that community. Lennox Farrell, a teacher and a leader in the protest against *Show Boat*, suggested in *Share* (1993) that the real and initial concerns affecting the production were about 'a *hierarchy* of rights: the rights of a producer to artistic freedom versus the rights of a community not to be hurt, not to have its children hurt by stereotypes, again.' The coalition fully recognized that artistic producers are not under any legal obligation to accurately portray the extent or nature of human suffering in every cultural production. But they also argued that they had a moral obligation to the community to not wilfully misrepresent history and to not perpetuate demeaning and stereotypical images of groups within that community. This was especially true when it came to mounting a production for a centre that had been built largely with the money of multiracial taxpayers, and a production that was intended to be used as an educational vehicle in the schools to teach students about racism (Coalition, 1993b).

The controversy over *Show Boat* highlights the tension between two competing rights: an individual's right to free speech, and the right of communities to be protected from harmful forms of speech and expression. But what constitutes *harm*? And who will decide what may (legally and ethically) be said or done in the public domain? Many groups, including Jews, have argued powerfully with respect to hate propaganda – for example, that the risk of not attending to hate groups is greater than the risk of regulating them. In the same way, women's groups and others have vigorously opposed the production and dissemination of pornography, arguing that pornography has the potential to cause serious harm to women and children. In each of these examples, freedom is not viewed as an absolute right, but rather is tempered with the notion of justice and the communal will to protect the rights and freedoms of those who are most vulnerable in society.

In the *Toronto Star*, Michele Landsberg (1993) asked: 'Why is it censorship to protest a demeaning and irrelevant theatrical production?' She observed that these protests had provided a valuable forum for public education and free speech. Similarly, Sol Littman, director of the Simon Wiesenthal Centre of Canada, wrote: 'The Black community has every right to protest what it sees as a racist vehicle' (1993).

From the perspective of Rick Salutin, the fact that the theatre was located in a public facility was central to the discussion. He accepted the principle of artistic freedom for artists, for artistic directors, and for theatres, but with this rider: 'not in the name of private profit when they are public institutions.' He pointed out that Drabinsky's private company had complete control of programming and profits in a municipal arts centre, in return for a set rent. He then posed the question: 'What kind of a way is that to run a public cultural facility?' (Salutin, 1993c: 26).

Richard Ouzounian (1993: 10, 11) drew a further kind of distinction. He said there is an important difference between a work that is allowed to exist on a library shelf, or on a video for a private VCR, and a work that is being performed by live actors in a publicly funded municipal theatre. He then argued that these different forms of art should be subject to different standards. Like Salutin, he did not support censorship of any kind on any work that has been written or recorded, and exists in those forms. Thus, we should not rewrite the original *Show Boat* created by Edna Ferber, Oscar Hammerstein, and Jerome Kern, which can be read in the privacy of one's home or watched on one's private VCR or television. But Ouzounian also believed that different criteria must be applied when a work is presented publicly. He defined 'publicly' in two senses of the word: first, when live actors have enacted a part in a contemporary situation, and second, when a production takes place in a public building.

To ask actors in the 1990s to step on stage and play roles in *Show Boat* and other 'classics' such as *The King and I, Flower Drum Song,* and *South Pacific* – all of which have through the passage of time become identified with offensive stereotypes – is problematic for today's actors and for multiracial audiences. As Ouzounian observed: 'I am all in favour of artistic freedom, I'm against boycotting artistic productions, but I'm also in favour of sensitivity to the feelings, thoughts and deeds of racial and sexual minorities and any other minority group that could be offended by works you are presenting in certain situations' (ibid.: 11).

Arguing from a similar perspective, Colin Taylor, artistic director of the WUM, observed that the opening of a civic performing arts centre is a highly symbolic event, and that in a community with a very large Black population, staging *Show Boat* in that circumstance seemed a 'grotesque failure of human empathy.' To produce this show in the 1990s was an act of 'gross insensitivity' on the part of both Livent and the appointed representatives of the people in North York. The possibility of giving pleasure to a significant number of North York citizens, whose taxes had helped build the centre, had been eliminated (Colin Taylor, 1993: 25).

In a somewhat analogous situation, a cultural production in New York was closed because it was offensive, yet, as the coalition pointed out, censorship was not raised as an issue in that situation. The play *And Jesus Was His Name,* a $24 million production (*Show Boat* cost only $8 million), was supposed to open in New York in 1993 but was cancelled after Jewish groups protested that it offended them. The co-chair of the coalition, Roger Rowe, argued that there were close parallels between the responses of the African-Canadian community to *Show Boat* and those of the Jewish community to *And Jesus Was His Name.* Each community perceived that the play in question perpetuated negative stereotypical images and distorted historical fact. In each community, leaders in major organizations issued condemnations. *And Jesus Was His Name* had played in Paris and was a quarter of the way through a thirty-city American tour when it was cancelled. The production was written by a French historian, Alain Decaux, who said he was deeply wounded by the accusations that his work was anti-Semitic (Rickards, 1993b).

Nourbese Philip (1993) suggests that those who argued that the protest against the play was an attempt to engage in censorship should remember 'that freedom of expression in this society is underwritten, not by the free flow of information, but by the fact that there are those who are powerful enough in society to make *their* voices, and *their* viewpoints heard' (66–7).

This point is demonstrated by the fact that in the case of the closing of *And Jesus Was His Name* in New York, there were no school board meetings; nor was there any prolonged debate in the press; nor were there protests or demonstrations. There was no need: the theatre simply stood empty for two weeks (ibid.).

The issue of censorship took an ironic twist when certain individuals attempted to actually buy tickets to see the production. In one case, a high school teacher with the Metropolitan Toronto Separate School Board, Lennox Farrell, was prevented from entering the theatre by the police. Farrell is a highly respected and active member of Toronto's African-Canadian community and is involved in many community organizations. At the time, he was a member of the Ontario Cabinet Round Table Committee on Anti-Racism, co-chair of the North York Black Education Committee, co-chair of the Ontario Anti-Racism Advisory Working Group, and chairperson of the Caribbean Cultural Committee that staged the Caribana festival. He was prevented by a police officer from entering the theatre to buy a ticket to attend the second performance of *Show Boat*. Initially, he was told that all 1,850 tickets had been sold out; but when he asked another person to sell him his ticket, the general manager, David Bednar, told him that he would not be allowed to see the show even if he possessed a ticket, as his presence was deemed to be 'objectionable.' Even the police officer seemed surprised, and was quoted as telling the general manager: 'You guys like to say that the protestors haven't seen the show, but when they want to buy a ticket to go in you won't allow them to do so.' On the following day Farrell received a call from Livent's executive vice president, Lynda Friendly, who said that she was prepared to personally escort him into the theatre. He indicated that if he couldn't attend the performance on his own, he would not go at all (Rickards, 1993c).

In the second case, Colin Rickards, the associate editor of *Share* at the time, tried to attend a preview performance. After purchasing his ticket, he was stopped from going into the auditorium by a police officer. He was then taken to the general manager, who indicated that he would not be able to attend, as his presence was deemed 'objectionable.' When *Share*'s managing editor questioned Livent the following day, their response was that Rickards had not been allowed to see the show because he had 'written critically' about *Show Boat*. Rickard's comment on this set of events: *'That's* "censorship"!' (1993d).

Representation, Identity, and Power

The polemical debates around *Show Boat*, and the politics of cultural difference, demonstrate that in a postmodern society questions of representation and identity assume a colossal significance, particularly for those groups which carry with them histories of diaspora, exclusion, and dispersion. For people of colour – and particularly for Black people in Canada, who have been labelled 'outsiders' and rendered invisible in terms of everyday discourses of positive recognition and affirmation – controlling the production and dissemination of negative images and racist representations becomes a stridently self-conscious strategy for challenging traditional Eurocentric cultural practices (Rutherford, 1990). As teacher Clem Marshall suggests, there is an intrinsic link between art and life, and '*Show Boat* as art has spilled into our lives' (1993).

Show Boat provided a testing ground for strategies to address issues of race, representation, identity, and resistance. Struggles over identity and power were the locus of the debate. The African-Canadian community was still in the process of developing an identity – a task made more difficult by the diversity of its members' backgrounds and by the systemic inequalities in Canadian society. As a result, the resources it could devote to protesting *Show Boat* were extremely limited. In comparison, Livent had almost limitless political and economic resources. The musical was sponsored the *Toronto Star*, CFTO-TV, CFRB radio, American Express, and Midland Walwyn, a brokerage house. Millions of advertising dollars were spent on promotions for *Show Boat*. Huge sums of money were required for enormous billboards, daily full-page newspaper ads, and radio and television promos, which were carried on different networks several times a day.

Advertising has a significant impact on public discourse. More and more, the commodity culture is penetrating every facet of daily life (Becker, 1994). In the case of *Show Boat* and other cultural productions examined as case studies in this book, mass advertising and its underlying corporate interests were critical elements in reinforcing the unequal power relations between those who opposed the cultural productions and those allied to the dominant culture. This is reflected in the fact that even the CBC became a vehicle for promoting *Show Boat*. CBC aired *Show Boat: Journey of an Epic Musical*, a documentary produced by Livent and narrated by James Earl Jones. The *Globe and Mail*'s television critic, Liam Lacey (1993), suggested that the documentary was essentially a slick, hour-long commercial. It is interesting to note that the 'documentary' manages to ignore the protest to the show. Lacey questioned the integrity of documentaries that are financed by the same people they are supposed to be about. 'If our public broadcaster cannot create programming about these super-musicals, which are neither politically or morally neutral, from a financially independent point of view, it should not cover them at all.'

The suit against the Ontario government by Livent was a further example of political and economic power being used to malign and discredit both the government and the members of the coalition. According to the co-chairs of the coalition, Jeff Henry and Roger Rowe, the lawsuit was totally without foundation: the coalition never received funding from the Ontario government. In *Share*, Jeff Henry wrote: 'The coalition has never received one penny from the Ontario Anti-Racism Secretariat. What transpired – during the seven months of the protest ... was that we collected money at our community meetings ... in order to subsidize whatever expenses we incurred' (1994a).

Given that the coalition was not incorporated, and had no infrastructure, it would not have qualified for any government funding. In point of fact, all through the controversy the Ontario government, including Premier Bob Rae and the Anti-Racism Secretariat, refused to intervene in the debate or articulate a position with respect to the production.

Much of the controversy revolved around the cultural and political identity of the Black community. In Canada, and specifically in Toronto, most Blacks are Caribbean immigrants. There is considerable evidence that people of Caribbean origin are marginalized in Canadian society as a result of racism and the stresses of the immigration experience. Moreover, Caribbean immigrants – specifically those from Jamaica (the largest subgroup of Caribbean people) – are being stigmatized as criminals and drug dealers (Frances Henry, 1994).

The position of African Canadians in southern Ontario is ambiguous. It is characterized by some degree of economic and political mobility for the small percentage of educated and skilled members of the community; by a small but growing middle class; and by a substantial working class. There is also strong evidence that an underclass is developing, particularly among the youth, many of whom were educated and socialized in Canada (ibid.). It is no accident that the protest over *Show Boat* was located among people attempting to establish a cultural and political identity in a new society. One of the main issues for immigrants, and especially migrants of colour, relates to their need to retain elements of their former ethnicity and culture while at the same time establishing themselves as Canadians. Also a factor here is their experience of having been colonized, powerless people in their countries of origin, whether those were Caribbean or African. The experience of colonialism has had a lasting impact on peoples of the Caribbean; and when they emigrate, their need to reestablish a cultural identity (a need that reflects but is also independent of the colonial experience) becomes a dominant concern.

Hall (1991) defines two kinds of identity evident in postmodern, fragmented societies. *Cultural* identity involves 'the recreation, the reconstruction of imaginary knowable places in the face of global postmodern which has, as it were, destroyed the identities of specific places ... So one understands the moment when people reach for these groundings ... and the reach for those groundings is what I call ethnicity' (35–6). Whereas *political* identity 'often requires the need to make conscious commitments. Thus it may be necessary to momentarily abandon the multiplicity of cultural identities for more simple ones around which political lines have been drawn. You need all the folks together, under one hat, carrying one banner, saying we this, for the purpose of this fight, we are all the same, just black and just here' (in Grossberg, 1992: 380).

For Hall and other researchers in Britain, a common Black political identity has emerged as a result of the displacement of identity under colonial conditions in the Caribbean, the more recently learned multiplicity of identities shaped by the forces of postcolonial historical and economic conditions, and the need to rearticulate identity when, once again, Caribbean people leave to migrate to their 'mother' countries. The identification as 'Black' and, in more recent times, 'African-Canadian' is the political signifier for sameness and solidarity.

It is only through a true commitment to a political identity that protest and perhaps meaningful socio-political change can be accomplished. The affective commitment to that Black African-Canadian identity turned, however briefly, into a social movement: the Coalition to Stop

Showboat. The coalition in fact became a major symbol for the community, which united however briefly under one banner. It also led to an alliance with the *Miss Saigon* protesters.

This commitment on the part of the *Show Boat* protesters and the majority of the African-Canadian population, which supported them, was one of the most important outcomes of the *Show Boat* controversy. It united a fractionalized community around a single theme: African-Canadian attempts to counteract the power, force, and insensitivity of a theatre company.

Yet many commentators, following the lead of Garth Drabinsky, focused on the failure of the protest – 'It was only 40 misguided people ...' (Drabinsky, in Goldstein, 1995) – and discounted its effectiveness. Its successes have been poorly understood and are rarely discussed in the public discourse, which still occasionally surfaces in the media.

For the African-Canadian community, the protest was a major symbol of togetherness and solidarity: the common political identity of 'Black' served to undermine some of the differences within the community. In the face of political and cultural agency and power, this community succeeded in 'overriding' concerns such as social class, country of origin, gender, and skin colour, and demonstrating its essential sameness. The protest highlighted how important it was for minority groups to defend with vigilance the integrity of their historical experience.

Tension in Jewish–Black Relations[6]

The production of *Show Boat* had serious repercussions in terms of relations between the Black and Jewish communities in Toronto. In this, the catalyst was Livent's attempt to introduce *Show Boat* into the school system as an 'educational vehicle.' Stephnie Payne, North York's only Black trustee, introduced a motion to the board to prevent the organizing of school trips to the play and the distribution of educational materials in the schools. Her concern that exposure to the play would cause pain to Black children and would not positively contribute to the learning of children of any colour was later to find strong support in the Black community and among many Black and White educators. The issue for the Jewish community was not the motion itself, but rather the comment by Payne that White men, particularly Jewish men, have a history of portraying Blacks in an unfavourable way.

Payne made the remark in an interview with CTV News that was supposed to focus on why this play was so problematic. She made a public apology the following day, in which she acknowledged the offensive nature of her comment; this did not prevent an immediate and angry response from the Jewish community. Members of the Jewish community felt deeply wounded by what they perceived as a slur. They were further incensed by a number of editorials and other articles that appeared soon after in *Share*, the largest newspaper in Toronto's Black community. Leaders in the Jewish community felt that many of the these articles demonstrated the existence of Black anti-Semitism. Of particular concern was an editorial by *Share*'s publisher, Arnold A. Auguste, that appeared on 1 April 1993:

The book on which the musical is based is written by a Jew. The musical was written, scored and produced by Jews – I mean someone who is Jewish actually sat down and wrote about 'niggers.' Someone who is Jewish is producing it here in our city, and a Jewish mayor is opening the doors of one of our most prestigious theatres with it, with not as much as a second thought to the effect of the words – and what the show represents – must mean to us ... Maybe it is that Jews are so consumed by their own memories, grief and anguish over the Holocaust, that they have little attention to spare for the suffering of anyone else.

In a response, which *Share* published the following week, Gerda Frieberg, Ontario regional chair of the Canadian Jewish Congress, asked:

How is the Jewishness of these individuals relevant? The producer and the mayor who are bringing Show Boat to North York did not engage in prior consultation with the Jewish community. It is unfair to say the least, to put the onus of responsibility collectively on the Jewish community because you object to the actions of a number of individuals who happen to be Jewish. Would you feel it right for the entire Black community to be attacked if a particular person, who happens to be Black, does something of which others disapprove? (Frieberg 1993)

These two quotations accurately reflect the huge distance that existed between the two groups. Contemporary life in Canada (and the United States) does not routinely bring Blacks and Jews together. This isolation leads to the development of stereotypes, untested assumptions, and attitudes of moral certainty about the 'other.'

Jews and Blacks in North America do not understand each others' fears and vulnerabilities, hopes and aspirations. The debate around *Show Boat* revealed a failure on the part of both groups to grasp the power of memory and the impact of those historical experiences which continue to shape the perceptions, beliefs, and actions of each group today. Moreover, the perspectives of the two Canadian communities are strongly influenced by the relationships between Blacks and Jews in the United States. Each group receives its information about the other through the American media.

African Canadians have failed to recognize the effect on the Jewish people of 2,000 years of degradation, persecution, expulsions, and massacres. They do not acknowledge the profound hatred that was aimed at Jews – a hatred that permeated European culture for many centuries and that culminated in the Holocaust. Because they focus on the current status and position of the Canadian Jewish community, Blacks have been unable to understand the Jews' collective psyche: that as a people they are deeply concerned about the potential for new forms and expressions of hatred, and possess a preoccupation with group death. Jews worry that their good situation will not last. Too often in history, they lived in countries where they were assimilated and achieved an elevated socio-economic position, only to face outbreaks of virulent anti-Semitism that threatened their very survival as a people.

Similarly, Jews have failed to recognize the power of remembrance for Blacks, whose memories are of slavery and systematic cultural destruction, and who must live as a racial minority in a society in which colour defines person and position.

Jews, as well as other White North Americans, have limited knowledge of Black American history. This is largely due to the continued erasure of, and silence about, Black history.

The horrific events of the Holocaust have long been examined and memorialized in fiction, film, television, theatre, music, and the scholarly literature; as a result, they have become imprinted on the public consciousness and popular culture in a way that the African genocide has not. In North America there are many Holocaust museums but no museums dedicated to the history and memories of those 15 million Africans who were part of 'the Middle Passage' and its 400-year legacy, which continues to affect Blacks today (Nourbese Philip, 1993).

Members of the Jewish community who dismissed the concerns of African Canadians about *Show Boat* were in all likelihood unable to relate to the pain and anger felt by many African Canadians within the context of their present, marginalized status in Canada. The decision to mount the play brought to the surface the stresses and misunderstandings that in recent years have characterized relations between Blacks and Jews in Toronto and other North American communities. It revealed how very differently the Jewish and Black communities view the world. Both communities were reflecting a lack of knowledge about the fundamental similarities and differences in their histories and in their present lives. This does much to explain the significant differences in their responses to *Show Boat*. According to Charles Mills (1994): 'Blacks worry about their actual conditions and fear for the present; Jews worry about their history and fear for the future ... Racism is a bacterium, potentially curable but presently deadly; anti-Semitism is a virus, potentially deadly but presently contained.'

Roger Rowe, who was co-chair of the Coalition Against Show Boat, observed that Arnold Auguste and many others in the Black community perceive that members of the Jewish community are so absorbed in their own experience of victimhood, of anti-Semitism, and in their terrible memories of the Holocaust, that they are unable or unwilling to relate to the current suffering experienced by members of other minority groups. He also points out that it was not Blacks who first raised the issue of the Jewish identity of those involved with *Show Boat*; it was, he suggests, Garth Drabinsky himself, who referred to his Jewishness and to his personal suffering as a minority (Foster, 1993c) as an indication of his sensitivity to issues of racism and as a reason for trusting him not to produce a racist show.

But many Blacks find it difficult to understand how members of the Jewish community can characterize themselves as a persecuted minority when 'the reality is that members of the Jewish community have virtually achieved total integration and "Honourary White Status" in North American society, and wield political and economic influence disproportionate to the size of the group' (Rowe, 1995).

The Jewish community's perceived reluctance to acknowledge its position of White privilege, or its access to and integration with the mainstream of Canadian life (Jews are well represented in the hierarchies of business, education, justice, the arts, and the media), and its perceived reticence about using its influence and power to support Blacks in their struggle for social, economic, and political equality, are seen as significant factors in the growing polarization between the two communities. *Show Boat* merely underscored this sense of failed expectations.

How is it, then, that the two communities, which historically have shared the common burdens of subjugation, segregation, expulsion, and genocide, have come to such a point of divergence? This is a huge and complex subject, and one that this analysis cannot possibly address adequately (but see West, 1993; Lerner and West, 1995).

Briefly, it *can* be said that relations between Jews and Blacks are characterized by highly contradictory and strongly ambivalent feelings. There is distrust mixed with a desire for acceptance; there are deep-seated resentments combined with strong expectations. Both groups expect more from each other than they do from Whites or gentiles. Barbara Smith (1984) argues that their common experience with oppression, bigotry, and injustice leads to the feeling that each other's communities should 'know better' than to be racist or anti-Semitic.

This is not to suggest that in the history of the two communities in North America, there have been no effective coalitions. As Cornel West (1993) reminds us: 'There was no *"golden age"* in which Blacks and Jews were free of tension and friction. Yet there was a *better* age when the common histories of oppression and degradation of both groups served as a springboard for genuine empathy and principled alliances' (71).

Together, the two communities fought for civil rights (1910–67) and mutual empowerment. However, West suggests, this period of co-operation and collaboration is often 'downplayed by Blacks and romanticized by Jews' (ibid.). Blacks downplay this era because they see Jews as having enjoyed incredible social, economic, and political mobility during this time, while they themselves were continuing to struggle with institutionalized racism in every area of their lives (Lerner and West, 1995).

On the other hand, Jews tend to romanticize this time of alliance because their present status as a community that 'has made it' unsettles their long-held self-image as a people who are compassionate, just, and 'their brother's keeper.'

The differences noted above are exacerbated by divergent experiences in the area of cultural production. For the past fifty years, Jews in North America have had a significant presence in all aspects of the arts and popular culture (Rogin, 1996). They are culturally successful and influential in terms of 'high' culture; for example, they are strongly represented in academic institutions, hold positions of power and influence in cultural institutions such as museums and galleries, and hold high-level positions in publishing, the film industry, and television (Lerner and West, 1995). Blacks, on the other hand, continue (as is demonstrated throughout this book) to be greatly underrepresented in all these cultural industries.

In both the Black and Jewish communities, all these factors strongly influenced responses to the controversy over *Show Boat*. The discourses of each community reflected their ambivalence toward each other. Distrust was mixed with the desire for acceptance; and resentment was mixed with expectation.

The authors of this book do not believe that the protest against *Show Boat* was driven by anti-Semitism. But at the same time, it can be said that without question one consequence of this musical production was to exacerbate both anti-Semitism and Black racism in the Toronto community.

Conclusions

The production of *Show Boat* in Toronto was an important watershed in relations between the African-Canadian community and the mainstream of society. Perhaps more than any other event in the recent history of this city, it placed cultural racism on the public agenda.

This case study demonstrated how cultural racism functions and the powerful impact it has on both the dominant culture and those groups which are marginalized within a society. It demonstrated how invisible cultural racism is to White people and how acutely present it is in the lives and experiences of people of colour. It also showed how racism in the arts can mutate as it permeates other arenas such as the media, education, government agencies, and the marketplace.

The *Show Boat* controversy continues to reverberate; its many significant consequences are still being felt in the Black community, the Jewish community, the United Way, the media, boards of education, municipal and provincial government agencies, and other cultural agencies. The production was a clear example of how the cultural and economic power of individuals and institutions converges to marginalize, exclude, and silence people of colour.

Show Boat was an example of political, economic, social, and cultural power being held by an élite group of cultural producers within the dominant culture. This power translated into hegemonic control over members of a minority group as they resisted a cultural production that they perceived as harmful to their community. Livent was able to use its cultural, political, and economic power in a number of strategic ways.

• It was able to influence the municipality of North York to give it absolute managerial control of the performing arts centre without a tendering process.

- It was able to draw upon its considerable economic resources to make the production happen despite the protest.
- Its access to the media was almost unlimited: Drabinsky and his associates were constantly being quoted in articles about this event; many articles by Livent personnel were readily published; and the electronic media ran continuous promotions and aired several specials.
- It mounted a civil suit against the government of Ontario, claiming that its antiracism directorate had provided grants to groups affiliated with the Coalition to Stop Show Boat.
- It denied access to a preview of the production to an associate editor of a newspaper and to a respected member of the African-Canadian community.

The mobilization and resistance of the African-Canadian community was an act of empowerment: an assertion of its right to control the production of racist images and discourse; a declaration of its intention to resist, dissent against, and challenge traditional hegemonic practices in cultural production; a reclamation of its history; and an affirmation of its members' identity as Canadians who also have roots in other cultures. The protest offered this community an opportunity to unite around a common set of objectives in ways that it had rarely attempted before. The repercussions of this are still being heard in the community, which has since created an umbrella group to further the goals and aims of African Canadians living in this country.

With the protest around *Show Boat*, the politics of cultural difference asserted itself in a new way. The entire long episode demonstrated the schism between multiculturalism as an ideology, a public discourse, and a national identity, and the lived reality of African Canadians, whose experiences are defined by the constructs of a Eurocentric, monocultural society.

Notes

1 There are approximately 450,000 persons of African descent in Canada (see Frances Henry, 1994).
2 George Elliott Clarke pointed to the problem with the poster that featured a white family waving to a docking riverboat. In the illustration Blacks were largely an imperceptible and undefined blur. 'Their invisibility emphasizes that *Show Boat* is a white dream in which Blacks are mainly incidental – mere figures of convenience' (1994: 36).

3 Similar Caribbean-based festivals take place in Brooklyn, Miami, and Boston, and elsewhere in the United States, but these are attended primarily by Blacks, with little participation by Whites.

4 Our monitoring and analysis of the media coverage of *Show Boat* is not an exhaustive study, but represents the majority of articles published on the subject.

5 Some of the Black organizations supporting the protest were the Jamaican Canadian Association, the Black Business and Professional Association, the Black Educator's Work Group, Black Artists in Action, the Canadian Congress of Black Women, and the African Canadian Heritage Association.

6 This issue created considerable controversy and concern in both communities. We provide a very brief overview, but it is not our intention to analyse in detail the complex history of relations between these two communities.

References

Adilman, Sid. 1993a. 'Do Show Boat Foes Know about the King and Anna?' *Toronto Star.* 18 May.

– 1993b. 'New York Critics Proclaim Show Boat as See Worthy.' *Toronto Star.* 23 October.

Alton, Robert. 1993. 'Time to Put Show Boat in Dry Dock.' *Globe and Mail.* 12 March. A21.

Anderson, Scott. 1993. 'Show Boat Drifts Up the Creek.' *Eye Weekly.* 20 May.

Auguste, Arnold. 1993. Editorial: 'Don't Want to Be Your "Niggers" Anymore.' *Share.* 1 April. 8.

Barnard, Linda. 1993. 'Missing the Boat.' *Toronto Sun.* 2 May. 73.

Becker, Carol, ed. 1994. *The Subversive Imagination: Artists, Society and Social Responsibility.* New York and London: Routledge.

Berton, Pierre. 1993. 'Let's Not Scrub Show Boat Too Clean.' *Toronto Star.* 20 March. 20.

Black Educators' Working Group. 1993. Letter to Premier Bob Rae. 18 June.

Blenman, Rober. 1996. Review of *Show Boat. Afro News Vancouver.* March. 10.

'Drabinsky Slams Show Boat Foes.' 1994. *Canadian Jewish News.*

Chong, Gordon. 1994. 'Show Boat's a Must-See for Our Society.' *Toronto Sun.* 16 July. 12.

Clarke, George Elliott. 1994. 'The Problem with Show Boat.' *Possibilitiis.* 1(2). 36–7.

Coalition to Stop Show Boat. 1993a. Mission Statement.

– 1993b. Press Release: Reply to Garth Drabinsky. 11 March.

Corbey, Raymond. 1995. 'Ethnographic Showcases.' In Jan Pieterse and Bhikhu Parekh, eds. *The Decolonization of Imagination: Culture, Knowledge and Power.* London: Zed Books.

Coren, Michael. 1995. 'Livent Court Case Really about Government Accountability.' *Globe and Mail*. 30 January. C3.

DeMott, Benjamin. 1995. 'Put on a Happy Face: Masking the Differences
between Whites and Blacks.' *Harper's*. September.

Drabinsky, Garth. 1993a. 'I Do Not Intend to Cancel Show Boat.' *Toronto Star*. 2
May.

– 1993b. Written statement submitted to a meeting of the North York Board of
Education. 12 May.

– 1994. 'Show Boat Exploited for Political Gain.' *Toronto Star*. 15 February. A17.

Duberman, Martin Baum. 1988. *Paul Robeson: A Biography*. New York: Knopf.

Essed, Philomena. 1991. *Everyday Racism: Reports from Women of Two Cultures*.
Claremont, Cal.: Hunter House.

'Ethnic Notions.' 1986. Video recording. Marlon Riggs. California Newsreel.

Farrell, Lennox. 1993. 'Artistic Freedom vs. Right Not to Be Hurt. *Share*. 29 April.

Farrell, V.W. 1993. Letter to the Editor: 'Staging Show Boat Is Power Play.' *Share*.
6 May. 9.

Ferber, Edna. 1926. *Show Boat*. Garden City, N.Y.: Country Life Press.

Foner, Eric. 1983. 'The New View of Reconstruction.' *American Heritage*. 34. 10–
15.

Foster, Cecil. 1993a. 'Son Says Robeson Would Have Fought Show Boat.' *Now
Magazine*. 6 August–1 September. 24.

– 1993b. 'Harmony Lost over Musical.' *Globe and Mail*. 19 October.

– 1993c. 'Rocking the Boat.' *Toronto Life*. November. 49–56.

Fotheringham, Allan. 1993. 'A Resounding Attack on Racism.' *Toronto Sun*. 19
October.

Franklin, John Hope. 1994. *Reconstruction after the Civil War*. 2nd ed. Chicago:
University of Chicago Press.

Frieberg, Gerda. 1993. Letter. *Share*. 8 April.

Fung, Richard. 1994. Interview.

Goddard, Peter. 1993. 'Artists, Officials Are Rallying to Sink Show Boat.' *Toronto
Star*. 27 February.

Goldberg, David. 1993. *Racist Culture: Philosophy and Politics of Meaning*. Oxford,
U.K., and Cambridge, Mass.: Blackwell.

Goldfarb, Martin. 1993. 'Anti-Semitism Is Wrong Weapon.' *Toronto Star*. 28 May.
A25.

Goldstein, Lorrie. 1993. 'Brothers under the Skin.' *Toronto Sun*. 25 May.

– 1995. 'Drabinsky Dares to Be Different.' *Toronto Sun*. 16 June.

Gombu, Phinjo. 1993. 'Show Boat Gets Bottom Billing.' *Toronto Star*. 14 April.

Graham, Renee. 1993. 'We Are What We Eat and the Box It Comes In.' *Toronto
Star*. 30 January. B5.

Grossberg, Laurence. 1992. *We Gotta Get Out of This Place: Popular Conservatism and Postmodern Culture*. New York: Routledge.

Gwyn, Richard. 1993. 'Show Boat Uproar Surprises Only the Insensitive.' *Toronto Star*. 28 April. A17.

Hall, Stuart. 1991. 'Old and New Identities: Old and New Ethnicities.' In A. King, ed. *Culture, Globalization and the World System*. Binghamton, N.Y.: Department of Art History. 19–40.

Handler, Richard. 1986. 'On Authenticity.' *Anthropology Today*. 2(1). 2–4.

Hanlon, Michael. 1993. 'An Unfortunate Choice Says Show Veteran.' *Toronto Star*. 15 April. A11.

Harris, Al. 1993. 'Mel Lastman Has Show Boat-itis.' *Share*. 6 May.

Henry, Frances. 1994. *Caribbean Diaspora in Toronto: Learning to Live with Racism*. Toronto: University of Toronto Press.

Henry, Frances, and Carol Tator. 1993. 'Listen to What Blacks Are Saying.' *Toronto Star*. 28 May. A25.

Henry, Jeff. 1994a. 'Jeff Henry Tells It Like It Was.' *Share*. 6 October.

– 1994b. 'Show Boat Protest Watershed for Blacks.' *Toronto Star*. 15 November.

Ijaz, Ahmed. 1993. 'Educators against Show Boat.' *Share*. 27 May.

Johnson, Adrian. Interview. 1993.

Jordan, Glenn, and Chris Weedon. 1995. *Cultural Politics: Class, Gender, Race, and the Postmodern World*. Oxford: Blackwell.

Kirchhoff, H.J. 1993. 'Show Boat Just Keeps Rollin' Along.' *Globe and Mail*. 18 October. C1.

Krivel, Peter. 1993. 'Show Boat Boycott Fails.' *Toronto Star*. 20 May. A2.

Lacey, Liam. 1993. 'CBC's Documentary Doublespeak.' *Globe and Mail*. 21 November, A12.

Landsberg, Michelle. 1993. 'Blacks, Jews Must Join Forces to Sink Show Boat.' *Toronto Star*. 12 June. H1.

Lee, Angela. 1993. 'Only White Sensibilities Matter.' *Toronto Star*. 28 May. A25.

Lerner, Michael, and Cornel West. 1995. *Jews and Blacks: Let the Healing Begin*. New York: Putnam.

Littler, William. 1993. 'Show Boat Set the Standard for Musicals.' *Toronto Star*. 16 October. J14.

Littman, Sol. 1993. 'Victims Can Be Racists Too: Blacks Have Right to Proclaim Their Fears over Show Boat.' *Toronto Star*. 22 June. A17.

Maharaj, Raynier. 1993. 'Pointless to Sink Show Boat.' *Toronto Sun*. 11 January.

Marshall, Clem. 1993. 'Racism and Popular Culture.' Lecture. York University. 10 November.

Mills, Charles. 1994. 'Race and the City.' Lecture. University of Toronto. 2 May.

Mitchell, Timothy. 1988. *Colonising Egypt*. New York: Cambridge University Press.

Moloney, Paul. 1994. 'Board Quietly Boycotts Show Boat.' *Toronto Star.* 6 July.

Morrison, Toni. 1992. *Playing in the Dark: Whiteness and the Literary Imagination.* Cambridge, Mass.: Harvard University Press.

Nourbese Philip, Marlene. 1992. *Frontiers: Essays and Writings on Racism and Culture.* Stratford, Ont.: Mercury Press.

– 1993. *Showing Grit: Showboating North of the 44th Parallel.* Toronto: Poui Publications.

Ouzounian, Richard. 1993. 'Racism and the Arts.' *Metro Word.* 10, 11, 25, 26.

Paltiel, Rudy. 1993. 'Sold-Out Show Boat Preview.' *Globe and Mail.* 5 October.

Payne, Robert. 1993. 'Show Boat Sails to Disaster.' *Toronto Sun.* 14 March. 14.

Pieterse, Jan. 1992. *White on Black: Images of Africa and Black in Western Popular Culture.* London, U.K., and New Haven, Conn.: Yale University Press.

Rable, George. 1984. 'But There Was No Peace: The Role of Violence in the Politics of Reconstruction.' In John Franklin, ed. *Reconstruction.* Athens: University of Georgia Press.

Rickards, Colin. 1993a. 'Show Boat's Many Sanitized Versions.' *Share.* 6 May.

– 1993b. 'Protests Put an End to Anti-Semitic Show.' *Share.* 3 June.

– 1993c. 'Farrell Bounced from Show Boat.' *Share* 14 October. 1.

– 1993d. 'Conduct and Presence Deemed Objectionable. *Share.* 14 October. 7.

Richmond, Norman Otis. 1993. 'The Hidden History of Black Resistance.' *Toronto Star.* 15 June. A19.

Robeson, Paul. 1958. *Here I Stand.* Boston: Beacon Press.

Rogin, Michael. 1996. *Blackface, White Noise: Jewish Immigrants in the Hollywood Melting Pot.* Berkeley: University of California Press.

Rowe, Roger. 1995. '*Show Boat.*' A draft paper in preparation.

Rutherford, Jonathan. 1990. *Identity: Community Cultural Differences.* London: Lawrence & Wishart.

Salutin, Rick. 1993a. 'Time to Put Show Boat in Dry Dock.' *Globe and Mail.* 12 March.

– 1993a. 'Is Show Boat a Metaphorical Fit?' *Globe and Mail.* 19 March. B1.

– 1993b. 'Racism in the Arts.' *Metro Word.* May. 10, 11, 25, 26.

– 1994. 'More Magic Media Moments.' *Globe and Mail.* 11 March. C1.

Slinger, Joey. 1993a. 'Show Boat Sails into Politically Correct Storm.' *Toronto Star.* 23 February. A1, A4.

– 1993b. 'How Show Boat Becomes a Slow Boat to Controversy.' *Toronto Star.* 16 March.

– 1993c. 'Show Boat Sponsorship Casts Shadow over the Star.' *Toronto Star.* 20 April. A2.

Smith, Barbara. 1984. 'Between a Rock and Hard Place: Relationships between Black and Jewish Women.' In E. Bulkin, M. Bruce Pratt, and B. Smith, *Yours in Struggle.* Brooklyn: Long Haul Press. 65–88.

Stam, Robert. 1993. 'From Stereotype to Discourse.' *Cine-Action*. Fall: 23. 12–29.

Taylor, Colin. 1993. 'Racism in the Arts.' *The Metro Word*. May. 10, 11, 25, 26.

Taylor, Donald. 1981. 'Stereotypes and Intergroup Relations.' In R.C. Gardner and R. Kalin, eds. *A Canadian Social Psychology of Ethnic Relations*. Toronto: Methuen. 151–69.

Taylor, Kate. 1993a. 'Trustees Protests against Show Boat.' *Globe and Mail*. 24 February. C43.

– 1993b. 'Bey Balks at Show Boat Audition.' *Globe and Mail*. 10 March.

– 1993c. 'A Private and Public Duet.' *Globe and Mail*. 16 October.

– 1993d. 'The Single Minded Approach.' *Globe and Mail*. 25 October.

Thorsell, William. 1993a. 'Show Boat's Murky Racial Waters Gets Muddier Still.' *Globe and Mail*. 17 April.

– 1993b. 'In America's Bazaar of Competing Interests, Power Is the Only Currency.' *Globe and Mail*. 16 October.

– 1996. 'Angels in America Has Powerful Parallels in Canada.' *Globe and Mail*. 28 September.

Toronto Star. 1993. Editorial: 'Compromise on Show Boat.' 17 April. D2.

– 1994. Editorial: 'Show Boat Shuffle.' 10 October. A12.

Toronto Sun. 1993a. Editorial. 8 April.

– 1993b. Editorial. 20 May.

Valpy, Michael. 1993. 'The Storm around Show Boat.' *Globe and Mail*. 12 March. 2.

– 1993. 'Surely There's Something Better Than Show Boat.' *Globe and Mail*. 19 October.

van Dijk, Teun. 1991. *Racism and the Press*. London: Routledge.

Walker, William. 1994. 'Public Agency Cash Fuelled Racism Row.' *Toronto Star*. 27 September.

Walkom, Thomas. 1994. *Rae Days: The Rise and Follies of the NDP*. Toronto: Key Porter.

West, Cornel. 1990. 'The New Cultural Politics of Difference.' In R. Ferguson, ed. *Out There: Marginalization and Contemporary Culture*. New York: New Museum of Contemporary Art.

– 1993. *Race Matters*. Boston: Beacon.

Wetherell, Margaret, and Jonathan Potter. 1992. *Mapping the Language of Racism*. New York: Columbia University Press.

Worthington, Peter. 1993. 'Foolish Lies about Show Boat.' *Toronto Sun*. 20 May.

8

Revisiting Central Themes and Tensions

Framework of the Case Studies

We have used a case study approach to examine the construction of identities and differences within systems of cultural production as processes of inclusion and exclusion, marginalization and erasure, power and resistance. In particular, we have used case studies to explore the relationship between escalating racial tensions in Canada and the struggle over cultural representation in both popular and high culture. The overarching theme of this book is that there is a crisis in representation in which the traditional modes of cultural production are no longer acceptable to many marginalized groups in Canadian society (which is not to suggest they ever were acceptable). As a result, there is now greater scrutiny, criticism, and contestation surrounding the role, function, and meaning of cultural institutions.

The case studies provided compelling evidence that despite the ideological foundations of democratic liberalism, and despite a legislative framework based on multiculturalism, social inequality continues to operate and to be reproduced and legitimated through culture. Racism in culture and cultural production is reflected in belief systems, norms and codes of behaviour, and literary and artistic expressions. It is embedded in the values and meanings, policies and practices of powerful cultural institutions that frame cultural projects and undertakings – institutions that include theatres, museums, art galleries, publishing houses, unions, the print and electronic media, advertising, and cultural funding agencies. Racism in cultural production is buttressed by the lack of access and equity in other public institutions such as government, education, and the police.

Each case study showed that there exists a huge chasm between the rhetoric of a national identity that is imagined as pluralistic, inclusive, accommodating, and benevolent, and the lived reality of ethno-racial minorities, for whom society is characterized by the forces of racism and monoculturalism. Canadian society embraces the processes of 'otherness,' which heighten differences created not only by race and ethnicity, but also by gender, sexual orientation, and other, less visible characteristics.

At the level of cultural production and public discourse, all of this creates an ideological climate that seems natural to those who are emersed in it, but also contains unchallenged assumptions about how the world is and ought to be (Hall and Neitz, 1993). Cultural production is one way that society gives voice to racism and recycles ideas, images, and beliefs about Canada's people of colour. Each of the cultural events discussed in this book provides many striking examples of how various forms of cultural production create, reinforce, and reproduce racism. Taken collectively, these cultural processes show how ethno-racial minorities are positioned outside the 'imagined community' or 'national culture' of Canadian society (Mackey, 1995).

Each case study in this book has been framed from a postmodernist cultural studies perspective. All forms of cultural production must be understood in terms of how they were produced, by whom, for whom, for what means, at what historical moment, and with what social, economic, and political impact (Jordan and Weedon, 1995; Hall and Neitz, 1993). We have utilized a cultural studies approach in order to push the cultural analysis beyond the boundaries of the specific exhibits, texts, scripts, and events, and to establish the relationship between the cultural activities undertaken and the values, norms, and power relations operating within these cultural arenas, institutions, and systems.

In this chapter we will examine some of the recurring themes, issues, and tensions that we identified in the case studies.

Construction of Identity as 'Otherness': Racist Imagery and Discourse

Stereotyping within the Cultural Productions

Race as a concept is socially constructed on the assumption that certain visible phenotypical differences signify moral, intellectual, and social inferiority. Racial stereotyping and misrepresentation are critical concerns in a culturally pluralistic and multiracial society. Throughout the

past two centuries, North American society has consistently incorporated demeaning images of Blacks, 'Orientals,' and First Nations people (among others), into its cultural productions and systems of
representation. The replaying of these negative images has made it
significantly harder for marginalized groups to access economic and
political power.

Images are ideological. To view an exhibit of paintings or cultural artifacts, or to listen to a radio station, or to read a piece of literature, or to
watch a theatrical performance, is to encounter a cultural event or experience that has been created through an interactive process of ideas,
beliefs, dispositions, and meanings that are rooted in a set of social and
political conditions. This process does more than shape how people
think about themselves in relation to difference; it also influences how
the mainstream represents and constructs 'others,' and how White
Canadians think about themselves.

The dominant culture entrenches its power and preserves its hegemony when well-funded, highly publicized cultural productions consistently depict a narrow range of images of racial minorities. Uncritical
audiences accept these misrepresentations and leave the theatre or art
exhibition with certain perceptions toward a minority group more
deeply entrenched. These distorted perceptions make their way into the
day-to-day practices of social and cultural institutions largely because
they go unchallenged.

To many White audiences *Miss Saigon* is a sad but appealing love
story. It contains reassuring images and tells a familiar albeit mythical
story designed to calm the anxieties of Americans about Asians. Kyo
Maclear (1993) suggests that the love story of *Miss Saigon* follows a popular formula used in many cultural works, including *Madame Chrysanthemum* (novel), *Madama Butterfly* (opera) and, *South Pacific* (musical).
The implicit message in each of these works is that 'Asian women, and
the countries they represent, are destined to be dominated' (33). Maclear
provides a synopsis of this narrative: 'Tall white man meets poor young
Asian girl (bargirl, geisha girl, prostitute). They fall in love overnight.
White man leaves. Marries white woman. Asian woman has child. Tries
to get white man to come back. Fails. Kills herself to save child from the
life she led – the great sacrifice. Heroic white man returns to bring child
home to America. The end' (33).

As this book's case studies show, the images created and presented by
mainstream writers, producers, directors, curators, broadcasters, and so
on are not the images that African or Asian Canadians would present of
themselves. Those who belong to the dominant culture can feel secure in

the wide spectrum of representations in which they see themselves in society's cultural productions, and in the curricula of educational systems; the sensitivity of minorities to negative images is directly linked to their feelings of exclusion and 'otherness' within these areas.

Stereotyping helps to construct 'otherness' by drawing boundaries around 'us' and 'them.' The differences between the in-group and the out-group are charged with value, meaning, and social consequences. Although stereotypes, which are based on simplification, generalization, and denial of individuality, have little basis in reality, they nevertheless have significant social impact. When minorities have no power to control, resist, produce, or disseminate other more real and positive images in the public domain, stereotypes can and do increase their vulnerability in terms of their social, economic, and political participation in the mainstream of society.

Stereotypes are part of the psychological and social fabric of society. Situated in the midst of historic processes, these images become invisibly embedded in the fabric of the dominant culture and in the lives of marginalized groups. Stereotypes thus become markers of social boundaries, reminding minorities who they are and where they belong. Role patterns are established, and imprinted on the dominant and minority cultures so that from them there is little escape (Pieterse, 1992).

While the most overtly offensive attributes of the Black characters in the earlier productions of *Show Boat* were 'sanitized' in the Livent production, Jo, Queenie, and Julie still functioned as ethnic markers (Nourbese Philip, 1993). They were there to serve the interests and needs of Whites in the central narrative, and to provide a colourful and entertaining backdrop. The Black characters were one-dimensional; the audience learned little or nothing about their real thoughts or feelings. They sang and danced and remained stoical to their assigned fate.

In the same way, the Asian characters portrayed in *Miss Saigon* were also one-dimensional figures serving the purpose of perpetuating American ideology. They were constructed as the 'other.' The only sympathetic Asian character in the play was Kim, who like Julie in *Show Boat*, had to sacrifice both her body and her life to further the interests of the White characters. But she was *never* angry. Her suffering and stoicism made her sympathetic, but also nonthreatening to the White audience, which had come to be entertained.

Both plays illustrated that stereotyping cloaked in musical theatre format is a subtle but highly effective medium for refurbishing stereotypes of both women and minorities. In the case of *Miss Saigon*, the romantic tragedy replayed a popular theme in Western cultural idioms and reflected a 'minefield of vested interests' fraught with stigmatizing meanings (Cohen, 1992: 92).

The Western fascination with the 'Orient' is reflected in all aspects of North American cultural production. The notion of Orientalism is infused with racist myths and stereotypes that have persisted since the eighteenth century. The cultural image of the Orient is based on a system of categorization – of ordering the world through a discourse in which the 'Orient' becomes the primitive 'other' and the antithesis of the 'civilized' West (Said, 1993).

Into the Heart of Africa presented images and objects resonating with hidden meanings and untold narratives. Blacks were portrayed as objects and Whites as the saviours of civilization. The Blacks were on show as 'primitives,' 'uncivilized,' unaware of technological advances. The booty of the soldiers and the religious 'exotica' were presented from the colonial perspective. The lens of the camera held by the missionary or colonizer captured the 'object' – the Zulu man with a sword thrust into his heart, the African women washing clothes, the frightened young woman being physically forced to have her picture taken by a White male photographer. These images were nothing more than objects. These people were without names, without stories, without voices, and thus were rendered powerless, passive, and silent.

The struggle for a Black/dance music radio station echoed yet another theme. Here, the listening audience for radio was assumed to be a White audience that would have no real interest in hearing music or commentary reflecting Black culture. This, even though much if not most North American music has African-American roots. As a result of these assumptions, the erasure and stereotyping of Blacks on Canadian airwaves was allowed to continue unchallenged. In the decision it made, the CRTC demonstrated a lack of concern for issues of access and equity in broadcasting, despite the commitment to diversity and multiculturalism written into its own cultural policies. This case study demonstrated that the CRTC sees no public role for itself in ensuring that ethno-racial communities, who traditionally have been ignored, erased, and silenced, have greater access to the broadcasting industry.

In White cultural works, oppressed people are almost never portrayed as angry or defiant – as *resisting*. Black or Asian bodies are manipulated in order that White characters can reinforce their own identity. But for this to happen, those Black bodies must remain on the margins, and represented in superficial terms, as 'ready and willing to be acted upon for the salvation of the White soul' (Carby, 1993: 245). As is demonstrated in the exhibit at the ROM, 'Black souls serve as white man's artifact' (Stam, 1993: 19).

Racist Discourse

Racist discourse refers to how society gives voice to racism (Wetherell and Potter, 1992). It includes explanations, narratives, codes of meanings, and accounts, which have the effect of establishing, sustaining, and reinforcing oppressive power relations. It is a set of social practices that favour the in-group and denigrate the out-group, and that categorize, evaluate, and differentiate between groups. Cultural racism is a discursive practice. According to Fiske (1994), 'there is a discourse of racism that advances the interests of whites and that has an identifiable repertoire of words, images, and practices through which racial power is applied ... Discourse does not represent the world; it acts in and upon the world' (5).

The discourse of modern cultural racism is framed and hidden within traditional, humanistic, liberal democratic values such as freedom of expression, rights, individualism, universalism, equality, national unity, and Canadian identity. Within this social and political discourse, race is deemed to be irrelevant. So-called 'liberals' deny or dismiss the cumulative impact of humiliations and exclusions embedded in daily discourse, systems of representation, organizational policies, and institutional practices.

Each case study explored the racist discourse contained within the cultural productions at hand, as well as the processes by which that production was rationalized. Racist discourse was analysed in the context of how these processes establish, entrench, and reproduce cultural forms of marginalization and exclusion. However, dominant discourse is an elusive concept, because it is often hidden within the mythical norms that define 'Canadianness' – as White, male, heterosexual, Christian, and English-speaking. Dominant discourse is so elusive by nature that it can easily mask its racialized ideas. Explicitly derogatory statements, slurs, and epithets are rarely used in public discourse, especially by the cultural élite represented in the case studies. Instead that élite presents itself as the defender of traditional democratic principles, cultural values, and liberal ideals. Its members argue that the values passed on to us by our Anglo-European heritage are at risk of being lost. The appeal therefore is not to prejudice, but to the preservation of national harmony and unity, and in defence of the values of history, truth, universalism, and freedom of expression. The rhetoric of racism is woven invisibly into the everyday, commonsense notions that make up what gets defined as reality (Essed, 1990; Lorde, 1984).

Each of the cultural productions analysed in this book reflected a struggle between those with privilege, power, and voice, and those who are seeking to gain control over the of images and systems of representation that misrepresent, marginalize, and exclude them. The controversy over the Writing Thru Race Conference was largely fuelled by the need of First Nations writers and writers of colour to speak out about racism in the Canadian literary world. The White literary establishment responded by an attempting to silence this debate. A well-known critic complained that including minority writers on Canada Council literary juries would bias their decisions. Fourteen White Canadian authors, members of the Writers Union of Canada, wrote in February 1994 that fellow members should 'shut the f--k up' on the issue of racial equity (Clarke, 1994). Protesters demonstrating at *Miss Saigon*, *Show Boat* and *Into the Heart of Africa* faced similar hostility, often combined with arrogant disdain. These negative responses came from the media, cultural critics, audiences, and (perhaps most importantly) authorities in cultural institutions.

Seven months after *Into the Heart of Africa* opened, the exhibition's curator was still failing to acknowledge that different interpretations of the exhibition were legitimate, or to demonstrate any sensitivity to the pain felt in the African-Canadian community. Three years after *Into the Heart of Africa* closed, T. Cuyler Young, the former director of the ROM, wrote about what he had 'learned' from the protest. He commented (1993) that the controversy was really about a small group of radicals motivated by an unstated personal political agenda. He maintained that only rarely is there a need to consult with individuals and groups from outside the museum about particular exhibitions. He stressed that in interacting with these groups, 'you listen carefully and endeavour to sort the wheat from the chaff' (186). In a postscript to the article, Young noted that the problems experienced by the ROM with the Black community resurfaced with another cultural production, *Show Boat*, and commented: '*Thoughtful* (authors' italics) Toronto newspaper columnists have quite rightly compared the new dust-up to the crisis over *Into the Heart of Africa* ... the producer of the show and the United Way have stood firm' (ibid.: 188).

Garth Drabinsky continually referred to the *Show Boat* protesters as 'extremists,' 'intellectually dishonest,' and 'irresponsible and bigoted,' and as 'exploiting the empathy of our tolerant society' (Drabinsky, 1993, quoted in Salutin, 1994: C1). He described the activities of the protesters as being akin to the Nazis' book burning during the Holocaust (1994).

Despite the disappointment and frustration felt by the Black community, *and* by the applicants, with the CRTC's repeated refusal to license a Black radio station, few labelled the commission's stance as racist. However, Howard McCurdy, then MP for Windsor, suggested that the decision was racist, and Keith Spicer in his dissenting statement implicitly accused the majority of commissioners of racialized decision-making.

Racist Discourse Hidden in Liberal Democratic Concepts of Truth, Universalism, History, and Freedom of Expression

Democratic liberalism is distinguished by a belief in the rights of the individual, the power of reason, tolerance of difference, and commitment to equality. Yet there is a fundamental dissonance in Canadian liberal democratic society, in the sense that two apparently conflicting sets of values are at play and must be reconciled. One set of values stresses the commitment of a democratic society to the egalitarian values of fairness, justice, and equality. Conflicting with these liberal values are those attitudes and behaviours, policies and practices that result in the different negative treatment of people of colour and other marginalized groups (Henry et al., 1995). Despite the centrality of liberal principles and humanistic values, the fundamental assumptions of most Western cultural institutions continue to mask practices of prejudice, discrimination and racism (Jordan and Weedon, 1995). The liberal paradox is that even while modernity commits itself progressively to the ideals and principles of equality, tolerance, and freedom, racial identities and new forms of racism and exclusion are proliferating (Goldberg, 1993).

We have seen these tensions play out in the cultural productions and events described in each of the case studies. More specifically, we have seen contested within the cultural arena the notions of truth, universalism, history, and freedom of expression.

One Truth versus Multiple Truths

There exists within society a relentless need to establish what is 'truth.' 'Truth' is discovered within a system of practices required for producting, distributing, and articulating the dominant belief systems of particular societies (Berger, 1992). Michel Foucault refers to this as the 'regime of truth,' which is rooted in the system of power that produced it. Each society 'has its ... general politics of truth: that is, the types of discourse it harbours and causes to function as true ... and what counts for truth' (in Berger, 1992: 80). In the postmodern world there is no single absolute truth; rather, there are different versions of events, each of which carries particular social implications. Truths differ across histories and cultures. There can also be different interpretations of truth among diverse interest groups within the same culture: 'Each of us lives in a narrative, a story in which we are characters and tellers. No one's story is the *whole* story, and in the various lights shed by our various stories, different truths will seem self-evident and different courses of action will seem obviously called for' (Fish, 1994: 74).

The media typically help to interpret events. People adopt or reject these interpretations as truth. For example, phone-in radio talk shows disseminate different versions of events and hence create truth. Throughout the efforts to establish a Black music station, some acknowledged that such a station could help to shape the truth about the experiences and rich cultural contributions of Canada's racial minority communities – specifically the African-Canadian community.

The controversy over *Into the Heart of Africa* was an example of contrasting discourses about truth coming into focus. In her approach, the curator was seeking to deconstruct the truth claims made by the colonizers of Africa. She used irony to create a distance between what the colonizer saw with respect to the objects collected by the missionaries and soldiers, and the 'real' meaning of the photographs and artifacts. However, the Coalition for Truth About Africa, and others in the African-Canadian communities, wanted a different interpretation of the historical meanings of these objects, one that would be more congruent with their understanding of truth. Their sense of truth told them that the exhibition was characterized by misrepresentations, omissions, and erasures. It followed, they felt, that they had a right and responsibility to express their views and disseminate these understandings (Mackey, 1995).

Universalism

Universalism is based on the premise that there exists a superior level of human understanding that transcends all human cultural and national boundaries. Good art, literature, and music are viewed as being timeless. Universalism is perceived an essential quality of expression and has always been valued in aesthetic production. However, from the perspective of both women and people of colour, the content and parameters of the 'universal' are never all-inclusive.

In the last few decades there have been significant shifts in the processes and criteria through which cultural products are understood and evaluated. The values venerated as 'universal' have been exposed as Anglo-Eurocentric values disseminated globally through colonialism and supported by the literary and artistic canons. Universalism is based on the premise that while human nature is essentially the same everywhere, some cultures are more highly developed than others.

As a result of this assumption, mainstream art history is constructed as a singular universal art history that is determined and realized by the West (Araeen, 1991). Creativity and innovation are seen as the products of *Western* artists. Thus, the organizers of the tour of the Barnes Exhibit were able to eliminate all the art forms created by the 'others' from the touring exhibit. Glenn Lowry, the AGO's director at the time, articulated a Eurocentric perspective when he suggested that the absence of the art of other cultures in this exhibition was not really a significant concern, since European art possesses a universal quality that presents the essence of all visual arts (Drainie, 1994). In the same vein, Christopher Hume dismissed concerns about the omission of African, Chinese, and Japanese art when he noted that while it was unfortunate that African masks don't have the 'mass appeal of a Renoir or a Picasso ... it doesn't make the gallery racist' (1994).

In all of these commentaries it is being expressed clearly that non-Western, non-European cultures can never be part of the corpus of great aesthetic works. Moreover, the anticipated and targeted audience of these important cultural events is clearly assumed to be White and of European descent.

Art galleries such as the AGO appear to be strongly influenced by the concept of 'primitivism' which has been integral to art historical scholarship and discourse for almost 150 years. The concept of primitivism has resulted in a system of categorization whereby 'White art' is seen as the only authentic art (Li, 1994; Araeen, 1991). It is within this context that the AGO could rationalize mounting an exhibition devoid of any examples of the art that was such a significant aspect of Dr Barnes's collection. There was not a single African sculpture, Chinese painting, or Native-American piece, nor were there any examples of African-American art. The absence of these also contradicted the philosophy and legacy of Barnes himself, who believed in the importance of revealing how art forms from different cultural traditions are related to one another. The exhibition instead chose to follow established tradition, glorifying the history of art through the prism of Western culture, thereby ignoring the contributions of the world's oldest cultures.

From this perspective, artists of European background are more likely to produce masterpieces, while artists of non-European descent produce only 'ethnic art.' A two-tiered art world is thus created: on the upper tier are mainly White, male artists with names, an identity, and a history; while on the lower sits the anonymous 'primitive' artist. This lack of representation of the art of other cultures reflects how Eurocentric aesthetic standards, values, and norms determine what constitutes a 'masterpiece.' Works of art become racialized when they are systematically assessed from the perspective of a racially based cultural hierarchy that maintains and preserves the artistic standards that flow from the dominant group (Li, 1994). These assumptions and principles may in part explain why the AGO had never, until after the Barnes Exhibit, mounted exhibitions focusing on work of the African-Canadian or Asian-Canadian artistic communities, despite the efforts of both groups to have their aesthetic contributions represented in the art gallery.

In terms of literary works, the concept of universalism justifies the teaching of a canon that is largely devoid of works by non-European and female writers. Toni Morrison (1989) poses a critical question about the Western canon: 'What intellectual feats had to be performed by the author or his critic to erase me from a society seething with my presence ...?' (12).

Taylor (1994: 18) cites the American writer Saul Bellow as suggesting: 'When the Zulus produce a Tolstoy, we will read him.' The underlying ethnocentric assumption is that 'we' can invoke 'our' standards to judge the contributions of all cultures and civilizations, and that their work rarely meets the test of these universal criteria.

In the Canadian context, the privileging of Eurocentric thought, traditions, and values explains why, until recent years, writers of colour were absent from the writers' union, publishing houses, and distribution markets. Nourbese Philip (1992) provides a critique of universalism, in the context of the denial and rejection it demands in relation to one's own culture: 'The novel, poetry, Shakespeare – all came (to the Caribbean) as cultural appendages to the Empire, expressing 'universal' values – the limpid objectivity of Eliot which meant that the little Black girl in the Caribbean should be able to feel exactly what he was feeling, when he wrote about cats, frogs and Prufrock. And surely that same child whose childhood boundaries were constant sunshine, black skins and mangos could understand about Wordsworth's field of daffodils' (100).

Many of those who organized and/or participated in the Writing Thru Race Conference would likely support Margaret Atwood (1997) when she suggests that a canon is merely an often-duplicated list, while a classic is a work that is read, reread, explored for meaning over a long period of time; 'and what one generation finds meaningful, the next may find puzzling, absurd, or even tedious' (xii).

We find an attachment to the notion of universalism throughout this book's case studies in the grounding assumptions of the dominant culture's literary and cultural critics. It seems that these people feel confident that they are operating from a position of 'objectivity' and 'neutrality,' and resist recognizing that every critic has a point of view, a terrain to which he or she is attached, a disciplinary/professional, ethno-racial, and gendered lens through which is filtered a set of understandings and perspectives. Those with White privilege often have little interest in self-reflection, which requires not only listening to the 'others' but also attending to their views and concerns, and confronting the troubling questions that are then raised.

One History versus Multiple Versions of History

In almost all of the case studies, the cultural producers raised issues of historical representation, authenticity, and truth and suggested that their work reflected and captured authentic and important historical events. They also accused the protesters of trying to revise or ignore history. Thus, one of the key questions arising in the controversies over *Show Boat*, *Miss Saigon*, and *Into the Heart of Africa* was *Whose history is it anyway?*

Racism in a cultural production works in part by distorting and sanitizing the history of the culture and society it is subjugating (Jordan and Weedon, 1995). Critics of *Into the Heart of Africa* argued that the only history learned, and the only experience acknowledged, was that of the missionaries and colonizers. The central narrative totally excluded the stories, experiences, perceptions, and voices of the Africans. The presentation of the 'booty' and 'exotica' collected by the soldiers and missionaries seemed to matter more than the story of how these things were gathered and possessed.

According to the exhibition's critics, what was missing from the museum's discourse was an analysis of the social, economic and political processes through which these objects became part of the museum's collection (Itwaru and Ksonek, 1994). Nowhere in the exhibition was there an opportunity for the African voice to challenge the racist commentary or offer alternative interpretations of the images being presented.

In the case of *Show Boat*, as the controversy escalated, Livent and many cultural critics challenged the protesters' credibility by arguing that the musical was based on an authentic and important period of American history. (Livent had originally intended to develop resource packages for the schools in order to educate students about this history.) The Coalition Against Show Boat rejected the claim that the musical was an 'authentic' retelling of the history of the period.

The coalition contended that the musical virtually excluded any reference to the catastrophic events and oppressive social conditions of the era in which it was set. There was virtually no mention that the play took place in the aftermath of more than two hundred years of slavery. None of the violence and oppression that was experienced by African Americans during and after the Reconstruction was represented in either the story or the characters. Also absent was the story of the political and social mobilization of the African-American community and their resistance to subjugation.

In a similar manner, *Miss Saigon* was based largely on a Eurocentric construction of historical events. It relied on sugar-coated clichés to explain the complex historical, political, and social realities that underpinned the Vietman War. In *Miss Saigon*, it was White men who acted and who did heroic deeds, and their story was portrayed with sympathy and understanding. But the historical account of the Vietnamese people and their horrific experiences was censored. Kyo Maclear (1993) comments that the real issue for the Asian community involved in the protest against *Miss Saigon* was the misrepresentation of the social context, which was steeped in racism, military and economic imperialism, and class oppression. He observes that *Miss Saigon* failed to deal with the key issues of the conflict: the political and historical causes of the war; the Vietnamese perspective on American intervention; North Vietnamese nationalism; the complexities of Vietnamese culture; and the deaths of two million Vietnamese people.

In both of these musical productions, the spectacle, the entertainment value, the story, assumed priority over authentic historical accounts. The producers relied on familiar music, spirited singing and dancing, and lavish set designs (including a full-sized helicopter) to distract the audience from disturbing historical events, and politically and culturally challenging issues.

Cultural Appropriation versus Freedom of Expression

Cultural appropriation was a critical issue in all of the case studies. It is important here to explain how the concept of cultural appropriation is understood and how attitudes toward it have been fixed. Since there are no clear boundaries between one set of cultural values, norms, and practices and the next, most cultural groups engage in some form of appropriation. Often this sharing and synthesis is positive; at other times it is part of a process of establishing cultural hegemony.

As Fung (1997) argues, the critique of cultural appropriation is 'first and foremost a strategy to redress historical inequities by raising questions about who benefits from controlling cultural resources' (98). The central issues are related to the pervasiveness of racist imagery, the erasure of the histories, stories, and voices of First Nations people and people of colour, unrestrained commercialization, the lack of access to cultural institutions, and the deficiency of resources for nonmainstream artists to produce and distribute cultural works. From the perspective of those who opposed *Into the Heart of Africa*, the ROM's exhibition of cultural artifacts was a prime example of cultural appropriation. The objects belonging to Africans had been taken by the colonizers; the histories and meanings of these artifacts had then been appropriated by the museum. At each stage, control of the possessions was assumed by members of the dominant culture. In the process, the true meaning of these artifacts in the lives of African peoples was decontextualized and lost. African voices and their interpretations of these events were silenced.

In the case study of the Barnes Exhibit, the relationship between European artists and artists of 'primitive' cultures was shown to be this: The Western artist admires and appropriates certain elements of the culture of the 'others,' while maintaining complete control over *how* those elements are applied in the Western context. The so-called primitive artists serve as a vehicle for new ideas and approaches in the Western art world. At no time do people from those civilizations become active subjects in defining or shaping art history.

Racism in mainstream art does not, then, totally deny the presence of the art forms produced by the 'others.' What it *does* do is appropriate visual ideas and images, which then come to be labelled 'primitive art.'

By applying their own interpretations of these works, and by imposing their own cultural assumptions about the peoples who produced these 'objects,' White Western artists, curators, historians, and art critics have helped erase the contributions of African, Asian, Caribbean, and First Nations artists.

A significant concern identified in the case study of the Writing Thru Race Conference was that White writers were interpreting the histories, experiences, and images of First Nations peoples and people of colour. Writers of colour and First Nations writers encounter significant barriers in the publishing industry based on their cultural and racial identities; but at the same time, mainstream writers often benefit materially by appropriating the traditions, stories, and forms of 'others.'

First Nations writers and writers of colour have argued that those in the creative stream of the dominant culture must learn to understand the difference between honest expansion into the world of the imagination and plundering someone else's imagination (Lorde, 1984). Jeanette Armstrong poses this challenge to mainstream writers: 'Imagine interpreting for us your own people's thinking toward us, instead of interpreting for us our thinking, our lives, our stories. We wish to know, and you need to understand, why it is that you want to own our stories, our art ... our ceremonies' (in Mackey, 1996: vii).

From a historic perspective, the possibility of writing, publishing, and profiting from another group's history and culture is closely tied to relations of property, power, and privilege.

The demonstrations and cultural critiques against *Miss Saigon* and *Show Boat* were based on the premise that cultural appropriation must be understood in the context of how the histories, images, and voices of Asian and African North Americans have been misrepresented, marginalized, and silenced by the dominant culture. The Coalition Against Show Boat and Asian ReVisions contended that the contributions of their communities had been obliterated from North Americans' social and cultural memory.

Both *Miss Saigon* and *Show Boat* were based on narratives and representations that people of colour saw not as neutral but as harmful. The protesters contended that freedom of expression was not the issue at hand. The suggestion that it was ironic, in that freedom of expression was being limited to those White writers, composers, and impresarios who already had power to exercise.

In both of these theatrical productions, as well as in the other case studies, cultural producers failed to understand the implications of being labelled Black or Asian in North America society. White cultural producers have been preoccupied with representing the reality of these groups, yet these groups' recorded social memories have been represented mainly in relation to Eurocentric cultural perspectives.

Freedom of Expression versus the Right of Minorities to Contest Cultural Practices

Freedom of expression is a cherished value in liberal democracies. Unjustified censorship contradicts both the spirit and the essence of freedom. Both minority and majority populations support the precept and the ideal of this freedom. However, in the way the limits of free expression are perceived, there is a significant gap between those who have power and those who are powerless.

In many of the case studies, demands by African Canadians, Asian Canadians, and other minority communities for greater sensitivity, accountability, and accessibility in cultural productions were met with a barrage of criticism and racist discourse from commentators in both the cultural élite and the media. Protests by people of colour against negative images and misrepresentations, which they believed were harmful to their communities and contrary to the principles of a pluralistic, inclusive society, were characterized as undemocratic. Many cultural critics viewed the protests as a threat to the harmony, unity, and viability of a multicultural society (see the discussion of the media that follows in this chapter).

The Coalition to Stop Show Boat strongly denied the premise – articulated by Livent and much of the media – that to call for a boycott of the play was to condone censorship. The coalition argued that it was really questioning whether it was socially and ethically responsible to dedicate a publicly funded theatre (supported in part with African-Canadian tax dollars) with a play that was so objectionable to a significant number of people in the community.

The debate over freedom of expression can be seen as a struggle over the hierarchy of rights in a democratic society. The rights of those who produce and attend a cultural object or event should be weighed against the right of a community not to be harmed by that event.

However, the question remains as to what constitutes harm and what legally may be said or done in the public domain. Many groups have urged governments to establish clearer and broader legislative guidelines to deal with this issue. None of the freedoms guaranteed in Canada is absolute; all are tempered by measures designed to achieve justice and to protect minority rights.

Absent from all the public discourse about freedom of expression and censorship was the question of whether various cultural institutions – including the ROM, Livent, the media, the CRTC, and the writers' union – were not in themselves helping indirectly to limit freedom of expression. Not only did they try to ignore and discredit the concerns of those who opposed these cultural processes, but they also employed other institutional forces, such as the police and government, to attempt to stifle resistance and dissent.

For example, it can be argued that by consistently refusing to license a station featuring African-Canadian music and programming, the CRTC was engaging, albeit unwittingly, in regulatory censorship. In the same way, Livent's suit against the government of Ontario can be interpreted as an attempt to silence or censor dissent and criticism. These examples suggest that a kind of myopia exists whereby 'censorship' as a category of punitive suppression may be utilized only by those who already have power and recognition. In other words, it is only the White cultural élite that has the force and the sense of entitlement that it takes to arouse outrage at the withdrawal of freedom of expression. As a consequence, members of communities that already feel themselves victims of ongoing exclusion and silencing are doubly jeopardized – in the second instance by the premise that they are contributing to censorship (Galleano, 1994).

Nourbese Philip (1993) suggests that those who argue that the protest against *Show Boat* was an attempt to restrain freedom of expression failed to recognize that this freedom is measured not by the 'free flow of information,' but rather by the power people have to make their voices heard (667). Who has that power? Judging by the case studies of *Show Boat, Into the Heart of Africa*, the Barnes Exhibit, and the CRTC, it is clear that it was the cultural producers, the cultural agencies, and the media that controlled the discourse.

Art as Consumer Product versus Art as a Vehicle for Self-Discovery

Few will dispute that Canadian society was built and sustained by European settlers, who introduced two official languages, as well as systems of governance, property ownership, and law and order. The values that support these systems may be referred to as 'traditional values'; they include individualism, authority, status, conformity, subordination, dominance, objectification, Eurocentrism, and racism.

As is demonstrated in the case studies, these values are also implanted in the philosophy and practices of the world of art. Unquestionably, capitalism tells us that the arts have a market. A work of art is a commodity, the value of which is measured less in terms of its value to the creator than by its market price. This product-oriented approach is the foundation of the economic organization of postmodern societies.

As North American cultural producers increasingly strive to control global markets and global culture in the name of 'universalism,' the gap between the 'art' and 'entertainment' worlds is narrowing. In other words, mass culture and high culture are merging (Fiske, 1994).

For any product to succeed in a market-oriented society – whether it be a museum exhibition, a theatrical production, a literary work, or a syndicated program on a broadcast network – it must respond to consumer tastes, attitudes, and needs. A consumer's concepts of beauty, excellence, worth, and entertainment are all relevant marketing factors. Yet 'beautiful,' 'entertaining,' 'amusing,' 'valuable,' and 'distasteful' are not immutable concepts: they exist within a social context, and are influenced by a historical and ideological frame of reference. In any society, aesthetic values are transmitted through many agents, including social institutions. The reproduction of society is dependent on the values of the community, because it is from the perspective of these values that cultural products are evaluated and that an exchange value is attached to them.

There are always those whose art, for political and economic reasons, remains on the margins. Art that does not measure up to traditional 'standards' of excellence fails to make it to the marketplace. For these artists there is little possibility of sharing in the wealth. Art deemed 'too political' is also sometimes excluded from the marketplace. Thus it can be said that the cultural products available in a marketplace, as well as in important institutions, are an indication of society's prevailing values. The continued absence from the public culture of art produced by artists of diverse ethno-racial backgrounds is related to the belief held by decision-makers that consumers will not buy these products. In other words, an ethnocentric society relies on the dominant culture's values to define 'good' art, its marketability, and its 'entertainment' value.

Culture is increasingly constituted by commerce, and the commodity culture is instrumental in shaping and defining systems of cultural representation and structures of cultural meaning (Becker, 1994; Rosler, 1994). The consumption of culture can be an individual or a collective experience. In either case, it involves constructing meanings in a process of interpretation that to some degree involves social identity and social relations. How signifying practices are interpreted by audiences, spectators, and critics will depend greatly on the social context from which they are seen or read.

The commodity-consumer approach to the arts emphasizes the power of cultural producers to limit or eliminate racial and cultural diversity from every stage of cultural production. Capitalism requires controlled diversity – a diversity that is both determined and limited by the needs of its mode of production. Art as commodity requires that cultural producers identify their market and strategically construct their consumer and/or audience (Fiske, 1994).

However, audiences and viewers, readers and users do not simply absorb cultural material mindlessly. Producers of culture need to shape the cultural production or event to please a targeted public. It follows that if the production is to be successful, those involved in the production process need to understand the shared ideological assumptions of the intended audience. Contemporary political discourse is framed in a recognition of the heterogeneity of Canadians, and celebrates these differences; yet cultural practices still focus sharply on a specialized audience, a cultural élite drawn largely from the White community. And this élite shares to a certain degree certain common interests and desires.

The case studies of *Show Boat, Miss Saigon, Into the Heart of Africa*, and the Barnes Exhibit illustrate how in each case the dominant narrative was developed from the perspective of a White, Eurocentric gaze. This perspective influenced every stage of the production process. The memories, histories, experiences, thoughts, and feelings of people of colour within the narrative were removed from the centre and placed on the margins. Those involved in the production process envisioned a White audience and shaped the content, form, promotions, and marketing to this audience.

Access to Resources versus Control of Those Resources by Cultural Institutions

One aspect of the struggle over culture and cultural production relates to access to resources. It takes resources to produce plays, own radio stations, develop exhibitions, and publish and market books. Poet Lillian Allen (1992) explains that the issue of access revolves around First Nations peoples, Asians, Blacks, and other cultural and linguistic communities being excluded from resources, services, programs, and decision-making processes of mainstream arts and cultural organizations. Allen defines the goal of access as to enable all cultural communities to be partners in the process of cultural production. This means creating new and relevant programs, facilitating full and equal access to existing programs, and ensuring that diverse cultures are well represented in cultural institutions.

The case of the Writing Thru Race Conference illustrated that publishing houses, distribution companies, literary and cultural critics (in both the media and academic institutions), the writers' union, public-funding agencies, bookstores, and libraries all form part of the institutional foundation for writing. Without these supports, writers have to finance and publish themselves, and they are unlikely to find many readers this way. There are numerous cultural and racial barriers in the publishing system that block First Nations writers and writers of colour from crucial resources.

Racial and cultural politics affect how publishers and funders view the work of First Nations writers and writers of colour. Their work is labelled 'new,' 'hyphenated,' 'immigrant,' and 'ethnic,' and rarely is there reference to the 'Canadian-ness' of the writing. For example, in its first sixteen years the Women's Press never published a work by a woman of colour. Until the Women's Press was reorganized, writers of colour relied almost entirely on presses and publications within their own communities. Scholarly journals and cultural magazines also contribute to this 'racism by omission' (Bannerji, 1993).

The enormous controversy surrounding Writing Thru Race Conference, and the withdrawal of government funding from it, also demonstrated the obstacles blocking the path for writers of colour. The participants in the conference were seeking a safe and secure space where they could gather to address the pressing issue of 'race' as it connects with all aspects of the literary world. Yet from the perspective of many journalists and cultural critics, this conference was a significant threat to the social order and cohesiveness of Canada.

The lack of access to cultural institutions manifests itself in a number of ways. In the case study of *Into the Heart of Africa*, lack of access took the form of the assumptions the ROM made about the respective roles of curators, anthropologists, and cultural communities in developing exhibitions and programs. The ROM supported the traditional stance, which holds that museum professionals should be the arbiters in all matters dealing with museum practices. ROM officials rejected the more contemporary, inclusive approach that some museums have now taken, which involves incorporating the community as an important resource and holds that curators have a responsibility to involve communities in a meaningful way in the planning and implementation of new programs and exhibitions.

The ROM denied the African-Canadian community access by engaging in token outreach and superficial consultations, and by ignoring the huge reservoir of expertise in the community. The words of the ROM's former director, T. Cuyler Young (1993), reinforce this point: 'You consult only when you think there is a good reason to do so, which I suspect will be rarely' (184).

The ROM officials seemed offended by the Black community's attempts to participate in an exhibition that was so connected with their own sense of identity and history. The curator, executive director, and board of trustees were never really willing to acknowledge that different interpretations of the exhibition were valid. Instead, they interpreted the protest as a challenge to their institutional authority and as a threat to the 'intellectual honesty, scientific integrity and academic freedom' of the museum (John McNeil, former acting director of the ROM, quoted in Nourbese Philip, 1992: 103).

Another, more overt expression of exclusion was seen in the attempt by museum officials to suppress the protest by drawing upon the resources and forces of other institutions. The use of heavily armed police to control the demonstration, and the legal suit by the museum against the protesters (which was eventually dropped), served to isolate and marginalize the community. The fact that this was the first exhibition in the ROM's history dealing with African or Caribbean culture only strengthened the alienation that the community was already feeling toward this cultural institution.

The Politics of Empowerment versus the Politics of Control

Each case study in this book reflects a crisis in cultural representation and a response to it from two perspectives: first, that of those cultural producers who exercise power from the centre of the dominant culture; and second, that of those who are located at the margins of culture, who are seeking access and equity in cultural production.

The cultural events examined in this book confirm the view that the margin is a site of resistance, possibility, and empowerment. The concept of empowerment suggests a spectrum of political activities ranging from individual acts of resistance to group and mass mobilizations that challenge existing power relations in society (Yuval-Davis, in Bhavnani and Phoenix, 1994).

Those who participated in acts of resistance included cultural activists, artists, writers, performers, and others from the various ethno-racial communities. The acts of resistance carried out by these various individuals and groups were attempts to demystify, deconstruct, and demobilize institutional power structures that were denying ethno-racial and other marginalized groups opportunities for participation. These challenges to cultural hegemony were commonly depicted by the cultural establishment as a threat to cherished democratic values; yet Toni Morrison (1992) reminds us that 'responding to culture – clarifying, explicating, valorizing, translating, transforming, criticizing is what artists everywhere do' (49).

In each case study, groups who were culturally misrepresented and degraded found themselves excluded from the dominant culture's different venues, and chose to contest established cultural traditions and practices. These groups all took up culture as a tool in the fight against marginalization, exclusion, and erasure. They used cultural production as a means to call on a liberal democratic society to live up to its promise of equality and justice for all.

The driving force in the protests against the ROM, the AGO, Livent, Mirvish Productions, the CRTC, and literary institutions was the need felt by ethno-racial groups to be recognized and respected; to be heard and listened to; to see themselves as equal participants in the production of culture; and to cross the boundaries that were keeping them outside the public culture.

Cornel West (1990) suggests that the new cultural politics of difference are not simply oppositional (in the sense of identifying exclusionary practices in mainstream cultural production); they are also driven by the aspirations and unrealized contributions of those individuals and communities who believe it necessary to expand the notions of culture, democracy, multiculturalism, and freedom of expression.

The struggle for recognition lies at the heart of the cultural politics of difference (Taylor, 1994), and is reflected in the discourses utilized by ethno-racial minorities. The protests around these cultural events were propelled by the need to reclaim subjectivity, identity, and history. People who do not see themselves represented on their own terms have no place 'to fix themselves,' moor themselves, berth themselves (Moure, 1994: 276) As Kyo Maclear (93) argues, the conflict over cultural productions such as *Miss Saigon* and *Show Boat* are about the need to establish a different kind of power from that emanating from the dominant culture: it is 'the power arising from critical thinking and collective action against prevailing ideologies in the entertainment industry' (5).

One of the recurring patterns seen in the struggle over representation is that the relationship in the world of arts between white cultural professionals and people of colour reproduces the symbolic basis of colonial domination (Butler, 1993). This process is described as 'the act of conceptualizing, inscribing, and interacting with "others" on terms not of their choosing; in making them into pliant objects and silenced subjects of our scripts and scenarios; in assuming the capacity to "represent" them' (Comaroff and Comaroff, 1991: 15).

In each of the case studies provided in this book, the interests of the cultural producers and cultural institutions collided with the interests of minority communities. Those who attempted to challenge or resist the power of the dominant culture were subjected to further acts of marginalization and exclusion.

In another context, Carl James (1994) makes a related point, observing that one's sense of self (as a racial minority) will always be situated within a set of meanings that are socially situated, and defined by systems of cultural representation: 'My race helps identify me. I cannot escape the media, the magazines and book images and information, etc., neither will my twelve year old son who has already begun to experience the hidden injuries of race. And whether or not I wish to represent the population of Blacks in Toronto, I am assigned the task ... That I am a professor does not make me immune to the stereotypes and concomitant issues and problems that go along with being a racial minority, and a Black person in particular, in this society' (51).

W.E.B. Dubois (1903) describes this phenomenon as one of 'double consciousness' and explains: 'It is a peculiar sensation ... this sense of looking at one's self through the eyes of others, of measuring one's soul by the tape of a world that looks on in amused contempt and pity' (3).

As the case studies in this book demonstrate, the dominant culture's élite does not willingly accept any kind of challenge to its power, control, and authority. As ethno-racial communities begin to deconstruct and resist the complex dynamics of racist ideology, racist discourse, and racist practices within cultural production, there is a backlash. The dominant culture defends itself in a variety of ways. This is a society that rejects resistance and critique yet at the same time promotes its tolerance and open-mindedness (Wallace, 1993). A kind of 'authoritative discourse' operates that 'seeks continually to pre-empt the space of radically opposed utterances and so prevent them from being uttered' (Asad, 1979: 621).

In view of this, the discourse of resistance used by those involved in the protests must be framed, and not just in symbolic language: it must also be linked to political actions. As Robert Labossiere explains. 'discourse must first exhibit power to affect the world around it' (1995: 17). In the case of the controversy over the Writing Thru Race Conference and other initiatives involving First Nations writers and writers of colour, it was not enough to gain the support and acknowledgment of White writers that racism is a significant factor in literary production. In addition, the conference attendees had to take the talk back to 'their own circles, teaching us that speech can become political by virtue of control over its location. Legitimizing discourse needs to be conducted and controlled by artists, who in claiming it for themselves, act like stakeholders they are instead of the clients they have been made out to be' (ibid.: 17).

Each of the cultural events analysed in this book created a community of interest, which in turn created a discourse around race, culture, difference, and rights that was more than symbolic: the discourse *itself* became an instrument of empowerment.

The Media: Silencing and Marginalizing Minority Dissent

This section of the chapter, the last, examines the role the media played in producing a public discourse for several of the events described in the book. Such an examination reveals a common pattern. Particular rhetorical devices were used to describe and analyse both the cultural events and the activities of the protesters. The press employed a discourse aimed at delegitimizing dissent and stifling debate. In the case of the Writing Thru Race Conference, *Into the Heart of Africa*, and *Show Boat*, the three Toronto newspapers created a 'media event' around the protests. The term 'media event' refers to print and broadcast coverage of a particular issue that 'is not a mere representation of what happened, but it has its own reality, which gathers up into itself the reality of the event that may or may not have preceded it' (Fiske, 1994: 2). This phenomenon suggests that it is no longer credible to rely on a clear relationship between a 'real' event and its mediated representation. Accordingly, it is not possible to argue that the 'real' is more important, more accurate, or more true than the representation.

The following are some of the standard rhetorical devices that were used by various journalists and editors in their critique of the protests.

Theme 1. Describing the protesters as 'extremists,' 'militants,' 'leftists,' 'zealots,' who are engaging in protest activities to further their own agendas, interests, and political goals. They are few in number and are not representative of the 'ordinary' members of the community. They are illogical and poorly informed.

Examples of this discursive strategy are many. Regarding *Into the Heart of Africa*, Christopher Hume (1990), art critic of the *Toronto Star*, wrote that 'either the protesters have not seen the show or they are deliberately distorting the truth to suit their own ends.' He went on to add: 'If the coalition members were better informed they would have realized the organizers of *Into the Heart of Africa* are on their side.' Christie Blatchford (1990), a feature writer in the *Toronto Sun*, concluded her condemnation of the coalition with the comment: 'Why are we so bloody eager to be held hostage by the ravers from the political left?' Bronwyn Drainie (1991) in the *Globe and Mail* referred to 'a small number of radical blacks' who viewed the exhibit as a 'perpetuation of old racist attitudes ... More moderate blacks, while not deeming the show racist in intent ...'

Journalists described the protesters against *Show Boat* with similar negative connotations. Michael Coren (1995) in the *Globe and Mail* called them 'unelected zealots.' Pierre Berton (1993) in the *Toronto Star* characterized the protesters' message as 'the silly argument' made by 'a small group of activists.' In the *Toronto Sun*, Allan Fotheringham (1993) referred to the coalition as 'the goofies who are screaming racism' and told them they should 'read some history.' He described them as 'instant experts who make a living out of protesting.' In the same newspaper, Linda Barnard (1993) attacked one of the key players in the protest against *Show Boat*, North York Board of Education trustee Stephnie Payne, asking rhetorically if she was 'a nasty, mean-spirited woman or ... simply dumb as a post.' An editorial in the same paper (1993) commented: 'We can't let them cook up some evil plot that this is something the Jews are doing to the blacks. Nonsense! It just goes to show how you have to check the hands for muck of those throwing the charge of racism. There really isn't much of a reason to pretend this is a major protest. What it is really is an excuse to agitate and get attention.'

Theme 2. Constructing the minority group as oppressor and accusing its members of engaging in 'reverse racism,' violating the rights of others.

Responding to the Writing Thru Race Conference, Richard Gwyn (1993) of the *Toronto Star* described the conference as 'an example of racism practised by those who suffer from it. All these noble intentions seem to be turning us into the hell of a "systematically racist society."' The *Star's* editorial of 5 April 1994 took a similar position, stating that 'reverse discrimination does not cure injustice, but rather feeds it.'

The *Star* described the protesters as 'becoming increasingly aggressive' (Platiel, 1993). This same kind of language was used by the *Toronto Sun*, which referred to the controversy as a 'race war in the making' (25 May 1993).

The *Globe and Mail's* editor-in-chief, William Thorsell (1993), wrote: 'The apparent issue is race – the allegation by some black people in Toronto that *Show Boat* demeans them. But the real issue is power. *Show Boat* is just a vehicle to advance the campaign of some blacks in Toronto for more power in the life in the city, in particular the City of North York.' Thorsell was inferring here that the desire for the power to exercise some control over racist representation is somehow negative and improper. Three years later, in response to a similar controversy, Thorsell (1996) wrote, 'In retrospect it was all the more clear that the struggle over *Show Boat* was not about race but power and protesters were using *Show Boat* as a vehicle in the contest for more power in the community at large.'

Theme 3. Alleging that the protesters are challenging the principles, values, and norms of a liberal democratic society (such as truth, rationality, freedom of expression, individualism, academic freedom, and the integrity of history).

In the *Globe and Mail*, Michael Valpy (1993a) suggested that the Coalition for the Truth About Africa, in trying to shut the ROM exhibition down, was proposing 'the death of memory, the death of education. Censorship.' Donna Laframboise (1990) in the *Toronto Star*, meanwhile, chastised the coalition for apparently believing that its interpretation was the one and only truth: 'There is something truly appalling about believing that only you have the right story.' Another *Toronto Star* journalist reported that the protesters 'seem to have willingly misread the exhibit' and that 'their attack on the exhibition challenges both academic freedom and the integrity of history' (Cayley, 1990). This writer seemed offended by the coalition's name, arguing that by calling themselves the 'Truth About Africa,' the protesters were contending that there was only one truth about Africa.

Robert Fulford (1990), the culture critic for the *Globe and Mail*, said of the Writing Thru Race Conference: 'Now the Writers Union of Canada wants to tell us that closed is open, limited is free, exclusion is inclusion and private is public. The old liberal pluralism holds that each of us has rights as an individual: this is the idea that has animated social progress for generations. The new multiculturalism ... focuses on the rights of groups.'

Theme 4. Trivializing and dismissing the concerns of minorities about racism in cultural production and other systemic forms of inequality, and alleging that minorities are hypersensitive about race.

Philip Marchand (1994b), a feature writer in the *Toronto Star*, noted that 'whatever the good effects the conference might have had for its participants, it is undeniably part of a recent trend toward intensifying racial and ethnic consciousness.' Drawing on the same theme, Richard Gwyn (1994) of the same paper commented: 'We are at risk of institutionalizing racism in Canada ... this often happens as a by-product of attempts to combat racism or to advantage the disadvantaged. But the effect of their actions can be to create a hyper-consciousness about race.' Sid Adilman (1990), the *Toronto Star*'s entertainment critic, dismissed the concerns of the African-Canadian community about the exhibition, noting that the museum's 'wishy-washy board stood inert in the face of loud protests by black activists against its superb exhibition.'

William Littler (1993), the same newspaper's music critic, wrote that the Coalition Against Show Boat was attempting to 'rewrite history.' The ubiquitous Pierre Berton (1993) suggested that 'a great fuss has been made about the use of the word "nigger."'

Theme 5. Implying that it is the actions of the protesters themselves that create the division, tension, and conflict, disturbing the harmony, cohesiveness, and stability of the society. These activities are also seen as linked to the policies of multiculturalism, which support the 'balkanization' of Canada.

An editorial in the *Globe and Mail* (1994) critiquing the Writing Thru Race Conference focused on the premise that the policy of multiculturalism is a powerful force underpinning the conference: 'As much as we share the revulsion to a publicly-funded racially exclusive conference ... it must be admitted this is entirely consistent with public policy.'

In the same paper Michael Valpy (1994) described the conference as advancing the notion of 'apartheid ... Why are the 800-some members of the union marching along with this cultural dismemberment of Canada?'

All these examples suggest that the press constructs a discursive pattern in which the following elements are found: (1) protesters are depicted as outsiders, or 'others'; (2) the pain experienced by the minority community is dismissed as irrelevant; (3) the existence of systemic racism is denied; (4) the motives of the protesters are belittled; (5) individual leaders are personally attacked; (6) the protesters' actions are equated with disruptive and dysfunctional forms of behaviour; (7) it is implied that the protesters have neither acquired 'Canadian' social values nor adopted 'Canadian' norms; and (8) expressions of dissent and resistance are described as threatening the social order, harmony, and equilibrium of Canadian society. This same discourse is also used by cultural institutions and cultural producers, as demonstrated throughout this book.

As is clear from the above discussion, most of the mainstream media coverage was critical of the protest groups and dismissive of their actions. However, it is important to stress that the media discourse, and that of institutional cultural authorities, was often markedly ambivalent and contradictory. It seems that critics, editors, and journalists are often of two minds. Attitudinal shifts are observable in the writing of the journalists we have quoted. For example, Valpy was totally dismissive of the concerns of First Nations writers and writers of colour at the Writing Thru Race Conference, but later he wrote concerning *Show Boat* that 'history is going to remember the insensitivity of the Centre's opening, not the artistic merit of what took place there' (1993b). In her coverage of the controversy over *Into the Heart of Africa*, Bronwyn Drainie provided two very different commentaries (Mackey, 1995). In an early piece, she wrote: 'Unfortunately what thoughtful white Canadians see as an ironic examination of our great-grandparents' dubious and racist role in bringing Christianity, Commerce, and Civilization to "the dark continent," black Canadians see as a celebration of colonialism and an unambiguous demonstration of white superiority over native Africans and their cultures' (Drainie, 1990).

Several months later we note a rather radical shift in her analysis of the protest: 'But what many visitors saw as an ironic and self-searching examination of white Canadians' historical intolerance toward Africa was viewed by a small number of radical blacks in Toronto as a perpetuation of those old racist attitudes. The dubiously named Coalition for the Truth about Africa ... picketed outside the ROM's doors for months ... More moderate blacks, while not deeming the show racist in intent ...' (Drainie, 1991).

Other writers exhibited similar kinds of contradictions in their analyses of these cultural controversies. What is clear, however, is that the issues of race and racism were largely invisible to the White institutional authorities within the press and other cultural institutions. Their own position of power and privilege, associated with *their* 'whiteness,' was ignored. Their beliefs, assumptions, and values were unmarked.

In this context, it is important to emphasize the influence of the media's ideological positions, narrative strategies, and image constructions on the formation of individual, group, and national identity. The implicit and explicit messages buried in the media discourse point to there being a deep divide in Canadian culture and identity, with some seeing our society as heterogeneous, as racially and culturally fragmented, and others asserting the dominant ideology, which is that Canadian society is homogeneous, unified, and harmonious. This tension is examined in the next chapter, Concluding Reflections.

References

Adilman, Sid. 1990. 'Bad Guys Discrediting Integrity of the Board.' *Toronto Star.* 24 December.

– 1993. 'New York Critics Proclaim Show Boat as See Worthy.' *Toronto Star.* 23 October.

Allen, Lillian. 1992. *First Steps on the Road to Cultural and Racial Equity.* Ministry of Culture and Communications. Province of Ontario.

Araeen, Rasheed. 1991. 'From Primitivism to Ethnic Arts.' In Susan Hiller, ed. *The Myth of Primitivism: Perspectives on Art.* London and New York: Routledge. 158–62.

Asad, Talal. 1979. 'Anthropology and the Analysis of Ideology.' *Man.* 14: 607– 27.

Atwood, Margaret. 1997. *The New Oxford Book of Canadian Short Stories in English.* 2nd ed. Toronto: Oxford University Press.

Bannerji, Hermani, ed. 1993. *Returning the Gaze: Essays on Racism, Feminism and Politics.* Toronto: Sister Vision.

Barnard, Linda. 1993. 'Missing the Boat,' *Toronto Sun.* 21 May. 73.

Becker, Carol. ed. 1994. *The Subversive Imagination: Artists, Society and Social Responsibility.* New York: Routledge.

Berger, Maurice. 1992. 'Are Art Museums Racists?' *How Art Becomes History.*
New York: HarperCollins.

Berton, Pierre. 1993. 'Let's Not Scrub Show Boat Too Clean.' *Toronto Star.* 20
March. K3.

Blatchford, Christie. 1990. 'A Surrender to Vile Harangues' *Toronto Sun.* 30
November. 5.

Butler, S. 1993. 'Contested Representations: Revisiting "Into the Heart of
Africa."' Master's thesis. Department of Anthropology. York University.

Carby, Hazel. 1993. 'Encoding White Resentment: *Grand Canyon* – a Narrative
for Our Times.' In C. McCarthy and W. Critchlow, eds. *Race, Identity, Representation in Education.* New York: Routledge. 236–50.

Cayley, David. 1990. 'Trouble Out of Africa.' *Toronto Star.* 10 August.

Clarke, George Elliott. 1994. 'After Ward.' *Possibilitiis.'* 1(2). 48.

Cohen, Philip. 1992. '"It's Racism What Dunnit:" Hidden Narratives in Theories
of Race.' In A. Rattansi and J. Donald, eds. *Race, Culture and Difference.* London: Open University Press. 62–104.

Comaroff, Jean, and John Comaroff. 1991. *Of Revelation and Revolution: Christianity, Colonialism and Consciousness in South Africa.* Chicago: University of Chicago Press.

Coren, Michael. 1995. 'Livent Court Case Really about Government Accountability.' *Globe and Mail.* 30 January.

Drabinsky, Garth. 1993. 'I Do Not Intend to Cancel Show Boat.' *Toronto Star.* 2
May. D4.

– 1994. 'Show Boat Exploited for Political Gain.' *Toronto Star.* 15 February.
A17.

Drainie, Bronwyn. 1990. 'Black Groups Protest African Show at "Racist Ontario
Museum."' *Globe and Mail.* 24 March.

– 1991. 'ROM Adds Insult to Injury in Debacle over African Show.' *Globe and
Mail.* 4. April.

Dubois, W.E.B. 1903 (1989). *The Souls of Black Folk.* New York: Bantam.

Essed, Philomena. 1990. *Everyday Racism: Reports from Women of Two Cultures.*
Clarmont, Cal.: Hunter House.

Ferguson, Russell, ed. 1990. *Out There: Marginalization and Contemporary Culture.*
Minneapolis: University of Minnesota Press.

Fish, Stanley. 1994. *There's No Such Thing as Free Speech ... and It's a Good Thing Too.*
New York and Oxford: Oxford University Press.

Fiske, John. 1994. *Media Matters: Everyday Culture and Political Change.* Minneapolis: University of Minnesota Press.

Fotheringham, Allan. 1993. 'A Resounding Attack on Racism?' *Toronto Sun.* 19
October. 12.

Fulford, Robert. 1994. 'George Orwell Call Your Office.' *Globe and Mail*. 30 March 30. C1.

Fung, Richard. 1997. *Fuse*. 'Working through Cultural Appropriation.' 20(2). Anniversary Issue. 95–103.

Galleano, Eduardo. 1994. In Carol Becker, ed. *The Subversive Imagination: Artists, Society and Social Responsibility*. New York and London: Routledge.

Globe and Mail. 1994. Editorial. 'Writing Thru Race.' 9 April.

Goldberg, David. 1993. *Racist Culture: Philosophy and the Politics of Meaning*. Oxford, U.K., and Cambridge, Mass.: Blackwell.

Goldstein, Lorrie. 1993. 'Brothers under One Skin.' *Toronto Sun*. 25 May. 12.

Gwyn, Richard. 1994. 'Good Intentions Pave Canada's Road to Racist Hell.' *Toronto Star*. 8 July.

Hall, John R., and Mary Jo Neitz. 1993. *Culture: Sociological Perspective*. Englewood Cliffs, N.J.: Prentice Hall.

Hall, John R., and Mary Jo Neitz. 1993. *Culture: Sociological Perspectives*. Englewood Cliffs, N.J.: Prentice Hall.

Henry, Frances, et al., 1995. *The Colour of Democracy: Racisms in Canadian Society*. Toronto: Harcourt Brace.

hooks, bell 1990. *Yearning: Race, Gender* and *Cultural Policies*. Toronto: Between the Lines.

Hume, Christopher. 1990. 'ROM Critics Confusing Content with Context.' *Toronto Star*. 19 May. H6.

– 1994. 'Racism Charges against AGO a Bizarre Spin on Barnes Show.' *Toronto Star*. 15 December. H6.

Itwaru, Arnold, and Natasha Ksonek. 1994. *Closed Entrances: Canadian Culture and Imperialism*. Toronto: TSAR.

James, Carl. 1994. 'The Paradox of Power and Privilege: Race, Gender and Occupational Position.' *Canadian Woman Studies: Race and Gender*. 14(2). 47–51.

Jordan, Glenn, and Chris Weedon. 1995. *Cultural Politics: Class, Gender, Race and the Postmodern World*. Oxford, U.K., and Cambridge, Mass.: Blackwell.

Labossiere, Robert. 1995. 'A Newer Lacoon: Toward a Defence of Artists' Self-Determination through Public Arts Funding.' *Fuse*. 18(5). Special Issue.

Laframboise, Donna. 1990. 'ROM Protesters Miss Own Point.' *Toronto Star*. 22 October.

Li, Peter. 1994. 'A World Apart: The Multicultural World of Visible Minorities and the Art World of Canada.' *Canadian Review of Sociology and Anthropology*. 31(4). November.

Littler, William. 1993. 'Show Boat Set the Standard for Musicals.' *Toronto Star*. 16 October.

Lorde, Audre. 1984. *Sister Outsider*. Trumansbury, N.Y.: Crossing Press.

Mackey, Eva. 1995. 'Postmodernism and Cultural Politics in a Multicultural Nation: Contests over Truth in the *Into the Heart of Africa* Controversy.' *Public Culture.* 7(2). Winter. 403–48.

– 1996. 'Managing and Imaging Diversity: Multiculturalism and the Construction of National Identity in Canada.' D.Phil. thesis, Social Anthropology, University of Sussex.

Maclear, Kyo. 1993. 'Miss Saigon: Sex, Lies and Stereotypes': *Nikkei Voice.* 7(8). September.

Marchand, Philip. 1994a. 'Author Protest No-Whites Conference.' *Toronto Star.* 14 May.

– 1994b. 'Politics the Real CanLit Power Fuel.' *Toronto Star.* 5 July.

Morrison, Toni. 1989. 'Unspeakable Things Unspoken: The Afro-American Presence in American Literature.' *Michigan Quarterly Review.* 28(1). 1–34.

Moure, Erin. 1994. 'The Glow.' In R. Miki and Fred Wah, eds. *Colour an Issue. West Coast Line.* 13–14. Spring–Fall. 276–8.

Nourbese Philip, Marlene. 1992. *Frontiers: Essays and Writings on Racism and Culture.* Stratford, Ont. The Mercury Press.

– 1993. *Showing Grit: Showboating North of the 44th Parallel.* Toronto: Poui Publications.

Pieterse, Neverdeen Jan. 1992. *White on Black: Images of Africa and Blacks in Western Popular Culture.* London and New Haven: Yale University Press.

Platiel, Rudy. 1993. 'Sold-out Show Boat Preview Wins Praise.' *Globe and Mail.* 5 October.

Rosler, Martha. 1994. 'Place, Position, Power, Politics.' In Carol Becker, ed. *The Subversive Imagination: Artists, Society and Social Responsibility.* New York: Routledge.

Said, Edward. 1993. *Culture and Imperialism.* London: Chatto and Windus.

Salutin, Rick. 1994. 'More Magic Media Moments.' *Globe and Mail.* 11 March. 61.

Seidel, Gill. 1987. 'The White Discursive Order: The British New Right's Discourse on Cultural Racism with Particular Reference to the Salisbury Review.' In Iris Zavala, Teun van Dijk, and Myriam Diaz-Diocaretz, eds. *Approaches to Discourse, Poetics, and Psychiatry.* Amsterdam: John Benjamins Publishing. 39–66.

Stam, Robert. 1993. 'From Stereotype to Discourse.' *Cine-Action.* 23. Fall. 12–29.

Taylor, Charles. 1994. 'Examining the Politics of Recognition.' In Amy Gutman, ed. *Multiculturalism.* Princeton: Princeton University Press.

Thorsell, William. 1993. 'In America's Bazaar of Competing Interests, Power Is the Only Currency.' *Globe and Mail.* 16 October. D1.

– 1996. 'Angels in America Has Powerful Parallels in Canada.' *Globe and Mail.* 28 September.

Toronto Star. 1994, Editorial: 'Excluding Whites.' 5 April.

Toronto Sun. 1993. Editorial: 'Missing the Boat.' 8 April.

Valpy, Michael. 1993a. 'The Storm around Show Boat.' *Globe and Mail.* 12 March.

– 1993b. 'Surely There's Something Better than Show Boat.' *Globe and Mail.* 19 October.

– 1994. 'A Nasty Serving of Cultural Apartheid.' *Globe and Mail.* 8 April.

Wallace, Michele. 1993. 'Multiculturalism and Oppositionality.' In Cameron McCarthy and Warren Crichlow, eds. *Race, Identity and Representation in Education.* New York: Routledge.

West, Cornel. 1990. 'The Cultural Politics of Difference.' In Russell Ferguson, ed. *Out There: Marginalization and Contemporary Culture.* Minneapolis: University of Minnesota Press.

Wetherell, Margaret, and Jonathan Potter. 1992. *Mapping the Language of Racism.* New York: Columbia University Press.

Young, Robert. 1990. *White Mythologies: Writing, History and the West.* London and New York: Routledge.

Young, T. Cuyler. 1993. 'Into the Heart of Africa: The Director's Perspective.' Curator 36(3): 174–88.

Yuval-Davis, Nira. 1994. 'Women, Ethnicity and Empowerment.' In Kum-Kum Bhavnani and Ann Phoenix, eds. *Shifting Identities, Shifting Racism.* London: Sage. 179–97.

9

Concluding Reflections

What conclusions can be drawn from these case studies? How do the cultural politics of difference as analysed in each of the case studies influence our understanding of the values and practices of a society based on the principles of liberalism and multiculturalism? What new models or cultural paradigms do we require in order to create a society in which the hermetic seal dividing Canadians into 'them' and 'us' can be broken?

Canada Today, as Earlier in Its History, Is in a State of Cultural Crisis

The case studies, most notably the one discussing the Writing Thru Race Conference, suggest that Canada is in a state of cultural crisis. This cultural crisis is a result of many factors, not the least of which is Canada's persistent struggle with the question of national identity. In 1867 the Fathers of Confederation built a constitution around the principle of cultural duality, and this led directly to the recognition of an English Canada and French Canada. Cultural duality was a mechanism embedded in the constitution to protect Canadians against the tyranny of the majority.

From the start, then, the idea of 'hyphenated' Canadians was part of the national discourse. On the one hand there was English Canada, and on the other French Canada. When they created English Canada and French Canada, the Fathers of Confederation ignored the cultural plurality that existed even at that time. Aboriginal and other cultures were omitted from the national discourse and rendered invisible. Canada imagined a national culture built of a blend of English and French cultures, and an identity build on French and English values. Although set in the constitution, the promise to build a national identity failed. As a result, three types of citizens were recognized – English Canadians, French Canadians, and 'others' – but only two of these had constitutional rights.

Ever since Confederation, Canada has lacked a national public culture strong enough to unify its disparate and distinct parts – a national identity sufficiently unique to differentiate this country from (especially) its giant neighbour to the south.

National culture is a discourse that constructs meanings and influences 'our actions and our conceptions of ourselves' (Hall, 1992: 292). National culture defines identity by 'producing meanings about the nation with which we can identify; these are contained in the stories which are told about it, memories which connect its present with its past, and the images which are constructed of it' (ibid.: 282).

Throughout Canadian history, politicians have preferred to deal with regional economic disparity rather than the conflictual issue of national identity. Historically, the question of national identity has been addressed only when there is a perceived cultural crisis. One such moment was the Canadian government's approval of the recommendations of the Bilingualism and Biculturalism Report. Multiculturalism emerged as a result of that report.[1]

In 1982 the country was again at a crossroads, largely because of Quebec's efforts to assert its independence. Multiculturalism was 'constitutionalized' in section 27 of the Canadian Charter of Rights and Freedoms. Canadian cultural identity remained unresolved – a situation exacerbated by Quebec's objection to the Charter itself. Tensions between English Canada and French Canada mounted. The dream of a 'Canadian-ness' built on a unique blend of English and French cultures seemed in jeopardy; at least from the perspective of Quebec, separation was beginning to seem inevitable.

Since the 1960s the country's demographics have changed profoundly. Canada's population has become far more racially diverse. However, people of colour are still being excluded from full participation in Canadian society. Race and racism have thus been added to the debate on national identity.

Although the federal government has legitimated multiculturalism, issues strongly affecting people of colour are largely excluded from the constitutional debate. This was evident at both Meech Lake and Charlottetown. The doctrine of multiculturalism did not fundamentally alter the hegemonic influence of English and French Canada. Multiculturalism was seen as an approach that in certain contexts would allow for the recognition and celebration of cultural differences; but that celebration was to be contained within the framework of the dominant value systems of the two founding groups (Mackey, 1996; Goldberg, 1994; Walcott 1993).

Moreover, section 27 of the Charter of Rights and Freedoms provided no actionable 'multicultural rights' under the Constitution Act of 1982. That is, the doctrine of multiculturalism did not provide people of colour with any means of redressing the power imbalances that led to their marginalization. The multicultural identity enshrined in the constitution was not the same as that which characterized relations between the French and the English. In this sense, Canada constitutionalized 'otherness' under the label 'multiculturalism.'

The historical dominance of the two founding cultures, and the marginalization of 'others' despite the enactment of multiculturalism, forms the backdrop to contemporary questions of identity, culture, and nationhood. The huge gap between the ideal of multiculturalism and the present, actual state of inequality has provided fertile ground for contestation.

Culture Is a Contested Space in Which Minorities Demand to Be Included in the Redefinition of Canadian National Identity

The debate about national identity is basic to Canadian discourse. Canada's search for national unity is really a search for cultural stability; it is thought that cultural stability will lead to a stable and permanent cultural/national identity. Identity and representation are at the heart of any examination of Canadian culture. Issues of identity go beyond how individual artists see themselves or how their racial/cultural background – along with other social markers such as gender, class, and sexual orientation – affects their life and work. Each individual artist lives with a diversity of potentially conflicting identities. A person's gaze, voice, and behaviour are an amalgamation of these identities. Thus, an African-Canadian lesbian artist cannot ignore any one of her identities when she sees, feels, and interacts with the world. She speaks to more than one community, about more than one reality.

The quest for identity in the postmodern world is linked to the ways in which the cultural politics of difference are practised within local communities, and within the national and international arenas. As curator Pat Cruz suggests, discussions around multiculturalism and national identity 'reverberate and rage with words and weapons. As we sort fact from the fiction of our collective being, we seek to define ourselves' (Cruz, 1993).

Many observers today conclude that there is no fixed Canadian identity 'to which all immigrants must assimilate' (Kulyk Keefer, 1996: 181). The fact is that identity is both fluid and plural. Identity is always changing; it is not monolithic. Identity is not only linked to local communities but is also experiential: no individual can exist within a society without a bank of experience. These experiences organize the ways people understand themselves and their place in both the local community and in the mainstream culture.

The legacy of Canada's rupture from colonialism is still part of this experiential reality. Minorities continue to endure this harsh legacy, which presents a contradiction for many people of colour. Members of the dominant culture are free to move between their individual and collective identities; people of colour seem trapped within their collective, group identity. This group identity is defined and understood in the society in terms of stereotypes, and such patterns do not represent the ways people of colour understand or describe themselves. The discourse about culture and identity then raises questions about 'who should define whom, when, and how (McCarthy and Crichlow, 1993: xvi).

In Canada, the question of cultural identity is influenced by the cultural politics of difference – a politics shaped by the interplay of history, culture, and power. The fluidity of identity is driven by the fact that each individual is a synthesis not only of existing relations, but also of the history of these relations. Each person 'is the precis of the past' (Rutherford, 1990). 'Identity has no fixed origin but is a positioning' (Hall, 1992: 392). When minorities position their experiences within the larger discourse of Canadian identity, the dominant culture incorporates a perspective of minorities other than that which those minorities would choose to construct for themselves. More important, the dominant culture receives an image about itself, its identity, that is inconsistent with its own self-perception.

In the struggle for national identity, the dominant culture is reluctant to include the identities of 'others' that it has constructed, perpetuated, and used to its advantage. To discard 'otherness' would in a sense be to abandon the vehicle through which inequalities and power imbalances are legitimated. For many White Canadians, to accept ethno-racial minorities as active and full participants in the creation of a national identity would be to threaten the stability of Canadian culture. For the dominant culture, including people of colour in the redefinition of

Canadian-ness would mean acknowledging contemporary effects of racism and Canada's colonial past.

Canadians see themselves as egalitarians and have little difficulty rejecting blatant expressions of bigotry and overt manifestations of discrimination. They have little difficulty making symbolic gestures of inclusivity. Beyond this point, however, the struggles of people of colour are met with the arbitrary use of political, economic, and cultural institutional power in the interest of 'maintaining democracy.'

Minorities' Demands for Inclusion in the Redefinition of Canadian Culture Exacerbate the Anxieties of the Dominant Culture

Each of this book's case studies illustrates that minorities are seldom invited into the mainstream discourse of what defines Canadian national culture. The selected few are considered to be model minorities, who are constructed as being different from the rest of *them.* An example of such an individual is Neil Bissoondath, a writer whose views on multiculturalism support dominant cultural positions and therefore are deemed acceptable to the majority. In contrast, the diverse perspectives of writers of colour on issues related to cultural racism, racist discourse, and processes of exclusion are commonly dismissed, deflected, or ignored. In a liberal democracy, justice and equality is assumed to exist. As a result, ethno-racial minorities' demands for access and inclusion are seen as 'radical,' 'unreasonable,' and 'undemocratic,' and as a threat to cherished liberal democratic values.

Four of our case studies (*Into the Heart of Africa*, the Barnes Exhibit, *Show Boat*, and *Miss Saigon*), demonstrated that the struggle for inclusion passes through five distinct stages:[2]

I. Selection and staging of the event.
II. Resistance mounted by racial minorities.
III. Development of two distinct factions.
IV. Counter-resistance by the majority.
V. Immediate outcomes.

Stage I. Selection and Staging of the Event

At this first stage, the institution selects an event to produce that raises important questions about culture and cultural politics. The institution or agency plans, organizes, produces, and markets the event based on the potential audiences and economic gains it can generate. Cultural production is increasingly driven by commerce and the spread of commodity culture into every aspect of cultural life. Interinstitutional support is sought after (for example, from the media and boards of education) and the economic value of the event gains momentum. As West (1990) argues, the processes of commodification promote a view of culture in which people are seen as passive spectators/consumers.

The institutional actors are typically members of the White dominant culture, so it is not surprising that they are guided mainly by Eurocentric assumptions about the nature of public culture. Traditional cultural policies, norms, planning practices, and management processes guide this stage. When decision-makers and culturally élite authorities conceive of audiences for their work, people of colour and other marginalized communities are largely erased. Invisible barriers, the signifiers of identity (race, ethnicity, gender, class, and so on), function subliminally within institutional processes, eliminating certain groups from the imagined community of viewers.

The case studies demonstrate, however, that the institutional players and producers are recognizing more and more that there may be 'sensitive' issues relating to diversity. In four of the case studies, the institutions involved were able, during Stage I, to talk the language of 'multiculturalism' and 'diversity,' albeit in ways that did not significantly influence the cultural undertaking. Stage I sometimes ends with a decision to undertake some form of limited consultation in order to show 'sensitivity.'

Stage II. Resistance Mounted by Racial Minorities

The resistance effort commences in Stage II, when minorities begin to pose questions, identify concerns, challenge traditional authorities, and seek institutional accountability. Those engaged in resistance struggle to deconstruct the complex and invisible biases and barriers embedded in institutional and other power structures. However, resistance efforts are usually reactive and ad hoc, and lack permanent organizational structures. Typically, such movements have few financial resources and depend heavily on volunteers. Often there is no defined leadership, although one or two people are usually designated to speak on behalf of the group. As the group is ad hoc, it has no track record or history of success, nor does it have a public profile. It therefore must generate support for its cause from the ground up, relying on pamphlets, flyers, the ethnic media, community networks, and demonstrations to communicate and disseminate its message. The protesters generally lack access to institutional power structures such as the media, cultural regulatory agencies, government, and the economic establishment.

Stage III. Development of Two Distinct Factions

In Stage III, distinct factions are created. There is a clash in perceptions and in the claims made by each side as to the correctness of their respective positions. If any kind of consultation has been implemented, that process unravels. During this phase there is a struggle to define the issues, but there is also an unwillingness to listen to alternative perspectives. Positions become more polarized and entrenched; resentment, frustration, and anger escalate. The institutional players defend their projects, dismiss criticisms, and reject alternatives. At this stage there may be public confrontations and – in rare instances – violence.

Stage IV. Counter-resistance by the Majority

During this stage the institution fights back, wielding its power in order to maintain the status quo. When the institution decides to exercise its power, it does so with all of its diverse resources. The institution has the advantages of permanence, tradition, organizational and.administrative structures, expertise, authority, and high visibility. Connections and alliances with other power élites and access to the media become important enablers in suppressing the resistance. Once the resistance efforts are crushed, they seem to fade away.

Stage V. Immediate Outcomes

During this stage the resistance effort disappears. The minorities involved in the struggle retreat. The extent to which the resistance effort made any appreciable change is seldom recorded, and the institution records a victory.

In each case study, the purpose of the resistance effort was to achieve change and the institution's counter-resistance focused on containment and the maintenance of the status quo. One should note, however, that the resistance–counter-resistance process does not seem to move along a continuum; that is, the nature and extent of the counter-resistance is not necessarily related to the nature and extent of the resistance effort. Rather, the purpose of counter-resistance efforts is always to silence and remove all evidence of contestation.

The case study of the CRTC hearings demonstrates that institutions sometimes fail to consider their own policies and operating guidelines. Instead, the institution may seek support from other institutions (for example, the education system, the media, or the police) and then offer a post facto explanation, selectively maligning the leader of the resistance effort in order to suppress the opposition movement. None of this institutional behaviour is challenged in the aftermath; rarely do these actions become the subject of 'official scrutiny.' By official scrutiny is meant the process by which the acts and omissions of institutions are examined and the institution held accountable for its wrongs.

Racist Discourse Is Characteristic of Contemporary Identity Politics and Prevents Progress

The current state of racist discourse has its roots in the history of this country. Canada was created as an economic union, not a cultural one, and for that reason the issue of national identity was postponed. All attempts to deal with questions of identity have been in the context of constitutional and legal discourse. Now, with the country perceiving itself to be in cultural crisis, these unresolved issues have risen up.

The case studies show that the construction of 'otherness' has three interlocking components: 'otherness' provides the dominant White culture with unmarked, invisible privilege and power; issues are deflected in a way which suggests that the 'others' threaten the democratic fabric of Canadian society; and there is a reassertion of individual rights and identity over collective identity and group rights.

Each case study shows that this understanding of difference is operationalized by the various groups protesting images and representations made by the dominant group. To begin the process of deconstructing the many levels at which racist discourse operates, it is necessary, in the first instance, to return to the concept of an 'imagined' community, that is, a 'national culture' that conceives of citizenry as a social unit, as a collectivity of different groups bound together by common norms, ideologies, and structures.

The élite, intent on maintaining its power, asserts *its* claim on liberal values of 'truth,' 'universalism,' 'history,' 'free speech,' and 'artistic freedom,' and constructs a view of ethno-racial minorities who do not share these values as being outside the boundaries of the common culture. The social, economic, and political dislocations being experienced in postmodern societies such as Canada, the United States, the United Kingdom, Australia, and so on are shaking mainstream cultures to their core. Underlying the restoration of traditional values and neoconservative ideologies is a sense of loss of control, authority, and equilibrium. Challenges to existing notions of identity, tradition, truth, beauty, history, knowledge, and canonical art are seen as threatening, even dangerous. Order and stability are seen as the natural condition of the state; dissent is seen as disorder; the dissenters are an aberration to an otherwise unified, cohesive, harmonious society (Goldberg, 1994). In this social millieu, racist discourse becomes an essential tool for reasserting the power of the dominant culture.

When we deconstruct the issues and events around cultural production that frame the case studies, we uncover a relatively 'new' form of racism. This is not the overt racism found in bigoted individuals, nor is it the systemic racism inherent in the policies and practices of organizations and institutions. Rather, it is the racism embedded in representation, in discourse; it is the process of making and using meanings within a particular historic, social, and political context. Racist discourse is revealed in the rationalizations, justifications, categorizations, and allegations resorted to by the cultural authorities and decision-makers when their cultural productions are contested. Racist discourse is exposed in the ways in which cultural power-brokers refuse to give credence to, or even acknowledge, the voice of the 'others.'

Each of the cultural events discussed in this book provides a striking example of how the various forms of cultural production create, reinforce, and reproduce existing power relations and racism. In the cultural productions discussed in this book, people of colour were represented in ways that were not neutral; this was an expression of cultural power. The images, representations, and stereotypes contained in the productions helped White audiences understand what they *are* – not to imagine themselves as something other than what the 'others' represent. Through these images, White audiences were entertained without 'whiteness' being politicized. But those images were inaccurate and maligning, and helped preserve racism.

The case studies illustrated how individuals and communities have been attempting to shed those collective identities that the dominant culture has imposed. To free themselves of the shackles of these labels, they must define their own identities on their own terms. They need to speak, act, and create in the interests of their own hybrid and fluid identities as African Canadians, Chinese Canadian, Indo-Canadians, Aboriginal peoples, and so on. In this process, they must name the cultural practices they perceive as being harmful to them as individuals, as artists, and as communities.

The protests described in the case studies centred on the demands people of colour were making on the self-selected gatekeepers of Canadian culture. They were calling for the doors of cultural institutions and cultural spaces to open up. Writers, artists, actors, directors, and musicians of diverse racial and cultural backgrounds were insisting on their right to a place on the representational stage of Canadian culture (Mackey, 1995).

The polarization of the majority and minority communities has allowed little opportunity for dialogue. Little attempt is made to listen, understand, and resolve. This impasse creates further risks, both for people of colour and for the nation as a whole.

Racist discourse asserts that people of colour who challenge the system are antidemocratic, but this assertion makes little sense. Ethnoracial communities and artists of colour have as much interest in artistic freedom as anyone else. But artistic freedom and freedom of expression ought to work both ways. The antidemocratic argument in Canada is a rhetoric or discourse resorted to when the élites perceive a threat. It has become coded language for silencing certain voices.

Artists of colour want to be able to speak freely. They want to tell their stories. People of colour want to gain control over the production of images of themselves, as well as the power to alter these images. They advocate uncovering the partial 'truths' found in history. They advance the idea of a system of knowledge that incorporates the learnings and contributions of diverse cultures. These are the tools required to ensure that the promises of democracy work.

There is much agreement between the majority culture and ethnoracial minorities with respect to some of the basic tenets of liberalism; the disagreement has been over whether those liberal principles are operational in Canada, and whether racism and democracy can coexist. This question arises from the oppression and the history of being marginalized and silenced that is the experience of people of colour. Ethno-racial communities have begun in earnest to protest the negative collective identity imposed upon them by the Canadian cultural élite. The Canadian cultural élite has responded by reasserting its desire to find a single unitary Canadian identity based largely on universalism. In the universalist conception of identity, a hyphenated Canadian is problematic, because the hyphen signals less than full commitment to Canada as a nation.

The Politics of Difference Strengthens Democracy

The desire for democratic equality is the motivating force behind the struggle now occurring at the site of culture. The dominant culture's reactions to minorities' resistance efforts are perhaps best captured by the media's response to the Writing Thru Race Conference. Many people in the media argued that the support of the writers' union for such an event signalled that Canadian culture and artistic freedom in general were in danger of being dismantled.

It is perfectly legitimate for the media and citizens to question events. What is of interest here is the *nature* of the questions that were posed before and after the conference. The general view in the media was that any attempt by artists of colour to explore the issue of their own identity in Canada as defined through their experiences of racism, was fundamentally devisive, illegitimate, and undemocratic. By refusing to acknowledge the role that race and racism play in the lives of people of colour, cultural critics were reinforcing their power to influence perceptions.

For racism to be weakened as a force, it must be brought into the light and openly examined as a feature of the events and experiences it influences, even in the most subtle ways (Dyson, 1994). What was lacking in the rhetoric of cultural 'authorities' was a conceptualization of racism as deeply rooted. The critics were often unwilling or unable to move beyond their own experiential framework.

The collective values, assumptions, and beliefs operating beneath the coded language of liberalism and democracy remain invisible to members of the White dominant culture. Their position of White privilege allows them to erase or evade issues of race, racism, and power. Their rhetoric of pluralism and inclusion does not incorporate the material properties of exclusion. They are unable to 'imagine' racism as a pervasive reality that affects the daily minutiae of living, working, thinking, and feeling. They are unable to see the racism that is woven into everyday discourse, popular culture, and 'high' art.

The obvious contradiction in the position taken by the dominant cultural authorities to the protest was this: they were attempting to silence the resistance effort, even while claiming that free expression must be protected. Free expression presumably should grant people of colour the right to talk and write about their experiences of marginalization, discrimination, and exclusion. These experiences are a legitimate basis upon which to seek social and political progress.

Democracy requires empowerment; empowerment depends on equality; and equality requires meaningful participation. The health of a liberal democratic society rests on the right of all of its citizens to affect change and to contribute meaningfully, and on the fair distribution of wealth and power. Inclusiveness, then, is integral both to the notion of equality and to the strength of democracy.

Contested Views on Multiculturalism

In each of the events in the case studies, the cloak of multiculturalism was used to legitimize and justify the cultural event itself. In the ROM exhibition, the curator set out to examine and critique the 'ethnocentrism and cultural arrogance' of the Canadian missionaries and soldiers who went 'Into the Heart of Africa' (Cannizzo, 1990). *Miss Saigon* was set in Vietnam and its central narrative dealt with a cross-cultural and interracial 'love story.' In the competition for the Barnes Exhibit, one of the strategies the AGO used to distinguish itself from other cities was the multicultural composition of the Toronto community. In announcing Toronto as one of the sites for the travelling exhibition, the president of the Barnes Foundation emphasized the importance of this diversity as a factor. According to Livent and its supporters, *Show Boat* was an opportunity for people of different racial and cultural groups to learn about racism during this period of American history. Many of the opponents of the Writing Thru Race Conference argued that this gathering represented a threat to multicultural, democratic values, including respect for and tolerance of differences.

Over the last three decades, discourse about Canada's national identity has been framed within the debate over multiculturalism, which promises to recognize, respect, and value cultural racial differences. While multiculturalism is not the cause of Canada's cultural and identity crises, it has heightened the anxiety many mainstream Canadians feel when they face issues of culture and identity.

For these individuals, contemporary multiculturalism poses a threat to the way they have imagined and constructed Canadian identity. Their image of Canada is based on the notion of French-English duality – a duality that is what distinguishes this country most from others, particularly the United States. Many Canadians fear that multiculturalism will never provide a solution to the problem of national identity. Canadians want to resolve the French-English tensions without having to address the issue of multiculturalism. One recent analyst argued that in Canada, the 'state sanctioned proliferation of cultural *difference* itself is seen to be its defining characteristic' (Mackey, 1996: 11). If this view is indeed correct, then the influence of multiculturalism must be critically examined in the light of the issues identified in our analysis of cultural production.

In one of the ironies of postmodernist societies, the dominant discourse about multiculturalism has recently been expressed by a writer who is himself a person of colour. Neil Bissoondath in *Selling Illusions* (1994) posits that multiculturalism is a fundamentally flawed approach to Canada's cultural and racial diversity. Multiculturalism, he argues, is based on a heightened sense of ethnicity among groups, and recognition and support for the expression of these differences represents a serious threat to Euro-Canadian values. He favours a return to the paradigm of assimilation, or biculturalism, in which all immigrants are expected to give up their cultural/ethnic identity (at least in the public domain) and conform to the values, beliefs, traditions, and norms of the dominant culture, be it English or French. According to Bissoondath's analysis, in the ideal world (one in which multiculturalism is absent) the identity of all Canadians would be unhyphenated and all citizens would have equal rights, responsibilities, and entitlements. There would be only one common culture, in which everyone shared the same history, traditions, values, and norms.

In Bissoondath's analytical approach, multiculturalism represents a conceptual framework that supports symbolic, folkloric expressions of cultural identity (in the private domain), while at the same time bolstering the idea of an unhyphenated and unmarked, yet dominant, Anglo-Canadian culture (Mackey, 1996; Moodley, 1983). Simply put, from Bissoondath's perspective multiculturalism as anything else but symbolic multiculturalism is flawed.

By the late 1980s, two perspectives on multiculturalism had gained currency among people of colour, including artists. The first understood multiculturalism as a manifestation of the postmodernist reaction to the delegitimation of the state and the erosion of the hegemony of the dominant culture in advanced capitalist countries (Turner, 1994). Understood in this way, multiculturalism is part of a decentring process and is grounded in the organization of capital on a global scale; it has manifested itself in the development of transnational labour, commodity, and capital markets, and in corporate structures that have reduced the power of traditional political and social structures to control or protect social groups within the state. People all over the world have turned to ethnic and cultural identity as a means of mobilizing themselves in the defence of their social, political, and economic interests (ibid., 1994: 419).

A second perspective emerged in the late 1980s – a race-based critique of multiculturalism based on the premise that multiculturalism is a movement for social change. Those who support this view situate multiculturalism as a means of challenging the cultural hegemony of a dominant ethnic group or social class. Multiculturalism calls for the equal expression of minority cultures within a heterogeneous societal structure.

Many scholars and writers (Nourbese Philip, 1993; Goldberg, 1994; Mackey, 1996; and others) have identified as a major weakness in multiculturalism its failure to deal with the problems of systemic racism in Canada. This race-based critique points out how multiculturalism as ideology has provided a veneer for liberal-pluralist discourse, in which democratic values such as individualism, tolerance, and equality are espoused and supported without the core of the common culture being altered or the rights of people of colour being ensured. Artists of colour and First Nations artists have also engaged in a critique of multiculturalism. They see its inadequacies reflected in its failure to transform Canadian society – to dismantle systems of inequality and to diminish white power and privilege.

A race-based analysis asserts that multiculturalism fosters 'a festive aura of imagined consensus' (Moodley, 1983). Multiculturalism focuses on 'saris, samosas, and steel-bands' in order to defuse the 'three R's': 'resistance, rebellion and rejection' (Mullard, 1982). A little local colour is 'tolerated' and even encouraged, providing vibrancy and vitality to what remains as the 'core' culture. A cultural-racial hierarchy based on hegemonic Western values and principles is thereby maintained.

In a sense, a race-based analysis of multiculturalism leads to what has been called 'radical' or 'critical' multiculturalism (Shohat and Stam, 1994; Goldberg, 1994). Critical multiculturalism challenges the politcal and cultural hegemony of the dominant class or group. It calls for a profound restructuring and reconceptualization of the power relations between different cultural and racial communities based on the premise that communities and societies do not exist autonomously but are deeply woven together in a web of interrelationships. It follows that racial and cultural diversity is a significant aspect of all forms of public discourse and interaction.

Critical multiculturalism is distinguished from liberal pluralist discourse in that it is not about 'tolerance' or 'sensitivity' or 'understanding' of the 'others.' Pluralism is premised on a hierarchical order of cultures that under certain conditions 'allows' nondominant cultures to participate in the dominant culture. Critical multiculturalism moves away from this paradigm. It deals with empowerment and resistance to subjugation, with the social transformation of social, cultural, and economic institutions, and with the dismantling of dominant cultural hierarchies, structures, and systems of representation.

Critical multiculturalism imagines minority communities not as 'special interest groups' but rather as active and full participants who are at the core of a shared history. It represents a different axis, one that moves away from tolerance and accommodation toward equity and justice. This approach rejects the view that identities and communities are fixed sets of experiences, meanings, and practices. Instead, it sees identities as dynamic, fluid, multiple, and historically situated. This form of multiculturalism moves beyond the narrow understanding of identity politics, and provides for the possibility that alliances and affiliations can be formed based on mutual needs and shared objectives. Critical multiculturalism makes transformation possible as a reciprocal process that includes rather than excludes, and that does not rely on bounded communities. This model of multiculturalism calls for the restructuring and reconceptualization of power relations between communities, and for challenging the hierarchy that currently exists and makes some identities 'us' and the rest 'them' (Shohat and Stam, 1994; Goldberg, 1994). Multiculturalism, in this context, provides a framework for understanding that diversity can only be meaningful within the construct of social justice.

At the core of critical multiculturalism is a challenge to the type of politics of diversity that ignores the system of power and privilege which operates without restraint in the dominant culture. This 'old' form of 'symbolic' multiculturalism postulates that the White mainstream culture controls the distribution of knowledge, systems of representation, cultural and institutional practices, and social relations. Artists of colour are now employing the newer, more radical expression of multiculturalism to explain their experiences in Canadian society, and to bring to light that a collective identity has been imposed on them by the mainstream. As a result of this, levels of anxiety and cultural panic have been increasing among members of the dominant culture.

The case studies strongly suggest that there is now a clash between critical multiculturalism and symbolic multiculturalism. As McFarlane (1995) observes: 'The nation is under siege ... We are not who we used to be. The promise of nostalgia is vexed by forgetfulness ... The nation is perceived to operate "*within*" a crisis of representation and cannot adequately locate itself.'

This seige mentality is most evident in the public sphere. In the public arena racism has been eradicated from the pubic agenda. The antiracism initiatives of the late 1980s and early 1990s have been either significantly weakened or eliminated. Equality is being redefined, and is considered less and less to be the responsibility of the state. It is no longer linked to *group* oppression and disadvantage (Apple, 1993).

In Ontario, under the Progressive Conservative government and its 'Common Sense Revolution,' the struggle against 'racism' has been eliminated from government policies and swept off the political agenda. The provincial government agency that was responsible for overseeing antiracism policies and strategies for almost two decades has been discharged, and the Employment Equity Act has been rescinded. Human and financial resources delegated to various government and other public sector programs to address racial discrimination have been eliminated. The Harris government is using the language of enlightenment and liberal discourse (rationality, progress, equality, individual rights and responsibilities) to implement its program (Mackey, 1996) and to further marginalize minority groups.

At the federal level, the Reform Party has fuelled the expression of overt forms of racial bigotry, xenophobia, and Eurocentrism; meanwhile, the Liberal Party is doing less and less to challenge racism and providing fewer resources to address racial inequality in Canadian society.

In this reactionary environment, the rhetoric and imagery of cultural racism has been reconstructed and reasserted. Cultural productions such as those examined in this text give voice to racism, reproducing and reinforcing racist ideologies and discourse.

The Aftermath of the Struggle over the Six Cultural Productions

Despite all the efforts by cultural agencies and authorities to contain the challenges to their institutions and systems, there have been some gains. The struggle did produce some results, thereby demonstrating that while cultural systems are powerful and institutionalized, they are not immutable. In most cases the changes have been symbolic and cosmetic rather than structural and systemic. Some of the initiatives have been ad hoc interventions that have barely touched the organizational and cultural life of the institution. In most instances, change has *not* been incorporated into mission statements, policies, programs and services, systems of management and governance, communications, professional training and development, and so on. 'Consciousness-raising' and 'consultation' tend to be the primary focus of change efforts. However, these objectives are generally perceived as ends in themselves rather than as preliminary steps.

Even so, we believe that the oppositional cultural politics described in these cases studies have begun to make a difference. A new language of cultural criticism is evolving. As can be seen in the examples described below, resourceful, creative, and resilient individuals and groups are slowly gaining access to cultural institutions and their resources. We would note, with a degree of caution, some of the more positive recent developments.

The Art Gallery of Ontario

In recent years, the AGO has taken a few limited steps toward presenting non-Eurocentric forms of art. Their mission statement incorporates the language of diversity and accessibility as it relates to audiences. Members of senior staff are articulating a commitment to globalizing the gallery's perspectives to allow for multiple voices and multiple narratives; as examples they cite programs such as those contingent with Black History Month and the Chinese Mid-Autumn Festival. There has been a slight increase in the number of exhibitions featuring artists of colour. These include two recent exhibitions, one featuring the work of a Korean artist, the other a Nigerian-born artist. In the summer of 1997 the AGO presented 'Entering the Millennium; A Spiritual Dialogue,' which explored the subject of spirituality at the end of the millennium from a diasporic African North American perspective.

The gallery has also formed a partnership with the Ontario Council of Agencies Serving Immigrants. Among the goals of this partnership are to foster meaningful relationships between ethnocultural communities and the AGO; to work toward making the AGO accessible to a broad range of communities, interests, and values; to work toward breaking down systemic barriers; and to support diverse cultural and artistic practices.

Although the AGO's board of directors does not reflect Toronto's diversity, the gallery's hiring practices are improving: it now has an assistant curator who is Black, and a curator of European art who is of Chinese origin; minorities are also represented in the design department.

The Royal Ontario Museum

The controversy surrounding *Into the Heart of Africa* has 'sensitized' the ROM staff to the need for greater consultation with and outreach to Toronto's diverse communities. According to a key respondent, the ROM now does community consultation on all exhibits and programs that 'deal with ethnocultural subject matter.' These kinds of outreach activities have informed its recent Asian exhibitions. For example, the Korean community was consulted on the Korea permanent gallery. Also, a group called 'Friends of South Asia and the ROM' has been formed whose objective is to raise money in this community to hire a south Asian curator.

In another recent initiative, African and African-Canadian scholars were called on to examine the African collections, since the museum does not have an African specialist curator. Similarly, a First Nations artist was consulted on the museum's reinterpretation of its Haida and Nitska crest poles.

However, there has been little progress with respect to more diverse representation at the staff level. According to museum spokespersons this is because of a provincial hiring freeze. When short-term and contractually limited positions become available, the museum now advertises these positions in nontraditional media sources (in the past it relied solely on the *Globe and Mail*). Two endowed curator positions have been filled: one individual is Chinese; the other is European but is bilingual in a Chinese language.

The museum claims that it is trying to involve people in a more meaningful way, but there is little evidence of structural change in the staffing, management, or governance of this institution.

Literature

We begin this brief overview of positive signs of change in terms of Canadian writers by quoting George Elliott Clarke. In describing the 'Awakening' in Canadian writing, he observes: 'A fresh breeze is blowing' through the halls of Canadian literature. The doors and windows of the grand, old slightly musty, Victorian mansion are opening slowly to admit new accents and fresh scents. The world is making a home on the premises, and there's plenty of room' (1994: 48).

While there have almost always been First Nations writers and writers of colour telling their stories, it is only recently that they have begun to find mainstream publishers, council grants, unbiased literary criticism, access to the writer's union, and other supports and resources. As a result, there has been an huge outpouring of poetry, fiction, and nonfiction by First Nations, African-Canadian, Asian, and South Asian writers.

The Writing Thru Race Conference and other, earlier initiatives helped bring about significant changes in TWUC. The 1996 annual meeting of the union drew significantly larger numbers of Asian and Black members, although First Nations writers were reported to be absent. By the time of that gathering, the anger and backlash against the advocacy efforts of racial minority writers had significantly dissipated. In the same year, the Racial Minority Writers Committee of the union, with the support and sponsorship of the Cultural Human Resources Council, launched a new project to establish a professional skills mentoring program for trainees from First Nations and other racial minority communities.

Theatrical Productions

Productions by playwrights of colour, particularly African-Canadian writers, have recently proliferated. It must be noted that with one or two exceptions (such as Tomson Highway's *Dry Lips Ought to Move to Kapuskasing*, at the Royal Alex), this positive development is not reflected in the large, mainstream theatres, which continue to be dominated by American mega-musicals. Plays such as *Riot* by Andrew Moodie, which won the Chalmers Award, and Djanet Sears's *Harlem Duet* – to mention only two examples – are produced in small theatres that seat less than two hundred.[4]

There are more and more festivals celebrating the cultural contributions of hundreds of artists from diverse ethno-racial groups. Two examples: the Celebrating African Identity Conference and Festival, and the South Asian Desh Pardesh Conference and Festival. These forums provide cultural space to view, discuss, and mark the outpouring of creativity within the non-White artistic communities.

The CRTC Hearings for New FM Licence

Another round of CRTC hearings applications was held in the spring of 1997 for a vacant FM frequency. Ten applicants were competing for this last FM station. Two groups, Milestone Communications led by Denham Jolly, a local Black entrepreneur, and the J. Robert Wood group, were part of previous applications for FM frequencies but lost out to mainstream broadcasting groups. As discussed in the case study, both Milestone and the Robert Wood group wanted to reach out to a younger, more ethnically and racially diverse Toronto market. The Milestone group had deep roots in the Black community and was made up of all African Canadians. The Robert Wood group, which helped pioneer the idea of a Black music station, widened its focus to aim at 'the new mainstream,' and committed itself to employment equity. Another group, AllToronto, submitted a proposal to set up Toronto's first Aboriginal radio station. The major competitor in this round of applications was the CBC, which decided it needed to change its AM frequency to FM because of its limited reception in Toronto. The CRTC in its decision of 1997 granted the frequency to the CBC. Milestone Communications is said to be appealing this decision to Cabinet.

The Print Media

In the print media there have been modest signs of efforts to more accurately represent the contributions of ethno-racial minorities in the popular culture and the arts. The *Toronto Star* now has a 'diversity' editor and has made significant progress in some areas of its coverage. The paper is making a clear effort to 'mainstream' ethnically and racially diverse groups and individuals. It has begun to write about and photograph people of colour participating in the everyday life of Canadian society (attending leisure and sports events, winning prizes, speaking on issues that are of concern to all communities, and so on).

One of the most significant changes in the *Star* and the *Globe and Mail* is that both papers are using more freelance cultural critics from diverse racial and cultural backgrounds. We would argue that this has resulted in a deeper and richer form of cultural criticism than existed before.[3]

The *Toronto Sun* has taken one small step forward: under a new editor, it has started an initiative to involve the ethnic press by inviting contributions from these varied sources.

Seeking a New Vision and Discourse

These new undertakings provide a glimmer of hope. As we move toward the new millennium, it seems possible that Canada will transform its vision of its national identity. However, first a new discourse will have to be developed, one that provides spaces for meaningful exchange. If the dialogue is to be purposeful, it cannot be circumscribed. It cannot bar pain, anger, and passion. It cannot avoid the issues of race and racism. It cannot disclaim the existence of disparate social realities, different subjectivities, distinct histories, and diverse truths. In approaching this daunting challenge, the first step must involve a commitment to recognizing and including the stories and images of all Canadians.

From the very beginning, there was only one definition of 'Canadianness': a 'Canadian' was either a francophone or an anglophone. Canadians have 'imagined' a national culture built on these two elements. Moreover, Canadians have always believed that one day the question of national identity will be resolved. Throughout the history of this country, Canadians have found it difficult to articulate clearly a national consensus on the issue of identity. We have failed to develop inclusive processes and spaces within which this critical discussion can take place. Instead, exclusive categories of what constitutes 'legitimate' debate have been established that eliminate people who do not share 'national' ideals.

Critical multiculturalism is not 'the promised land' (Wallace, 1994: 259). But it does offer hope, and a means by which Canadian cultural institutions and systems can begin critically analysing and revisioning the values, priorities, and practices of contemporary culture. Critical or transformative multiculturalism can become a tool and strategy for cultural and institutional change. It can provide a mechanism for reshaping the collective consciousness of the nation, and help us sort out fact from fiction, and myth from reality. At the same time, however, it can be used as a technique for diverting, deflecting, and defusing demands for access, inclusion, and representation within the cultural landscape of this country.

Canadian society is constantly evolving. Our analysis of the controversies around the six cultural events that formed the substance of this text suggest that within public culture we must make a space for the multiple experiences, stories, voices, and creative responses that exist in all ethno-racial communities in Canadian society. We need to recognize that the rising political and cultural consciousness of minorities in this country offers the possibility for enhancing our national identity and strengthening our liberal democratic society.

Notes

1 Multiculturalism as a state policy had its official beginnings in 1971, when Prime Minister Pierre Trudeau announced in Parliament that his government had accepted the recommendations contained in Volume IV of the Royal Commission on Bilingualism and Biculturalism, published in 1967. This report recognized that Canada was a culturally and ethnically 'plural' society in that it contained Canadians of British and French origin, aboriginal peoples and 'others,' and recommended that its diversity be recognized and maintained. 'Multiculturalism within a bilingual framework commends itself to the government as the most suitable means of assuring the cultural freedom of Canadians' (Trudeau, 1971).

Since then, the policy has been enshrined in the Multiculturalism Act (1988), which committed the government to policies that would preserve and enhance the multicultural identity and heritage of Canadians, as well as achieve equality for all Canadians in the economic, social, cultural, and political life of Canada.

The Multiculturalism Act subsection 3(1)(c), says:

It is hereby declared to be the policy of the Government of Canada to promote the full and equitable participation of individuals and communities of all origins in the continuing evolution and shaping of all aspects of Canadian society and assist them in the elimination of any barrier to participation.

Subsection 3(2)(a) of the Act recognizes discrimination in Canadian society and articulates the federal government's commitment to ensuring that there are no unfair barriers to employment and career advancement. The Act commits federal institutions to take action to enhance the ability of individuals and communities to contribute to Canadian society by ensuring that government policies and programs respond to the needs of all Canadians.

2 The Writing Thru Race Conference and the application for a Black/dance music station followed a slightly different pattern; they were cultural events created to address existing cultural processes of exclusion and marginalization. They therefore represented stages II to V.

3 One example of how literary criticism is changing is the response of critics to the work of Dionne Brand. Regarding her collection of essays *Bread Out of Stone* (1994), which contained many pieces of writing that exactingly delineated the nature of Canadian racism and the worldwide legacy of colonialism,

Brand was largely dismissed and discredited as a serious writer. Critics referred to her as the 'angry black,' 'the ungrateful immigrant, the misandrogenous lesbian.' Her involvement in community activism meant that she was 'too political' to be seen as a serious writer by much of the literary establishment. Donna Bailey Nurse (1997) wrote in the *Globe and Mail* that 'the invective eclipsed discussion of the intensely lyrical quality of the essays.'

4 In the fall of 1997, after winning four Dora Mavor Moore Awards, *Harlem Duet* returned to a somewhat larger space.

References

Apple, Michael. 1993. 'Constructing the "Other": Rightist Reconstructions of Common Sense.' In C. McCarthy and W. Critchlow, eds. *Race, Identity and Representation in Education*. New York and London: Routledge. 24–39.

Bailey Nurse, Donna. 1997. 'Writer Packs Poetic Punch.' *Globe and Mail*. 29 April.

Bissoondath, Neil. 1994. *Selling Illusions: The Cult of Multiculturalism*. Toronto: Penguin.

Brand, Dionne. 1994. *Bread Out of Stone*. Toronto: Coach House Press.

Cannizzo, J. 1990. 'Into the Heart of a Controversy.' *Toronto Star*. 5 June. A17.

Clarke, George Elliott. 1994. 'After Word.' *Possibilitiis*. 1(2), 48.

Cruz, Pat. 1993. 'ArtTable: A Panel Discussion. 8 January 1992. Whitney Museum of American Art. New York: American Council for the Arts.

Dyson, Michael. 1994. 'Essentialism and the Complexities of Racial Identity.' 218–58. In David Goldberg, ed. *Multiculturalism: A Critical Reader*. Oxford, U.K. and Cambridge, Mass.: Blackwell.

Goldberg, David. ed. 1994. *Multiculturalism: A Critical Reader*. Cambridge, Mass.: Blackwell.

Hall, Stuart. 1992. 'The West and the Rest: Discourse and Power.' In Stuart Hall and Bram Gieben, eds. *Formations of Modernity*. Cambridge, U.K.: Polity Press, in association with Open University. 272–332.

Kulyk Keefer, Janice. 1996. 'Writing, Reading, Teaching Transcultural in Canada.' In H. Braum and W. Klooss, eds. *Multiculturalism in North America and Europe: Social Practices – Literary Visions*. Wissenschaftlicher Verlag Trier.

McCarthy, C., and W. Critchow. 1993. *Race, Identity and Representation in Education*. London: Routledge.

McFarlane, Scott. 1995. 'The Haunt of Race: Canada's Multicultural Act, the Politics of Incorporation and Writing Thru Race.' *Fuse* 18(3). 18–31.

Mackey, Eva. 1995. 'Postmodernism and Cultural Politics in a Multicultural Nation: Contests over Truth in the *Into the Heart of Africa* Controversy.' *Public Culture*. 7(2). Winter. 430–31.

– 1996. 'Managing and Imagining Diversity: Multiculturalism and the Construction of National Identity in Canada.' D.Phil. Social Anthropology, University of Sussex.

Moodley, Kogila. 1983. 'Canadian Multiculturalism as Ideology.' *Ethnic and Racial Studies*. 6(3). 320–31.

Mullard, Chris. 1982. 'Multiracial Education in Britain: From Assimilation to Cultural Pluralism.' In J. Tierney, ed. *Race, Migration and Schooling*. London: Holt, Rinehart and Winston.

Nourbese Philip, Marlene. 1993. *Frontiers: Selected Essays and Writings on Racism and Culture*. Stratford, Ont.: Mercury Press.

Rutherford, J., ed. 1990. *Identity: Community, Culture, and Difference*. London: Lawrence and Wishart.

Shohat, Ella, and Robert Stam. 1994. *Unthinking Eurocentrism: Multiculturalism and the Media*. London and New York: Routledge.

Trudeau, Pierre Elliott. 1971. Announcement of 'Federal Multicultural Policy.' *House of Commons Debates*. 8 October, pp. 8545–8.

Turner, Terence. 1994. In David Goldberg, ed. *Multiculturalism: A Critical Reader*. Cambridge, Mass.: Blackwell. 406–25.

Walcott, Rinaldo. 1993. 'Critiquing Canadian Multiculturalism: Towards an Anti-racist Agenda.' Masters thesis, Dept. of Education. York University.

Wallace, Michele. 1994. 'The Search for the "Good Enough" Mammy: Multiculturalism, Popular Culture, and Psychoanalysis.' In T. Goldberg, ed. *Multiculturalism: A Critical Reader*. Oxford: Blackwell.

West, Cornel. 1990. 'The New Politics of Difference.' In Russell Ferguson, ed. *Marginalization and Contemporary Culture*. Cambridge, Mass.: MIT Press.

Wetherell, Margaret, and Jonathon Potter. 1992. *Mapping the Language of Racism*. New York: Columbia University Press.

Glossary

aesthetics
This term is associated with the 'refined' appreciation of beauty in the arts. The object of study for aesthetics is the art object itself, detached from the historical–cultural context of its production. The study of aesthetics, or the analysis of what constitutes beauty, is a branch of philosophy.

agency
A term widely disseminated in the postmodernist literature. It generally refers to the disempowered and is used to describe the action involved in the attempt at empowerment. It places the emphasis on individuals in their own right. Individuals themselves are believed to make a difference, and not merely as members of groups or organizations.

appropriation
This term refers to rights to language, subject matter, and authority that are outside one's personal experience. It also refers to the process by which members of relatively privileged groups 'raid' the culture of marginalized groups, abstracting cultural practices or artifacts from their historically specific contexts (Dines and Humez)

anti-Semitism
This term describes unconscious or openly hostile attitudes and behaviour directed at individual Jews or the Jewish people, leading to social, economic, institutional, religious, cultural, or political discrimination. Anti-Semitism has also been expressed through acts of physical violence and through the organized destruction of entire communities.

assimilation
The process by which an individual or group completely adopts – or is absorbed by – the culture, values, and patterns of thought of another social, religious, linguistic, or national group.

cultural
artifact/object   This term refers to human-created objects of any kind, including books, visual art, theatre, television, and print media. Cultural studies scholars also use the term as a way of broadening the study of culture by including aspects that are not usually included, such as verbal, visual, and auditory forms of discourse.

colonialism   A process by which a foreign power dominates and exploits an indigenous group by appropriating its land and extracting the wealth from it while using the group as cheap labour. Racial doctrines are commonly invoked that reinforce patterns of superiority to justify the blatant exploitation of indigenous peoples. *Colonization* refers to a specific era of European expansion into overseas territories between the sixteenth and twentieth centuries, during which European states implanted settlements in distant territories, ultimately reaching a position of economic, military, political, and cultural hegemony in much of Asia, Africa, and the Americas.

commodify   To commodify something is to turn it into a commodity, that is, into an object or service that can be bought or sold in the marketplace.

cultural relativism   A school of thought premised on acceptance of cultural differences. The theory postulates that no hierarchy based on the superiority or inferiority of cultures should be presumed to exist within present or past human societies. Cultures are simply different from (i.e., not better than) each other. Geographic, historical, environmental, cognitive, and linguistic differences explain human cultural variation.

cultural studies   This term refers to the study of cultural practices, of systems of representation and communication, and of the relationship between culture and asymmetrical power relations. It is an interdisciplinary approach that draws from anthropology, sociology, history, semiotics (see below), literary, art, theatre, and film criticism, psychoanalysis, feminism, and Third World studies, to name only a few sources. This approach is used to critically examine the dominant culture and the role that mainstream cultural institutions and the media play in the legitimization, production, and entrenchment of systems of inequality. Cultural studies emphasizes the roles of both 'high' and popular culture in the transmission and reproduction of values. Cultural studies also examines the processes of resistance by which women, people of colour, and other marginalized groups are challenging hegemonic (see below) cultural practices.

culture   This term has many meanings and is used to refer to a number of different schools of thought. Anthropologists have traditionally defined culture as the totality of ideas, beliefs, values, knowledge, and language – as a learned, shared, and transmitted way of life of a people, a group, or a nation. For others, culture is a signifying system utilizing knowledge, artifacts, and symbols, through which a social order is communicated, reproduced, and experienced (Williams and Grossberg). In popular discourse, 'high' culture refers to artistic and intellectual development and to the works and activities that are their products.

deconstructionism This term refers to a mode of interpretation based on the assumption that texts/narratives/images do not have fixed meanings. Individual readers and viewers can be said to interpret the meanings of the texts as they read and works of art as they observe and examine them. It follows that there is no absolute 'centre' or system of ideas outside of the text that enables it to be comprehended and interpreted in a fixed or static manner.

discourse   Refers to the production of knowledge through language and social practices. This relates to the particular ways of producing meaning – to an interactive association between words and their denotative capacity and especially their connotative capacity.

dominant/
majority group   Refers to any group within a given society possessing the power and authority to preserve, sustain, and reproduce the prevailing distribution of cultural, social, economic, and political power, privilege, and resources.

encoding/
decoding   Terms developed by British cultural studies writer Stuart Hall in an article of the same name. Hall argues that meaning does not simply exist in a media text's codes but is the result of a complex relationship between particular audiences and texts. In this analysis, Hall proposes three possible audience

responses to the dominant ideology contained in media text's codes: *dominant reading* (accepting the preferred meaning); *negotiated reading* (accepting aspects of the preferred meaning but rejecting others); and *oppositional reading* (rejecting the preferred meaning (see Hall, in During, 1994).

equity
Refers to equality of access and outcome. An equity program is designed to remove barriers to equality by identifying and eliminating discriminatory policies and practices.

ethnic/
ethnocultural
group
Terms used to describe groups that share a common language, race, religion, or national origin. Everyone belongs to an ethnic group. In Canada there are a variety of ethnocultural groups among people of African, Asian, European, and indigenous American descent. Some Canadians experience discrimination because of ethnocultural affiliation (ethnicity, religion, nationality, language).

ethnicity
A social and political construct used by individuals and communities to define themselves and others. Ethnicity is also a process that can be changed over time both by social conditions and by individuals. Ethnicity tends to be based on a common culture, history, language, religion, and nationhood.

essentialism
(A) The practice of reducing the complex identity of a particular group to a series of simplified characteristics and denying individual qualities. (B) The simplistic reduction of an idea or process.

ethnocentrism
The tendency to view events, values, beliefs, practices, and experiences from the perspective of one's own group/culture; and the corresponding tendency to misunderstand or diminish other groups' values and practices, regarding them as inferior.

eurocentrism
Refers to a complex system of beliefs that upholds the supremacy of Europe's cultural values, ideas, and peoples. European culture is seen as the vehicle for progress toward liberalism and democracy. Eurocentrism minimizes the role of Europeans in maintaining the oppressive systems of colonialism and racism.

exclusion
The state of group disempowerment, degradation, and disenfranchisement maintained by systemic barriers and supported by an implicit ideology of ethnic or racial superiority.

hegemony	A concept first used by Gramsci in the 1930s and taken up in cultural studies, where it refers to the ability in certain historical periods of the dominant classes to maintain power over the economic, political, and cultural direction of a nation. In cultural studies, the concept of hegemony is often found in those analyses which seek to show how everyday meanings, representations, and activities are organized and made sense of in such a way as to maintain the power of the dominant group at the expense of nondominant groups.
hybridity	The recognition that no culture is pure and pristine. All cultures are constantly changing, and interacting with other cultures.
identity	A subjective sense of coherence, consistency, and continuity of self, rooted in both personal and group history.
ideology	A complex set of beliefs, perceptions, and assumptions that provide members of a group with an understanding and an explanation of their world. Ideology influences how people interpret social, cultural, political, and economic systems. It guides behaviour and provides a basis for making sense of the world, imparting meaning to life, instilling a common bond among group members, and explaining the reality of a situation. Ideology provides a framework for organizing and maintaining relations of power and dominance in society.
inclusiveness	Exists when disadvantaged communities and designated group members share power and decision-making at all levels in projects, programs, and institutions.
institutions	Organizational arrangements, structures, and practices, through which collective actions are taken (e.g., government, business, education, media, health and social services, and cultural institutions such as museums and galleries, publishing corporations, and theatres).
mainstream	The dominant culture, and the political, social, educational, cultural, and economic institutions through which power is maintained and reproduced.
marginalization	The process of restricting an individual, group, or community from participating in the decision-making processes, programs, activities, benefits, and resources of an institution or society. Marginalization is a form of exclusion that occurs when credentials, abilities, and interests are disregarded or ignored by the dominant culture.

multiculturalism   (A) A description of the composition of Canada both historically and currently, referring to the cultural and racial diversity of Canadian society. (B) An ideology which holds that
racial, cultural, religious, and linguistic diversity is an integral, beneficial, and necessary part of Canadian society and
identity. (C) A policy operating in various levels of government, including the federal government, and in various
social institutions (see *Radical/cultural multiculturalism*).

performance   Involves an individual or group of people interpreting an
existing tradition, and reinventing themselves in front of an
audience, or the public.

postmodernism   Originally related only to literary and art criticism and to the
abandonment of traditional cultural practices in favour of
more innovative forms of expression. It also led to the col-
lapse of rigid distinctions between high and mass or popular
culture. Later, it became also a paradigm for social change
(for example, change from the modernist view of society,
founded on the theories of the eighteenth-century Enlightenment. As a philosophy and discourse, it challenged authority
and power relations; and questioned traditional social values, as well as the fragmentation of individual identities by
social markers of difference such as race, gender, ethnicity,
and sexual orientation.

racism   An ideology (i.e., a complex and organized set of implicit
and explicit beliefs and values) that asserts the inherent
superiority of one racial group over another. It is manifested
in discriminatory practices that protect, sustain, or support
the power and privilege of the dominant culture. It is found
in organizational or institutionalized values, norms, structures, and programs, and also in individual thought and
behaviour patterns. The various elements of racism are commonly divided into the following categories: *individual racism, institutional racism, systemic/structural racism, and cultural
racism.*

racist discourse   Refers to the ways that society gives voice to racism, and
includes explanations, narratives, codes of meaning,
accounts, images, and social practices that have the effect of
establishing, sustaining, and reinforcing oppressive power
relations.

racist ideology   The whole range of concepts, ideas, images, symbols, and institutions that provide the framework of interpretation and meaning for racial thought in society. It creates and preserves a system of dominance based on race. It is communicated and reproduced through agencies of socialization (the family, school, religious doctrines, symbols and icons, images and discourse in art, music, and literature, media representations, and so on).

radical / critical
multiculturalism   A form of multiculturalism that calls for a radical restructuring of the power relations between ethno-racial communities and challenges the hierarchical structure of society. Radical multiculturalism focuses on empowering communities and transforming systems of representation, institutional and structural centres of power, and discourses. Multiculturalism in this context suggests that diversity can only be meaningful within the construct of social justice and equity.

reception theory   Theorists in cultural studies, and literary and media studies, focus on the role that audiences (readers of texts, critics of texts) play in understanding and deriving pleasure and meaning from texts. The role/interpretation of the reader/ viewer becomes central in this process. According to reception theory, a meaning should not be viewed as an immutable property of a text, but should be seen as the fruit of the relationship between the artistic work and its aesthetic realization by the reader/viewer.

reify   To make an abstraction concrete, thereby depriving it of its analytical power.

reflexivity   Involves critical thinking and rethinking about issues often taken for granted. Reflexivity also involves deconstructing feelings, events, situations, and experiences by peeling away the various levels of meaning attached to them through the passage of time.

representation   The process *and* the product of making signs stand for their meaning. It is the process of putting abstract ideological concepts into concrete forms (examples: representations of women, workers, Blacks). Representations include all kinds of imagery and discourse, and involve constructions of reality taken from specific social points of view. Representation is a social process of making sense within all available signifying systems: speech, writing, print, video, film, tape, and so on.

semiotics	The study of the ways in which languages and nonlinguistic symbolic systems operate to associate meanings with words, visual images, or objects. Semiotics examines *all* aspects of communication, focusing on *how* meaning is created rather than *what* the meaning is. Semiotics seeks to relate the production of meanings to other kinds of social productions and social relations.
stereotype	A false or generalized conception of a group that results in unconscious or conscious categorization of each member of that group, without regard for individual differences.
subjectivity	Encompasses unconscious and subconscious dimensions of the self, such as one's sense of who one is in relation to other people. It is the product of social and cultural systems that magnify differences. This concept has been used widely in literary and film criticism, which holds that narrative texts themselves produce through their codes an ideal 'viewing position,' from which the narrative is experienced by any viewer or reader.
text	Any product or work of art. 'Text' includes not only books, plays, and poetry, but also media representations, films, and visual art forms. Textual analysis involves studying how particular written or verbal cultural artifacts generate meaning, taking into account their social and political contexts.
universality	Refers to a level of understanding that transcends all human boundaries of culture and nation. Universalism is a critical quality of expression and comprehension traditionally valued in literature and art. Universality has, however, been defined in specific Eurocentric rather than truly universal terms. The Eurocentrically influenced notion of universality has been disseminated globally through the forces of colonialism.
whiteness	A social construction that has created a racial hierarchy that has shaped all of the social, cultural, educational, political, and economic institutions of society. Whiteness is linked to domination and is a form of race privilege that is invisible to White people who are not conscious of its power. Whiteness as defined within a cultural studies perspective is description, symbol, experience, and ideology.

References

Dines, Gail, and Jean Humez. eds. 1995. *Race, Gender, Class in the Media: A Text Reader*. Thousand Oaks, Ca.: Sage.

Grossberg, Lawrence. 1993. 'Cultural Studies and/in New Worlds.' In Cameron McCarthy and Warren Crichlow, eds. *Race, Identity, and Representation in Education*. New York: Routledge.

Hall, Stuart. 1993. 'Encoding, Decoding.' In Simon During, ed. *The Cultural Studies Reader*. New York: Routledge.

Williams, Raymond. 1976. *Keywords*. London: Fontana.

Index

Aboriginal(s), 12, 91, 97; art, 72; artists, 7; cultures, 72, 82; radio station (*AllToronto*), 266. *See also* First Nations
academic institutions, 233
academics, 12, 21, 25, 28
Adilman, Sid, 56, 240
advertising: and Barnes Exhibit, 70; and *Into the Heart of Africa*, 38, 59; and *Miss Saigon*, 153; and racism, 31, 214; and *Show Boat*, 153, 164, 179, 188, 194, 199–200; stereotypes of Blacks in, 164, 177, 178, 208n; and Toronto broadcasting, 121, 122, 123, 124
aesthetic(s), 14, 19; African, 77; and consumerism, 231; and dominant group, 72; Eurocentric, 4, 69, 72, 73, 98, 224; and 'excellence,' 68; First Nations, 98; mainstream Canadian, 95, and multiculturalism, 96; of 'others,' 33, 77; representations, 95–6, 104; standards, 80; and universalism, 223; values, 98; Western, 65
African(s), 37, 38, 41, 44–5, 46–7, 49, 50, 57, 60, 225, 226, 227, 241; and aesthetic awareness, 77; architec-

ture, 64; art, 64, 68, 69, 71, 72, 73, 74, 223; artifacts, 4, 36–40, 43–4, 46, 47, 48–9, 50, 222, 227; artists, 81, 82; culture, 64–5, 66; masks, 64, 71, 72, 76, 223; museum collections, 4, 264; music, 134; in photographs, 40, 45, 218; sculpture, 63, 65, 76, 223
African American(s), 64; art, 65, 66, 223; and art criticism, 78; artists, 66; community, 176; and identity, 137; and mainstream society, 187–8; music, 218; after Reconstruction, 184–5, 186, 226; and *Show Boat*, 186, 187, 188
African Canadian(s), 12, 159, 208n, 229; artists, 39, 122, 224; community and Black/dance music stations, 111, 112, 113, 122, 133, 134, 266; community and *Into the Heart of Africa*, 38, 39–40, 42, 43, 47, 48, 51, 56, 60, 220, 222, 234, 240; community and *Show Boat*, 163, 172, 180, 181, 188, 192, 195, 197, 201, 202, 207, 208; and identity, 199, 200, 201; and mainstream society, 187–8; music, 230; music professionals, 111; in Ontario, 200–1; writers, 39, 265